HISTORIC
COSTUMING

HISTORIC COSTUMING

By

NEVIL TRUMAN

With Additional Chapters by

RUTH M. GREEN

SECOND EDITION

LONDON
SIR ISAAC PITMAN & SONS LTD.

First impression 1936   *Seventh impression* 1947
Second impression 1936   *Eighth impression* 1949
Third impression 1937   *Ninth impression* 1952
Fourth impression 1940   *Tenth impression* 1956
Fifth impression 1944   *Eleventh impression* 1960
Sixth impression 1945   *Twelfth impression* 1962
Second edition 1966

SIR ISAAC PITMAN & SONS Ltd.
PITMAN HOUSE, PARKER STREET, KINGSWAY, LONDON, W.C.2
THE PITMAN PRESS, BATH
PITMAN HOUSE, BOUVERIE STREET, CARLTON, MELBOURNE
20-25 BECKETT'S BUILDINGS, PRESIDENT STREET, JOHANNESBURG

ASSOCIATED COMPANIES
PITMAN MEDICAL PUBLISHING COMPANY Ltd.
46 CHARLOTTE STREET, LONDON, W.I

PITMAN PUBLISHING CORPORATION
20 EAST 46TH STREET, NEW YORK, N.Y. 10017

SIR ISAAC PITMAN & SONS (CANADA) Ltd.
INCORPORATING THE COMMERCIAL TEXT BOOK COMPANY
PITMAN HOUSE, 381-383 CHURCH STREET, TORONTO

MADE IN GREAT BRITAIN AT THE PITMAN PRESS, BATH
F6—(G.122)

DEDICATED

TO

GEOFFREY WHITWORTH

FOUNDER AND DIRECTOR OF THE BRITISH DRAMA LEAGUE
TO WHOSE VISION AND ENTERPRISE THE STAGE OWES MUCH

FOREWORD

By SIR CHARLES B. COCHRAN

THEATRICAL producers and designers, whether professional or amateur, should have frequent cause to thank Mr. Nevil Truman for the great amount of research which he has undertaken in compiling this book.

Although in my work as a producer I have made it my business to have a working knowledge of the costume of most ages and countries, I cannot pretend to the exact knowledge of date and detail which Mr. Truman here supplies in a handy and compact work of reference.

It is right that these data should be available to the theatre in as accurate a form as possible, though I would venture to suggest that, for stage purposes, there are few instances of plays in which the very strictest historical accuracy is necessary. While I am always anxious to create on the stage the right atmosphere of period for an audience, this can often be done better by a slight departure from exactitude.

An audience, seeing a play, will not have Mr. Nevil Truman's knowledge of costume; it will, at best, have a rough and ready idea of "the sort of thing" that people wore at different epochs. Sometimes it may be better to indulge the popular conception, even if it is not accurate.

We may have a play about a historical event of which we know the exact date. Here, except in the case of leading personages with whose appearance and dress the man in the street is familiar through pictures, I would willingly allow my designer the rope of ten years either way, earlier or later. It might happen that the exactly right fashion was an extraordinarily ugly one from the point of view of the stage picture, or inconvenient for the actors, whereas a few years previously or subsequently the style of dress was better for the producer's purpose. As long as the general spirit and atmosphere of the time are created, and the stage effect is pleasing, the demands of the theatre are satisfied.

This must not be taken as ingratitude for the present author's carefully tabulated tables of dates and styles, a novel feature of this book which I highly commend and shall often find useful. One must know what is exactly right before one permits oneself a little licence.

The visual side of the stage, expressed in the lines and colours and lights with which the producer, aided by the scene-designer, the costumier-designer, and the electrician, paints his stage-picture, has always had a very strong appeal to me, and I could not say how many books on historic costume I have on my shelves—from small pamphlets to highly elaborate tomes.

Mr. Nevil Truman's book will, however, be a welcome addition and by no means the least highly valued and constantly consulted, as it should be by all workers in the Theatre.

I congratulate him and wish him the success which it richly deserves.

CHARLES B. COCHRAN

CONTENTS

PAGE

FOREWORD vi

CHAPTER I

INTRODUCTION, COSTUMES, COLOUR, AND PRODUCTIONS . . 1

The purpose behind the costume—General scope of the book—Rigid separation not possible because the fashions change imperceptibly

CHAPTER II

GREEKS, 550 B.C.–322 B.C. 3

Beautiful folds and graceful limbs—The chlamys, chiton, and tunic age

CHAPTER III

ROMANS, 509 B.C.–A.D. 324 7

Classic dignity—The period of the toga, tunic, and paenula

CHAPTER IV

SAXONS, 460–1066 11

The Bayeux Tapestry—Not as angular as they look—Tunic and hose clothe the entire man

CHAPTER V

NORMANS, 1066–1154 16

The dressing gown period—Woman lets her hair down, and long toed shoes are invented

CHAPTER VI

PLANTAGENETS, 1154–1272 20

Richer materials and brighter colours—The wimple, cross gartering, and furs come in

CHAPTER VII

THE THREE EDWARDS, 1272–1377 24

Men revolt and wear tight-fitting garments—Woman displays her hair and brings great beauty into the lines of her clothes

CHAPTER VIII

RICHARD OF BORDEAUX, 1377–99 29

Extravagance everywhere—Freak shapes for men while the dandies reign supreme

CHAPTER IX

THE THREE HENRIES, 1399–1461 34

The houppelande and leg of mutton sleeve devised—Women's hats become fantastic

CHAPTER X

PAGE

YORKIST, 1461–85 39

Women wear steeple hats with trailing veils—Low necks are affected by both sexes

CHAPTER XI

HENRY VII, 1485–1509 44

Dignity returns with the long gown, the handsome neck chain, and the gable hat

CHAPTER XII

TUDOR, 1509–58 49

Padding and pomp—History's most costly period in dress—Clothes are stiff with gold and jewels

CHAPTER XIII

SHAKESPEARE'S ENGLAND, 1558–1625 54

The cloak and rapier school—Man cuts a funny figure in doublet and trunkhose with a comic hat, starched ruff, and early Plus-Fours

CHAPTER XIV

THE MARTYR KING, 1625–49 59

The artists' reign—Silk and satin skirts, the Cavalier hat, and Vandyck collar bring great beauty into the service of clothing

CHAPTER XV

PURITANISM, 1649–60 64

A military dictator with no sense of humour makes everything dour and drear—No lace or ribbons relieve the monotony of the times—Plain leather and steeple hats command the day

CHAPTER XVI

RESTORATION, 1660–89 68

The King's return brings beauty in its train—The wig is created and the frock coat foreshadowed—Lely and Kneller immortalize the Stuart beauties

CHAPTER XVII

DUTCH WILLIAM, AND AFTER, 1689–1727 72

Dandies carry muffs, and woman stiffens her front and tight-laces—Panniers lend attraction to the scene

CHAPTER XVIII

GEORGE II, 1727–60 76

Flowered waistcoat and embroidered coat make man very gay—The muff grows larger, and Gainsborough paints the wasp-waisted, ribbon-capped women

CHAPTER XIX

THE MAN OF FASHION, 1760–1820 81

Man achieves even greater heights of style, and the modes change rapidly—The hoop is at last abandoned

CHAPTER XX

EMPIRE AND THE DANDIES, 1820–37 87

Man's last fling—Beau Brummel and the Regent introduce cleanliness as a novelty—Prince Florizel's famous buckle—Bucks and Beaux

CHAPTER XXI

THE CRINOLINE, 1850–60 93

The hoop again returns—The John Leech period—Little bonnet and round hat—A hideous outline, yet the Pre-Raphaelites did their best with it

CHAPTER XXII

GROSVENOR GALLERY, 1870–80 98

Oscar Wilde and the artists herald the dawn of the day of beauty, but the majority stand aside—The sage green and peacock feather period

CHAPTER XXIII

NOAH'S ARK, 1880–90 103

Buttons, buttons everywhere—The wasp waist returns, while bustle and train make women a curious shape—The Du Maurier period

CHAPTER XXIV

THE NINETIES, 1890–1900 107

Broad shoulders and tight waists eventually give way to a more graceful outline for women, while men remain figures of fun in a series of tubes

CHAPTER XXV

EDWARD VII, 1901–10 112

Freed from the rigid framework of Victorian dress, woman becomes more elegant and distinguished—Both style and cut are dashing and man is a dignified and effective foil to his womenfolk

CHAPTER XXVI

THE END OF AN EPOCH, 1910–20 118

Fashions become less formal and more comfortable

CHAPTER XXVII

PEACE AND WAR, 1920–45 123

New fashions spread more quickly than ever before but informality becomes more and more fashionable

CHAPTER XXVIII

THE POST-WAR WORLD, 1945–65 130

Good-quality clothes at low prices bring about what is in its way a social revolution and adolescent fashion assumes a new importance

CHAPTER XXIX

CLERGY AT MASS 135

The clergy remain the most conservative dressers in all ages and all climes—Their clothes have not changed since the Catacombs, and priests still wear an Italian workman's hat

CONTENTS

CHAPTER XXX

PAGE

CLERGY IN CHOIR AND STREET 139

Dress of the different religious orders and secular clergy varies at home and in church, and also out of doors, during different epochs

CHAPTER XXXI

ARMOUR FASHIONS SUMMARIZED 145

APPENDIX

THE EVOLUTION OF STYLES 151

INDEX 167

COLOUR PLATES

YORKIST LADIES, 1450 . . . . *Facing page* 38

TUDOR MERCHANT AND HIS WIFE, A . . . . . . " " 48

CHARLES I AND HIS QUEEN . . . . " " 58

CHARLES II AND HIS QUEEN . . . . " " 70

AT COURT, 1760 . . . . " " 80

BISHOPS . . . . " " 136

HISTORIC COSTUMING

CHAPTER I

COSTUMES, COLOUR, AND PRODUCTIONS

THE age-old story of this still mysterious world contains no pages more fascinating than those which reveal how men and women have clothed themselves, with what devices they have decorated their limbs, in what gay colours they have arrayed their bodies, and into what fantastic shapes they have twisted and twirled the forms their Creator gave them.

Ever since the day when Eve made a girdle from the leaves of the nearest tree, Woman has sought to attract and delight her Adam with similar tricks, and if to-day she no longer is content with the simple beauties of Nature and must call in to her aid the developments of an artificial and mechanical age, her aim is, nevertheless, the same as that of her first parent.

To-day clothes have returned to their first precedent. In Eden it was Woman who was the adorned and decorated one. Her spell of supremacy over Man was short-lived. Adam imitated her leafy garment and outshone her speedily. Taking another leaf from Nature's book, he gazed with awakened eyes on the animals and birds, and discovered that to the males were given the brightest colours, the gayest shapes, and the most impressive forms. Then for eighteen hundred years of the Christian Era Man was the more brilliantly costumed.

Woman, whilst she was but little behind in the race for sartorial supremacy, never outran her partner and won that race until the last of the Hanoverian Georges dazzled Europe with the massiveness of an intellect that could devise an eight-inch shoe buckle.

Prince Florizel also made fashionable the black suit—and men have mourned ever since—though whether for the suit or for the character of its inventor we leave the historians to decide.

Woman now heads the bill. Her shape alternately swells and slims, lengthens and diminishes, according as her fancy takes her—and Man in his sober duns, greys, and blacks, looks on admiringly. Perhaps the wheel will turn again. There are signs, in the cautious revival of colour and shape, that modern man is tired of being the uninteresting foil to woman, and we may yet see him again arrayed in all the glory of the rainbow.

Adown the procession of the ages flit many famous people. The history of costume conjures up for us the figures of great men and women. Indeed, it is impossible to separate the two. Who can think of Cardinal Wolsey without his bright red cape and biretta? Who remembers Queen Elizabeth without her great lace ruff? Verily, the clothes have become the symbols of the people; and the lesser has usurped the place of the greater. What is Wellington but a pair of boots, or Gladstone but a travelling bag? Raleigh with his cloak, Henry VIII with his falsely broad shoulders, King Charles with his feathered hat, Lord Byron with his open collar, James the First in his padded plus fours—we cannot recall the men without their clothes. The clothes *are* the men. They stamp their personalities upon us.

Then are not clothes a fascinating part of history and of life? Will not their study well repay us in forming a prelude to our understanding of human nature, without which knowledge it is impossible to advance far in the battle of life? Let us then to business.

As clear-cut a description of the different periods as is possible with such a complex and pliable subject as costume will be given. In order to make reference quick and easy, the dress of each reign or period will be summarized in tabular form in each chapter preceded by fuller descriptions and illustrations. It will thus be possible, once the descriptive matter has been mastered, for the reader to turn to the summary and immediately to grasp what is wanted without having to re-read the whole chapter, as is the custom with most costume books. Indeed, writers on this subject are notoriously vague, and it is by  no means easy to select the dress of a special epoch readily from current works. Writers have great reluctance to date the costumes sufficiently precisely. This springs partly from the undoubted fact that dress changes so imperceptibly and gradually—being advanced in the larger centres of population, and old-fashioned in the

WOMAN OF THE PERIOD OF ELIZABETH

country places—that it is never safe to dogmatize too severely as to what was or was not worn at any given date.

Nevertheless, the artist or actor is not expected to be an antiquary. He is expected to adopt a costume that is correct. I will give the normal type of dress of its date, without the "buts" and "ifs" of the archaeologist. The risk of dogmatizing must, therefore, be incurred in the interests of practicality. This risk is really slight when it is borne in mind that the purpose of the costume is to please those who see it, who are never so critical as the members of a learned society. People to-day, with the spread of education, know broadly what costumes are "right," and they naturally resent the production of a period play or the painting of a period picture that is not in the main correctly costumed. Bearing these points in mind, all that is necessary will be given.

We must remember that what the medieval mind loved above all things was colour. The people of the Middle Ages had a sound artistic sense that seems to have sprung naturally from

them. It was partly due, no doubt, to the fact that they were a race of craftsmen. The coming of the machine struck a deadly blow at craftsmanship, and men turned to the machine-made article which resulted in the machine-made mind. Luckily, there is to-day a revolt from the mastery of the machine and the domination of the trade designer. This is all to the good. We are returning to our earlier good taste, and the dressing of any play should be prepared on an ordered scheme of colour.

Have as much colour as you can by all means, but avoid harsh and clashing effects. The cast of a play may indeed be dressed in clashing colours, provided that they do not appear together on the stage. Lovely effects can be obtained by blending the minor characters in different shades of the same colour, whilst making the leading characters outstanding with vivid contrasts. Nothing looks better than to have retainers dressed alike, whilst medieval crowds may be as bright and variegated as possible, and little attention need be paid to avoiding clashing, if a goodly proportion of browns and greys are included for the menfolk. The right use of black as a foil and an accentuator should be recollected.

MAN OF THE PERIOD OF CHARLES I

In crowd work the producer should mark the places where he desires his supers to stand having regard to their dress colours. For this he must have full knowledge of the colours of the dresses that will be provided. He can then allot them in mind from the start, and it will be easy at each rehearsal to get the characters into the places they take for the actual performances.

CHAPTER II

THE GREEKS, 550 B.C.–322 B.C.

DURING the 2,500 years of Greece's power costume varied, and in the earlier period was so scanty as to be useless for stage purposes. The Greeks knew the advantage of sun and air reaching the skin, and their clothes were designed so as to allow for this, and also to give great freedom for athletic exercises—two points that we should do well to imitate to-day. The great Greek dramas of the classical period range from 550 B.C. to 322 B.C. It is this period which will be wanted for theatrical purposes and which is here described.

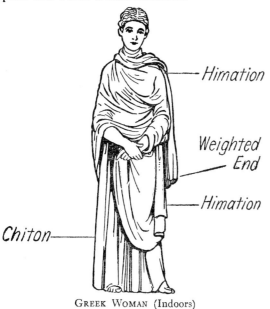

GREEK WOMAN (Indoors)

DRESS

The *Doric Chiton* (men and women) was a tunic made from a rectangle one foot longer than the wearer's height and of width twice the distance from finger tip to finger tip with arms outstretched. It was made of wool, and the favourite colours were purple, red, saffron, and blue. To adjust it, the extra foot in length was first folded over, then the long rectangle was folded in half and draped round the body with the fold on the left side. Back and front were caught together with pins at the shoulders, and it was girdled at the waist with a slight overhang there. Thus two loopholes were left at either side for the arms to pass through. The length was shortened by pulling it over the girdle to form a blouse called the Kolpos. The arms were left bare. The loose ends at the right side were not fastened together, but were left free for exercise; for theatre purposes these should be stitched together. The overfold may be embroidered with Greek Key and other designs and the loose end (on the left side) should be weighted with beads. This end should fall slightly lower than the overfold edge on the left side.

SLEEVE OF IONIC TUNIC

The *Ionic Chiton* (men and women) was a similar tunic without the overfold at the top, but made of linen or cotton, and larger and fuller, showing more folds. It was also distinguished by having sleeves made by holding the back and front of the chiton together at intervals with small pins at the arm openings. An overfold was sometimes, but rarely, added.

Skirts must not be worn under these tunics, as the limbs must show in outline, and the draping should be done with the greatest care. It was one of the chief duties of the slaves to adjust these beautifully.

The *Super Tunic* (men and women) reached to the waist and was worn for extra clothing. Generally speaking, the tunics of the men were shorter than those of the women.

The *Pallium* (men) was a large cloak worn by philosophers, who also wore the *Tribon*, a rough cloak of black or brown.

The *Peplum* (men and women) was about 4 yds. long by 2 yds. wide, and was passed twice round the body under the arms. It was then brought up over the shoulders, and secured by closely winding it about the body, or it was pulled over the head. The latter was the case when mourning.

Girdles (women) went across the shoulders and

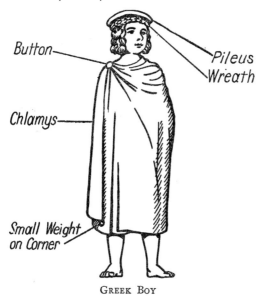

Button
Pileus
Wreath
Chlamys
Small Weight on Corner

GREEK BOY

breasts diagonally with the Ionic tunic, and round the hips several times. Later, they went round the body, higher than the waist and just below the breasts.

The *Himation* (men and women) was a large rectangle of white wool, draped over the left arm and shoulder, across the back, and under or over the right shoulder. Its weighted end was thrown over the left shoulder or the left forearm.

The *Chlamys* (men) was a small mantle for travelling, riding, and war, fastened by a fibula (pin-brooch) on the right shoulder, or in front. It was made of wool. It covered the left arm, leaving the right arm bare, and was often weighted at all four corners. It was extensively worn by youths. A good size is 5 ft. by 3 ft.

The *Diplois* (women) or doubled mantle was folded at a third of its width and caught up on the right shoulder with a brooch at some distance from the ends, which fell in zig-zag folds. It was wound tightly round the body under the left shoulder.

The *Peplos* (women) was a veil of woollen stuff that could envelop the whole figure if thrown over the head. It was a shawl with an overfold at the top, and was worn, with a girdle, beneath the left arm and fastened with tapes on the right shoulder so that the overfold covers the body to the waist. It was similar to the Doric Chiton.

The *Strophion* (women) was a kind of corset with three bands—one round the hips, one at the waist line, and one under the bust.

LENGTH OF TUNICS

Women wore their tunics to floor level and even below and had to walk with a pushing stride. Old men wore them to their feet, but younger men wore them shorter. The borders of the tunics and the corners of the cloaks were decorated, whilst spots, stars, and birds were often embroidered all over the fabric.

FEET

MEN. Sandals with leather, matting or felt soles, had a broad strap across the foot and a thong between the toes. Boots were high to the middle of the calf, laced up the front, and turned over at the top for the richer folk. Soft ornamented leather shoes were worn till about 480 B.C. Gilded sandals were worn by high ranks.

WOMEN. Sandals were also worn by the women, and had thick leather soles, ankle straps, and an ornamented piece on the instep. Coloured leather shoes, laced on the instep, were also used.

Peplos

Overfold of Peplos

Peplos

HAIR

MEN. The hair was short and curly and curling tongs were used if required, a finish being given by the use of a fillet round the head across the brow. Short beards were the mark of the older men.

WOMEN. The women's hair was waved and curled, and dressed in a knot of

GREEK GIRL

plaits or curls high above the nape of the neck and projecting well beyond it. It was *always* parted in the middle. Sometimes the hair was placed on a metal frame attached by bands over the head. White (not gold) bands round the hair are allowable, and girls may wear a wreath of flowers.

HATS
MEN

The *Petasus* (men) was a wide felt hat with a low round crown and ear flaps, to which tying strings were fastened. When not in use, it was borne on the shoulders at the back by the strings. It was only worn when travelling, and was similar to the medieval pilgrims' or palmers' hats made familiar by the opera *Tannhäuser*. The *Pileus* (men) was a tight-fitting cone-shaped hat.

HATS
WOMEN

The *Himation* (women) served the purpose of a hat when thrown over the head on the rare occasions when women travelled, a fold being carried from the body over the head. The women also wore dazzling veils of white cotton or other (then) expensive material. Actual hats are rare and can be ignored.

Tholia (sun hats) were worn when needed and were circular, with a small high crown as in the illustration.

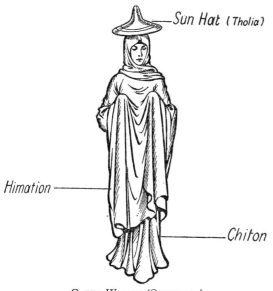

GREEK WOMAN (OUTDOORS)

JEWELLERY

The women wore a great profusion of jewels—

combs, pins, hair nets, and brooches, which were ornamented with gold mounts; bracelets of gold or silver; necklaces of beaded fringe on plain bands, armlets, anklets, etc. The Gold Room of the British Museum furnishes many excellent examples of this fine work. The men wore rings and sometimes carried walking sticks.

PEASANTS

The *Tunic* was short and plain with few folds (being scanty) and with short sleeves.

The *Cloak* was a rough oblong for travelling and wet weather.

The *Hood* had a short point, giving a "Gnome" effect, and was made from thick brown felt or cloth. Artisans and crowds can be bareheaded.

The *Carbatina* were of soft leather, put under the foot, but 2 in. wider all round so that the surrounding portions could be drawn up and over the foot by lacing to cover the toes and heel.

Puttees were linen straps swathed round the legs like modern puttees, but without the modern thin and regular strip.

GREEK ARTISAN

SLAVES

Slaves may be richly dressed, if their owners please, and should have closely cropped hair.

Courtesans carried hand mirrors. The Greeks used flame coloured wedding veils, held on by gold fillets in the key design, with a golden girdle, but no wedding ring was worn.

For *Dances*, garlands and wreaths were used, and the colour for funerals was white. In the military dances the men still wore the cuirass, crested helmet, and leg-greaves, made of gold, brass, steel, or tin. Skins of animals, sometimes gilded, were stretched over the cuirass and helmet. The armour should be worn over a short tunic, the greaves over the bare skin. The feet were either bare or sandalled. This armour was definitely old fashioned and retained for ceremonial dancing only. Every Greek was most wisely compelled to dance until he was thirty years old, this being another instance of the sound rules of physical culture then current. In war, bows and

THE PETASUS   PEASANT'S HOOD

arrows were used with spears, and swords were worn under the left armpit. Further light on the costume of the period may be gained at the British Museum—especially from the Elgin Marbles.

SUMMARY

MEN

Dress

Doric Chiton or Tunic.
Ionic Chiton or Tunic.
Super Tunic. Pallium—a large cloak. Peplum—an outer wrap. Tribon—Black or Brown Cloak.
Belt of leather.
Himation—an outdoor cloak.
Chlamys—a short cloak.

Legs

Bare.

Feet

Sandals. High-laced boots, soft leather shoes.

Hair

Curly and short. Fillet on head. Short beards.

Hats

Petasus of wide felt with cords.
Pileus—a tight round cap.

Jewels

Finger rings. Walking sticks. No armlets or anklets.

WOMEN

Dress

Doric Chiton or Tunic with overfold.
Ionic Chiton or Tunic without overfold, sleeved.
Super Tunic.
Peplum—an outer wrap.
Girdle.
Himation—an outdoor cloak.
Diplois—a doubled mantle.
Peplos—a shawl-veil, full length.
Strophion—a corset.

Feet

Sandals. Coloured leather laced shoes.

Hair

Waved or curled. Middle parting. White bands round. Knot at back.
Flower wreaths for girls.

Hats

Fold of the Himation.
White veil.
Hats very rare.
Tholia—sun hat.

Jewels

Gold and silver mounted bracelets, necklaces, pins, brooches.

PEASANTS

Dress

Chiton or Tunic, very plain.
Simple cloak.

Legs

Linen puttees.

Feet

Carbatina of soft leather.

Hair

Rough and short.

Hats

Hood of soft leather.

CHAPTER III

THE ROMANS, 509 B.C.–A.D. 324

THE Romans set great store on physical perfection in order to produce as perfect a race as possible for the good of the State, which was pre-eminent in the minds of the nation. Their dress, consequently, was loose and free, and whilst they were rather more fully clad than the Greeks, there was plenty of space allowed for sun and wind to reach the skin. Sports were often indulged in whilst the athletes were naked, and this also applied to the races and other games played during the great annual festival of the Saturnalia. The Romans, as the conquerors of the then known world, had great dignity and sense of power, and this was reflected in the lines of their dresses, which were flowing, dignified, and of full length. They had elaborate sumptuary rules—as to what colour and decoration might be worn by particular classes of people. The classes were clearly marked, being divided into the court circle of Patricians (the Nobles), the Government Officials, such as Senators, Magistrates, and Priests, and the Common People. In addition there were the military, by whom the people set much store, and the gladiators, who were the public entertainers, and who, though they might be popular, were an unfortunate class, being doomed to early decease.

The Roman Republic began in 509 B.C. and became an Empire in 31 B.C. It collapsed in A.D. 324 when Constantine the Great transferred his capital to Byzantium, which he renamed Constantinople, and the Sack of Rome put the finishing touch to this epoch. Cicero and Caesar flourished from 106 B.C. to 44 B.C. and it is this time that will be mostly in demand for stage purposes.

DRESS

The principal dress for men was the Tunic and the Toga; for women it was the Stola.

The *Tunic* (men). The Tunic can be seen to-day, scarcely altered from Roman days, in the Dalmatic worn by the deacon at High Mass. It was of wool, in its natural yellowish shade, but later sumptuary laws allowed colour. Its length was a matter of taste, but those who wore it to the feet with sleeves to the wrist were thought effeminate. Two pieces of material were sewn together at the sides and top to form a shirt with short sleeves. Normally it reached to the calf, or half way down the thigh. It was drawn up under a girdle, at option. The *Tunica Palmata*

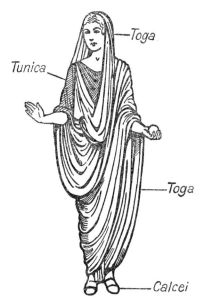

ROMAN LADY

worn by Generals at triumphs was covered by palms embroidered in gold. The *Tunica Laticlavia*, worn by Consuls, Senators, and Priests, had two broad bands (Clavi) of purple, which encircled the neck opening and ran down to the hem in front centre. Similar narrow bands from shoulder to hem, back and front, were allotted to the knights. No girdle was worn with the banded tunic.

The *Toga* (men) worn out of doors over the tunic, was a large cumbersome white woollen cloak. About eighteen feet by seven, it was semicircular in shape to enable its two ends just to clear the floor back and front. To wear, place the straight edge, at about a third of its length, on the left shoulder, letting the shorter end fall on the ground in front. Carry the rest of the straight edge across the back and under the right arm. Take the remainder (in front of the body), not at its edge, but about a third of the way down its depth, and let this upper part fall over the front. Gather the bulk now in front and carry it over the left shoulder. The fallen over straight edge now forms a kind of pocket (*sinus*) or loop which

ROMAN PRIESTESS   EMPEROR HADRIAN

can be tightened by pulling up the left shoulder piece. In this was kept the handkerchief, etc. Later the toga was made of silk. It was never used when mourning.

Under the Empire (31 B.C.–A.D. 476) togas were of scarlet, purple, and violet, but by law white was the correct hue.

The *Toga Praetexata*, worn by magistrates, priests, and censors, was bordered with purple. Freeborn boys under 14 years of age, girls till marriage, and the later Emperors wore this. The *Toga Picta* worn by generals was of purple cloth embroidered with gold stars, and was worn on state occasions also by Emperors and Consuls. The *Toga Candida* worn by candidates for public office was made pure white by chalking and as

much of the body as possible was exposed. The common toga, called *Toga Virilis*, as worn by all men, was of white wool. Children wore togas.

The *Lacerna* (men and women) was an outer mantle worn over the toga. At first it was brown or black and used only by the poor and soldiers. Later it was generally adopted and when red was called a Birrhus. It was short, sleeveless, open at the sides, and could have a hood called a Cucullus. It was fastened by a brooch on the right shoulder.

The *Paenula* (men and women) was a thick woollen travelling cloak, large and circular, with only a neck opening. It was like a full chasuble worn at Mass and was the origin of this vestment. Occasionally left open down the front, it was lifted over the arms each side. (Illustrated on page 120.)

The *Stola* (women) was an Ionic Chiton, i.e. a long tunic fastened along the upper arm by costly brooches to form sleeves. Long and loose, it was essentially an aristocratic garment. It differed from the Greek tunic in having a wide flounce (*instita*) at the bottom and was pulled up under the girdle at the hips. Three loops on each arm are enough. It need not have sleeves. It can be any colour and embroidered, the fabric being wool, silk, or linen.

The *Zona* (women) was a girdle wound round the body under the breasts and at the waist and hips, with long knotted ends hanging to the ground in front.

The *Palla* (women) was a shawl wrap worn over the Stola. It was a rectangle or square of wool worn across the back and over both arms.

The *Pallium* (women) was a cloth cloak with woven intertwining floral designs, bordered with fringe. Like the Palla, it could be placed over the head and was shawl-like.

The *Toga* (women) was worn only in early times by women; later it became the badge of freed slaves and prostitutes, so no respectable matrons would use it.

LEGS

The men's legs were bare and the women's legs did not show!

FEET

Sandals (men and women) of open leather work were worn in the house. A strap was passed between the big toe and the rest. There were about four fairly broad straps—loops on one side and ends on the other—tied at the top, and the "lacing" could be covered with a patterned leather or metal "tongue." In addition to these horizontal straps, there were two upright ones at the heel.

Soleae were slippers of leather or matting with straps, worn only in the house.

Calcei were street shoes covering the upper foot and laced or strapped with thongs fastened to the back and tied round the ankle. A second pair of straps, fixed to each side of the sole, was tied on the instep. Senators' shoes were cut higher and patricians' and magistrates' shoes were of the richest leather, ornamented with gold and silver.

The *Pero* was a boot of rough leather or untanned hide, worn in early times by senators. From 157 B.C. senators, however, wore high black boots with a silver or ivory "C" or crescent-shaped ornament above the heel behind the ankle.

Caligae were stout shoes with spiked soles for soldiers.

The colours yellow, white, and green were forbidden in men's shoes.

The *Phaecassium* (women) was a white leather boot covering the whole foot, tied with coloured silk straps. It was also worn by effeminate men.

HAIR

MEN. Hair was worn longer earlier; in the bulk of the period men's hair was short, curly or waved, and a short curled beard was common. The emperors, except Marcus Aurelius, were nearly all clean shaven. Priests wore a band of ribbon.

WOMAN. Hair was curled, waved, and false hair was dressed in broad plaits, whilst a band of ribbon was bound round maidens' heads, and the staid and respectable adult women, including priestesses.

The *Caul* (women) was a gold wire hair net, pearled, jewelled, and even embroidered—a fashion continually cropping up through the centuries.

HATS

Men mostly went bareheaded; the back of the toga could be drawn over the head.

The *Causia* was the same as the Greek

Petasus—a broad-brimmed, low-crowned hat with ear flaps, like a Pilgrim's hat of the Middle Ages. It was used when travelling by the upper classes.

The *Pileus* was a tightly fitting cone-shaped hat worn by the commoners and freed slaves, specially at the Saturnalia.

Laurel Wreaths (men) were awarded to the military for their triumphs, and Julius Caesar had special licence always to wear one.

Gold Coronets, high in the front, narrowing at the sides and back, were worn by emperors and kings.

Women wore diadems (*stephane*) set with

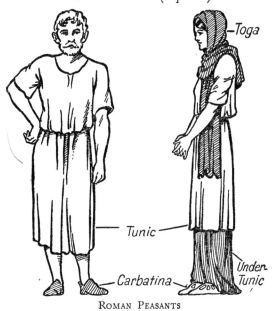

ROMAN PEASANTS

diamonds, sapphires, emeralds, opals, and garnets, and the younger ones used floral wreaths. The shawl garments were used as head coverings, but hats as such did not exist.

JEWELS

MEN. A signet ring was a man's sole jewel and intaglio rings were used as seals.

The *Bulla* (boys) was a golden ball hung on the necks of boys up to 14 years old, sometimes heart shaped and containing charms.

WOMEN. Great profusion of elaborate jewellery was worn by women—necklaces, bracelets, pins, nets, fillets, diadems, and long ear-rings set with stones. Twisted gold wire rings and armlets.

Serpent bracelets. Large-headed pins for the hair. The umbrella and fan may here be mentioned as carried by fashionable women.

PEASANTS

Peasants wore a plain tunic, and the *Toga Sordida* or *Pulla*, which was of black or brown with a *Hood* and *Cape* like those of the Greeks or the Medieval Englishman.

Carbatina were similar to the Grecian style, being of soft leather 2 in. wider than the foot, drawn up over it by lacing to cover heel and toe.

Reference to the British Museum will provide a flood of light on the costume, ornaments, and living habits of the Romans, who, like the Greeks, attached much importance to the value of physical development.

SUMMARY
MEN
Dress

Tunic—a woollen shirt.
Toga—a woollen cloak of many types for outdoors.
Lacerna—a dark outer mantle and optional hood.
Paenula—a travelling cloak.

Legs

Bare.

Feet

Sandals.
Soleae—house slippers.
Calcei—street shoes.
Pero—Patricians' shoes.
Caligae—Soldiers' spiked shoes.

Hair

Short curled hair and beard. Longer earlier. Emperors mostly clean shaven.

Hats

None generally.
Causia or Petasus—a broad-brimmed travel hat.
Pileus—cone shaped.
Back of the Toga.

Hats—contd.

Laurel wreaths for triumphs and Caesar.
Gold coronet for Emperors.

Jewels

Signet ring only. Intaglio rings as seals.
Bulla—gold pendant for boys.

WOMEN
Dress

Stola—a long tunic, with wide flounce, with or without sleeves.
Zona or Fascia—a girdle.
Palla—a shawl.
Pallium—a flowered cloak.
Toga—a cloak, in early times only.
Paenula—a travelling cloak.
Lacerna—a dark outer mantle.

Feet

Sandals.
Phaecassium—of white leather.
Shoes and slippers like men's, only finer.

Hair

Curled, waved, false, broad plaits.
Caul—a gold hair net.
Veil.

Hats

Diadems and wreaths.

Jewels

Rings, necklaces, bracelets, ear-rings, diadems, pins, nets, fillets. The umbrella and fan.

PEASANTS
Dress

Toga Sordida or Toga Pulla—brown or black cloak tunic.

Hat

Hood and Cape (see Greeks).

Feet

Carbatina (see Greeks).

CHAPTER IV

THE SAXONS, 460–1066

THE Saxons existed, for my purpose, from about A.D. 460 to A.D. 1066, and one immediately conjures up visions of the Bayeux Tapestry. Yet the Saxons and Normans were by no means as awkward as they look in that piece of needlework, and their reputation for angularity must be laid at the door of Queen Matilda and her ladies who made this embroidery. The Saxons were perpetually harried by invaders —Danes, Scots, Northmen, Normans—and it is a wonder they had time to devote to the niceties of dress at all.

The distinctive feature of Saxon clothes is the wrinkling of sleeves and legs. Both were made longer than the limbs they covered, so that the surplus could be pulled up. In this way more warmth was obtained as the material was, in effect, doubled by its folds.

Clothes were made from silk, linen, and wool, often fur lined and embroidered in gold. Colourings were simple, and tended to favour browns. Clothes were thick, and a somewhat stocky appearance was given to the figure owing to their volume. The shape of the body was not revealed as in later times.

Sir Walter Scott was a careful writer, and he has a brilliant passage descriptive of the costume of this period. The Anglo-Saxon aristocrat had "long yellow hair, equally divided on the top of his head and upon his brow, and combed down on each side to the length of his shoulders. His dress was a tunic of forest green, trimmed at the throat and cuffs with what was called minever, a kind of fur, inferior to ermine, and formed, it is believed, of the skins of the grey squirrel. This doublet hung unbuttoned over a close dress of scarlet, which was set tight to his body; he had breeches of the same, but they did not reach below the lower part of his thigh, leaving the knee exposed. His feet had sandals of the same fashion as the peasants, but of finer materials and secured in the front with gold clasps. He had bracelets of gold upon his arms, and a broad collar of the same precious metal about his neck . . .

Behind his seat was hung a scarlet cloth cloak, lined with fur, and a cap of the same material richly embroidered, which completed the dress of the opulent landowner when he chose to go forth."

From the word "Gunna" comes our modern "Gown." Sir Walter Scott has an equally in-

SAXON LADY

teresting passage about the Anglo-Saxon noblewoman.

"Her locks," he says, "were braided with gems, and being worn at full length intimated the noble and free born condition of the maiden." (Here I think Scott describes the hair of the younger women only, for, as I have written above, women's hair was nearly always carefully concealed under the head-rail.) "A golden chain, to which was attached a small reliquary, hung round her neck.

"She wore a bracelet on her arms, which were bare. Her dress was an under gown and kirtle of pale sea green silk, over which hung a loose robe, which reached to the ground, having very wide sleeves, which came down, however,

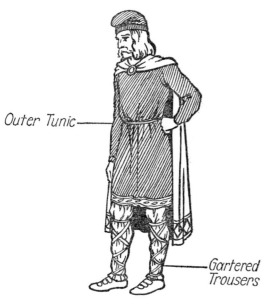

Outer Tunic——

——Gartered Trousers

SAXON NOBLE

very little below the elbow. This robe was crimson, and manufactured out of the finest wool. A veil of silk, interwoven with gold, was attached to the upper part of it, which could be, at the wearer's pleasure, either drawn over the face or bosom, after the Spanish fashion, or disposed as a sort of drapery round the shoulders."

Considering that Sir Walter Scott wrote over a century ago, when antiquarian questions received scant attention (apart from Classical ruins) it is surprising how accurate his description of Saxon costume is, and *Ivanhoe* throws quite a vivid light on the manners and customs of this period. Scott was, of course, the pioneer of the modern love for the antique and the respect for the work of our ancestors in Britain.

The moustaches of the men were grown as long as Nature allowed, and it was the absence of this feature that led King Harold's spies to assume that the clean shaven army of William the Conqueror were not soldiers but merely Monks. The Conqueror took a dislike to these over prolific hirsute adornments, and ordered the Saxons (or at any rate those about him) to be clean shaven.

DRESS

The *Under Tunic* (men) was of knee length and made of linen. The *Outer Tunic* (men) was of knee length, but had long sleeves that were wrinkled up over the arm, which they exceeded in length. It was slit at the sides from the hips downwards, to allow freedom.

The *Mantle* (men) was cut something like a chasuble—elliptical or circular, and was fastened on the right shoulder by a brooch or pin, or gathered through a ring. It was short and circular or long and straight.

The *Kirtle* (women) was an inner tunic with the same long sleeves, whilst the *Gunna* (women) was an outer tunic like the men's but had short sleeves. Its skirt was tucked into a belt on the right side.

It will be noted that the men's long sleeves alone were visible, whilst the women's short sleeves on the outer tunic showed and the longer sleeves of the kirtle also appeared from the elbow downwards. Thus the women revealed two sleeves, whilst the men showed only one.

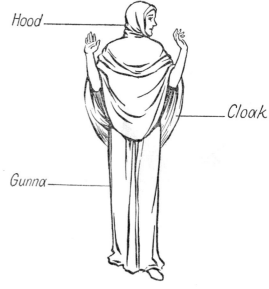

Hood——

——Cloak

Gunna——

SAXON PEASANT

There was not much difference in the cut of the tunics of the two sexes, but the women's were slightly longer. A *Girdle* or *Belt* encircled the waist.

LEGS

Trousers (men) were long and loose, rather full, and wrinkled in much the same way as the sleeves, but on a lesser scale. They were cross gartered to the knee and the trousers reached to mid thigh, from the foot. Cloth stockings with leather gaiters were, alternatively, worn.

FEET

Shoes (men) were low leather ones, with a fastening at the side or in front. Socks or stockings of cloth were worn. Commoners wore black, nobles coloured and embroidered, shoes.

Shoes (women) were tied or buckled at the ankles.

Leather Boots also worn.

HAIR

Hair (men) included a full beard with two-forked ends. The hair was long and unconfined, parted from crown to forehead, and curled in ringlets. A big moustache was included, and the whole presented a vivid contrast to the closely cropped Normans when they came over.

Hair (women) was loose or braided, whilst fillets of material were worn by the better classes,

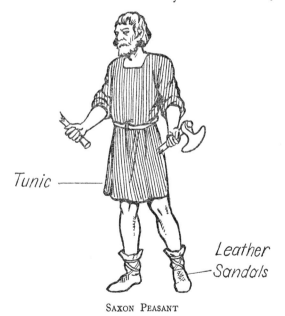

SAXON PEASANT

but often the hair was hidden under the head-rail (head covering). It was also worn in two plaits

hanging down on either side of the front of the body.

HATS

Caps (men) were made of skins or cloth and were small and pointed, not unlike a cap of liberty or a Greek cap.

The *Head-rail* (women), later to be called a

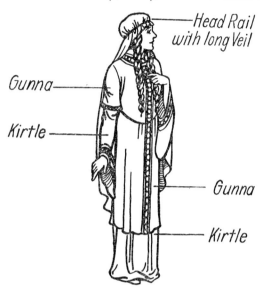

SAXON LADY

Wimple, was a large white linen or coloured square, about 2½ by ¾ yd. in size, which was drawn over the head from the left to the right shoulder, under the chin, and then around the back of the neck to the right shoulder. Over this was worn a circlet of gold, which was narrow. The same thing for an unmarried girl was called a *Snood*. It completely hid all hair from view, save where the long hanging plaits were worn.

JEWELS

Besides the golden circlet mentioned, the women wore large circular ear-rings, necklaces, rings, bracelets of the precious metals, and they were skilful embroideresses, working in threads, which harmonized with the coloured material of the kirtle or tunica. It was the desire to show this embroidery and colour to their best advantage that led to the custom of tucking up a corner of the gunna into the belt. The furs worn included sable, beaver, cat, fox, and lamb.

PEASANTS

The Saxon peasant wore clothes of the simplest cut possible, in view of the fact that his wife had to make them in her spare time. A sleeved, close jacket of skin reached from the throat to the knees, with a narrow neck opening just sufficient to admit the passage of the head without leaving too wide a gap to admit cold and wet. His sandals were bound with leathern thongs and a roll of leather was twisted round the legs to the calf, leaving the knees bare. This bandaging and cross gartering

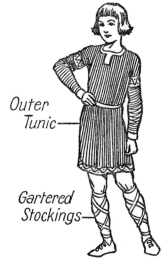

Outer
Tunic—

Gartered
Stockings—

SAXON YOUTH

of the legs, over stocking or trousers, is a distinctive feature of Saxon times.

GENERAL

The practice of making sleeves much too long and wrinkling them up was a practical one, for it gave additional warmth through the extra thickness, and in winter the hands could be withdrawn completely into the sleeve, which thus served the purpose of the modern glove.

The edges of the tunics can be embroidered in coloured thread or wool to form a border of decoration, and this border can be carried up around the slits that appeared at each side from the hip downward (for the men) to allow of freedom of movement, the tunic being rather closely fitting.

The Bayeux Tapestry is a good guide to the dresses, but some elementary knowledge of the clothes that were worn is necessary in order to distinguish the various garments from each other. Unfortunately, the Bayeux Tapestry is not easy to reproduce in illustration. The best illustrations of it are the enlarged coloured prints that may be seen in many museums in London and the country. The small photos of the Tapestry sold at the Victoria and Albert Museum will not serve the purpose of anyone making costumes in this style.

SUMMARY
MEN

Dress

> Under tunic.
> Outer tunic with long sleeves, slit at sides.
> Girdle.
> Mantle, circular or straight, fastened on shoulder.

Legs

> Trousers, long, loose, wrinkled, with cross garters, or cloth stockings with leather gaiters.

Feet

> Low leather shoes.
> Socks or stockings.

Hair

> Full bi-forked beard. Heavy moustache. Long, curled hair, mid parted.

Hats

> Skin or cloth "Liberty" caps.

WOMEN

Dress

> Kirtle—an inner tunic with long sleeves.
> Gunna—an outer tunic with short sleeves.
>   Skirt tucked into belt.
> Girdle.

Feet

> Shoes tied or buckled at ankles. Leather boots.

Jewels

Large round earrings, bracelets, rings, necklaces.

Hair

Loose or braided for youth and peasants.
Head-rail for the others, concealing hair.
Fillets of material.

Hats

Head-rail.
Circlets, mainly golden.

PEASANTS

Dress

Sleeved close tunic. Narrow neck opening.

Legs

Leather bandages, or cross gartering.

Feet

Leather sandals, thonged.

CHAPTER V

THE NORMANS, 1066–1154

OWING to the perpetual battles that William the Conqueror and his successors had to undertake in order to subdue a country that did not welcome the Normans,

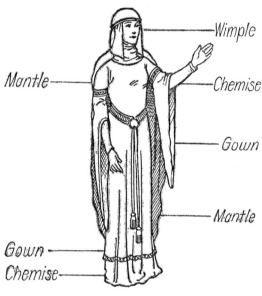

NORMAN LADY

there was little change in dress during the Norman period. Men's minds being upon war they were not inclined to waste time in designing costumes, and of what use was it for the ladies to think of something fresh when their lords were almost always on service?

The basis of the clothes was a shirt which was close fitting and reached to the ankles, but its simplicity was relieved by its having the edge banded and embroidered with gold, while the large hanging cloak added a decorative and spacious appearance to the costume. The cloak was fastened by a massive brooch, often of elaborate design, in precious metal or humbler substance. The type of design was similar to the well known (though earlier) Alfred jewel.

Clothes were lined and adorned with fur—

ermine, squirrel, marten, goat, and rabbit being favourites.

DRESS (William I)

The men seem to have taken over the ways of the women in the matter of the length of their tunic sleeves, for the outer tunic now has short sleeves, and the inner one, long sleeves. Both were knee length and embroidered.

The *Outer Tunic* (men) had short wide sleeves of elbow length, with embroidered edges. The *Inner Tunic* (men) was of white, with long wrinkled sleeves projecting over the hand if extended. This white tunic shows round the neck, where the wider opening of the outer tunic was V-shaped. This close neck hole was bordered with embroidery or it might be V-

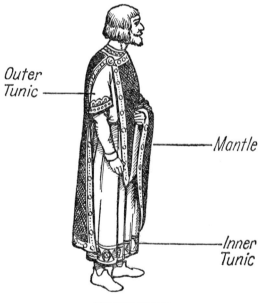

NORMAN NOBLE

shaped, about five inches deep. It was either belted or closely fitted the knees, and, if the latter, had slits at either side to allow free movement. The *Mantle* was a knee-length cape, rectangular or semi-circular, fastened on the right shoulder or in the front. It was like the Saxon mantle, except that it was slightly larger, and was kept together with a brooch. The women dressed like the Saxon women and the Norman men, in two tunics (the kirtle and the gunna), now called the chemise and the gown. The *Chemise* was of white linen, with a long skirt and long wrinkled sleeves.

The *Gown* had a loose elbow-length sleeve and a skirt of three-quarter length and often even longer.

DRESS (William II)

The men's tunic sleeves became so long that they were turned back over the wrists.

The women's tunics were laced up the back so as to make the front fit smoothly to the figure.

Cloaks (women) were lined with fur, and hung from the shoulders by straps across the bosom.

DRESS (1100–1150)

The *Bliaud* (women) was a long smock-like gown with a laced bodice of elastic fabric. The

NORMAN PEASANTS

skirt was full and straight, and was bound by a wide belt. *Girdles* were either a wide strip of cloth richly embroidered or a long silken rope wound round the waist, with tasselled ends, which

hung in front almost down to the hem of the gown. The pendulous cuff increased so much that the sleeve had to be knotted on itself to prevent it trailing on the ground. Clothes became longer.

LEGS

Chausses (men) were trousers of wool, tight to the ankle. The legs were wound to the knee with

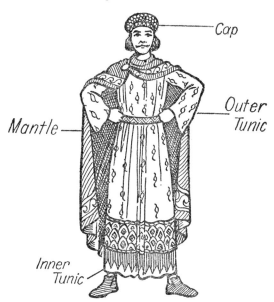

NORMAN NOBLE

strips of leather or cloth, which was sometimes banded at the knee and/or the ankle. Linen breeches, like pyjamas, were fastened with a running string at the hem.

There is much confusion in costume books between breeches and chausses. Breeches, no matter what their length, were always hung from the waist downwards, being fastened by a running string. They were close fitting, or loose, according to taste, and if loose were brought close to the leg by cross strapping from the knee to the ankle. The length varied from what were our modern "shorts" to ankle length. Shorts were loose enough to enable them to be caught up at the sides of the thighs and pinned to the upper waist line part.

Chausses were stockings and were drawn from the foot upwards, and this distinction between the two garments should make clear the different cut and use of the two. The hose gradually became longer and more closely fitting and were very wide at the thigh so that the breeches could be tucked into them. Old drawings show that these stockings were tied to the waist string of the breeches in front by a tape. Again, some drawings show that even when the "shorts" variety was adopted they could be gathered in at the knee to prevent draughts blowing upwards.

FEET

Shoes (men) were of black leather with narrow bands of embroidery along the top and down the instep. Red, yellow, blue, and green shoes were also used, and their tops rolled over to the ankle. In William II's day (1087-1100) the shoes became pointed, and were stuffed with wool at the point. In the reign of Stephen (1134-54) the tops of the shoes went much higher, and were rolled back so as to show the brilliant lining. Stockings, which became common about 1100, were made of say, which was a kind of worsted cloth.

HAIR

Hair (men) was, during the reign of William I, short, and clean shaven faces were *de rigueur*, but this custom only lasted a short time and the nation went back to the pre-Conquest customs of longer hair. By William II's time the hair and beard were worn quite long again.

Hair (women) was simply coiled at the back of the head, and in curls about the face. It was still hidden by the head-rail (now called a wimple). By Henry I's time (1100-35) the hair was no longer hidden, and long braids which were intertwined with coloured ribbons became fashionable. The ends might be bound with strips of silk instead, and about 1135 the wimple went out.

HATS

The *Hood* (men) was warm, and of cloth, but tight *Caps* of cloth were also worn. These were brimless or were peaked in the centre of the crown (the "Gnome" variety again).

The *Wimple* (women) was the Saxon head-rail. It was a square of material, generally white, which was wound round the head and throat. Some women preferred to expose the hair even in early Norman times, and this became normal in Henry I's time, when the wimple went out, about 1135.

Down to the end of the fourteenth century it was the common custom to be bareheaded—a healthy practice which has come again into fashion in our own times. Hoods were worn mainly when travelling and in inclement weather. The same applies to the wimple and it is not entirely necessary to provide headgear in order to be accurate. Hoods and wimples appear and reappear right down the centuries in varying forms and have lasted right down to the present day in academic and monastic dress. Conversely, it will be observed, as this treatise progresses, how in later centuries—the seventeenth and eighteenth— the reverse principle was adopted and instead of men and women going bareheaded out of doors, they actually wore their hats indoors as well as outside.

PEASANTS

For the peasants, canvas and fustian were popular. As in all ages, the peasants disregarded the extremes of fashion when they were exaggerated in cut. This is only to be expected; firstly, because they had not the money to spend on the latest fashions, and, secondly, because such exaggerations nearly always got in the way during work, and only the rich, who had little manual work to perform, could tolerate such clothes. This refers specially to the points appended to clothes and shoes, and to the extreme length of dresses.

Hats and caps were of felt. Trousers were loose.

GENERAL

Costume in Norman times was in the main quite simple for all classes. The rich imported fabrics, and adorned the native English woollens with needlework, pearls, and other precious stones, a fashion that followed the more advanced culture across the Channel. It should be borne in mind, however much we are inclined to resent the Norman invasion, that Norman culture and Norman learning were definitely in advance of the Saxon, and though the Conqueror's methods were stern, he and his descendants introduced many benefits in government and living.

In stage work this distinction between the cultured Norman and the less polished Saxon can be made with advantage.

The Crusades had a reflex effect in the introduction, by the returning warriors, of Eastern fabrics and decorations, and the lengthening of dresses, which became voluminous, like those of the East.

The Girdle comes into great prominence during the first half of the twelfth century, and may be said to be a distinguishing mark of this period. Mittens were in use. The wimple is sometimes known as the couvre-chef. The favourite colours of early Norman times were red, blue, and green.

With the advent of the long sleeves, which touched the ground, men found a way out of the difficulty of being unable to use their hands by making a slit in the sleeve at the place where the opening ought to be, that is, at the elbow, through which the arm was put, the rest of the sleeve hanging down. This interesting relic still remains in the academic gowns of masters in our universities.

When braids came into fashion, those women who were not well favoured by Nature did not shrink from using artificial plaits for the purpose.

Macbeth is sometimes costumed in early Norman style, though that usually adopted is a kind of legendary British and Saxon combined. Its main features are described in the chapter on the Saxons; but for the braided hair, and the long sweeping sleeves customary for Lady Macbeth and her womenfolk, the Norman dresses are sufficiently accurate. Indeed, there was at first little change between the Saxon and the Conqueror's fashions.

In fastening the ample cloaks to the shoulders large circular brooches or rings should be used. These give scope for fine decorative touches.

Deep borders of ornament on the tunics were embroidered, woven, or appliquéd at the neck, wrists, and hem, and sometimes there was also a band of decoration round the upper arm.

SUMMARY
MEN
Dress

Outer tunic with short sleeves.
Inner tunic with long sleeves.
Mantle, fastened on shoulder.
Belt.

Legs

Chausses—wool trousers.
Leather or cloth bandages.
Breeches—tight or loose, long or short.

Feet

Leather shoes, black or coloured and embroidered.
Later they have high rolled tops.

Hair

William I—clean shaven.
William II—long hair and beard.

Hats

Hood—gnome-like.
Cap—peaked in centre, brimless.

WOMEN
Dress

Chemise—long skirt and sleeves, white linen	} William I
Gown—elbow sleeves	
Cloaks—fur lined, straps on shoulders	} William II
Bliaud—a smock-gown, laced	
Girdles	} 1100–1150
Long knotted sleeves to gowns	

Feet

As men.

Hair

Coiled at back, curls in front—hidden by wimple (William I and II).
Long braids (1100–1150).

Hats

Wimple till 1135 round head and throat.

PEASANTS
Dress

Fustian or canvas.
Hats and caps of felt.
Loose trousers.

CHAPTER VI

THE PLANTAGENETS, 1154–1272

I NOW deal with the period from 1154 to 1272—the reigns of Kings Henry II, Richard I, John, and Henry III. The constant travels of Richard I in the Crusades familiarized his people

DOCTOR AND NURSE

with the gorgeous fabrics of the East, and great luxury resulted. They brought back with them the Dalmatica. Another factor was the wearing of steel armour that readily rusted in every shower. To obviate rust the Surcoat was invented to cover the armour. It is in this period that the Capuchon, or hood, first appears, and it lasts through many centuries in one form or another; indeed, for a long time it remained almost unchanged, and we may say that it has persisted to our own day in the clothes of the monks and friars.

Garments became more voluminous and were embroidered. A favourite pattern was that of circles overlapping each other, which appeared on garments and shoes; when on the latter the embroidery was in gold.

Many new materials appeared. Among these were Burnet, a brown cloth; Bysine, a fine cloth of cotton or flax for mantles; Ray, a striped Flemish cloth; and Damask, which took its name from the city of its origin—Damascus. It was the rich stuff that is known by that name even to-day. Peasants wore a coarse brown cloth called Burel, a thicker cloth called Byrrhus, sheepskin leather named Basil, and a rough cloth termed Brocella. It is curious that all these names begin with the same letter.

Under Henry III, when the Crusaders returned, the Eastern materials came into rapid vogue, and had many delightful names, such as Baudekin, Checklatoun, Ciclatoun, and Tissue. All these were silk woven with gold thread and many coloured. Sarcinet was a thinner silk. The Tennysonian "Samite" was a similar gold-woven silk, rather like Satin. Gauze was known. Gowns and mantles were brought over from Italy,

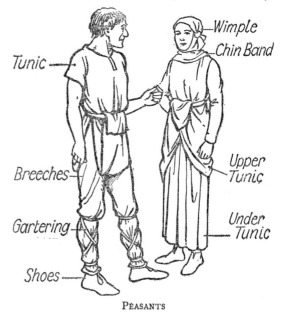

PEASANTS

and all were richly lined with fur, for the badly heated rooms of the period were cold and draughty.

The effect of all this sudden magnificence

tended to make the gayer folk try to wear everything at once, and this caused garments to become
both numerous and bulky; indeed the age is
known as the age of draperies. At the same time,
the cut was simple and dignified on the whole,
and did not attain to the fantastic shapes made
fashionable by the clever and artistic Richard of
Bordeaux.

DRESS (HENRY II AND RICHARD I)
MEN

The *Dalmatica* was shirt-like, being a loose-
sleeved, full-length tunic, worn over the *Under-
tunic*, which was of equal length, but had close-
fitting, tight sleeves.

The *Mantle* was worn over all, and was voluminous and made from fine Flemish cloths or
rich Italian silks.

DRESS (JOHN)
MEN

The *Surcoat*, which came into prominence first
in King John's reign, was a full-length garment,
sleeveless, and with wide arm-openings. It had

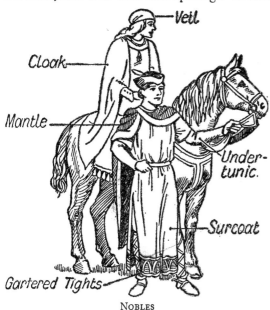

NOBLES

a slit from the bottom edge to the waist in front
to give freedom in walking and riding. (This slit
may be omitted.) Not yet are coats of arms em-
blazoned on the surcoat. It was belted in leather

3—(G.122)

with a buckle and a long tongue falling in front.
The whole was worn over

The *Long Tunic*, which reached to just below
the knees and had sleeves, either tight or loose.

The *Capa* was a large mantle with a hood that
could be drawn over the head when needed. It
was made of wool.

The *Balandrana* could be worn over all these,

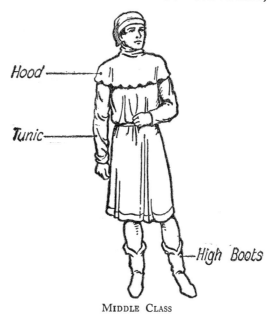

MIDDLE CLASS

and was simply a large cloak. It was worn, as
the hood was, when travelling.

DRESS (HENRY III)
MEN

The *Surcoat*, which first appeared in John's
reign, now became fashionable, and was as already
described under that reign. It was worn over

The *Tunic*, which was either tight-sleeved or
loose-sleeved, as in the previous reign, and was
of full length. The sleeves, if loose, should flow.

The *Cloak* was circular, fur-lined, and made of
silk. It should be capacious. The furs in vogue
were marten, beaver, badger, sable, and squirrel.

The *Capuchon* was a hood attached to a short
cape that covered the shoulders, fitting neatly over
the chest, arms, and back. Its bottom edge was
sometimes cut in semi-circles.

The short *Upper Tunic*, which is common to

all reigns, was worn more especially by older men and was Tabard-shaped; that is, it was slit right down each side, it fell straightly down back and front, and was gathered in by a belt, so that many folds appeared.

Dress (Women of all Reigns)

The *Gown* was loose, with sleeves cut close from the elbow to the wrist, at which appeared a row of small buttons. The sleeves should extend well below the wrists, so that wrinkles appear throughout their length.

The *Belt* was in silk or leather, with a good buckle and long tongue like those of the men.

The *Aumônière* came in during Henry III's time, and was a silk or cloth bag hung from the belt at the left side.

The *Mantle* was a long cloak simply cut, left open in front, and tied across the chest by cords, which were attached to the mantle by handsome metal clasps.

Legs

The *Men* wore breeches, but, owing to the length of the tunics, these did not show. Stockings appeared in the earlier reigns, and in Henry III's time close-fitting tights came in.

Feet

The *Men* wore shoes that were slightly pointed in the earlier reigns, but in Henry III's time these became much sharper, the point, of course, extending in front either from the big or the middle toe. Boots with folding tops lined with silk of contrasting colour, laced up the side, were worn.

The *Women's* shoes were similar, but the points were shorter. They should be of leather and well-fitting. Another version is a rather blunt toe, long enough to be bent back over the foot. They were fastened by one button above the ankle. High boots to the calf may be used. Both kinds were rolled over at the top.

Hair

The *Men* were generally clean shaven, though a few had short beards. The hair was curled, and occasionally a fillet was worn over the brow.

The *Women's* hair, though much hidden by the wimple, was more elaborate in treatment. It was parted in the middle, and the plaits were gathered into two bags, one each side of the face. These

were sometimes again covered by the *Couvre-Chef*, which was a veil. These bags could be richly jewelled or netted in an elaborate pattern.

Hats
Men

The *Men* wore tall crowned hats with brims which were turned up at the back and which ran forward to a point at the front. A long quill was stuck into the side. You will recognize from this description and that of the Capuchon that we have reached the age of Robin Hood of Sherwood Forest. *Conical caps* were also worn. They were of the sugar-loaf variety and were not too tall. The *coif* (really a peasant's cap) was worn by the better class when hunting, probably because as it was close fitting it did not catch the wind. Further, it could not be wrenched off when the hunters were passing under trees in the forest. The coif was white and fitted the head closely. It came down at the back and was tied under the chin with strings or it was without strings. The coif lasts well into Jacobean times as part of a judge's official dress.

Hats
Women

The *Wimple* and *Chin Band* (women) was in two pieces of white linen. One was bound round the forehead and secured by the other, which went under the chin. They were pinned together at the top. The former should be pinned at the back. This is a most becoming fashion, especially for older folk with double chins. It is seen to-day in most of the orders of nuns, though many of them have spoilt its beauty by unduly stiffening and starching the wimple and chin band.

Peasants

Peasants wore, as usual, the always serviceable tunic and hose, with a coif or hood. It was a neat and warm dress that did not get in the way when the peasants were at work. They also wore breeches, which were loose and full to the knee, and tied round the waist with a string. The hose were fastened to the breeches by similar strings tied to the waist.

For their feet the peasants wore what were oddly called *Startups* or *Peros*. We came across the Pero in the chapter on Roman dress, and it is the same thing in this reign. They were high shoes, laced in the front, and the soles were pegged with wooden pegs that were similar, in principle, to those used in modern football boots. Considering the normal state of the floor of the living rooms in this period a little elevation from it was quite desirable! The rushes covered many unpleasant things!

GLOVES

Gloves were of gauntlet type. The wealthy had the backs richly jewelled. This custom led in time to the back being embroidered instead of jewelled, though the bishops retained their jewelled gloves to comparatively recent times. The poor had to be content with woollen mittens.

During the Crusades, with so many men away from home, there was little incentive to the women to dress themselves radiantly, and their costumes changed but little; but with the return of the warriors things took on a brighter hue. Cut, colour, and fabric became more elaborate and more gay.

In Henry II's time tights were fastened with cross garterings, which ended in a tassel below the knee. Shoes were of coloured leather, not black, and had golden stripes or patterns upon them.

SUMMARY

MEN

Dress

Dalmatica — long sleeved Undertunic — tight sleeved Mantle—voluminous	Henry II and Richard I
Belted surcoat Very long tunic Capa—large hooded mantle Balandrana—wide cloak	John
Surcoat—leather belted Tunic—tight or loose sleeved Cloak—fur lined, circular Capuchon—hood and cape	Henry III
Short upper tunic, Tabard shape Gloves	All reigns

Legs

Breeches—did not show ⎫ Richard I
Stockings—hardly seen ⎬ and John
Tights—close fitting (Henry III).

Feet

Shoes slightly pointed (Richard I and John).
Shoes sharply pointed (Henry III).
Boots, side laced, silk lined.

Hair

Clean shaven. Short beards sometimes.
Hair curled, sometimes a fillet on brow.

Hats

Tall crowned, brim turned up at back and pointed at front.
Conical caps.
Coif when hunting.

WOMEN

Dress

Gown—loose with sleeves close from elbow to wrist and long row of buttons.
Belt—silk or leather.
Aumônière—a bag at the belt (Henry III).
Mantle—long cloak, open in front, cords across chest, fur lined.
Gloves—jewelled.

Feet

Shoes less pointed than men's. Well fitting in leather.
High boots.

Hair

Middle parting.
Two hair nets at sides over bags, jewelled sometimes.

Hats

Wimple and chin band.
Couvre-chef—a veil.

PEASANTS

Dress

Tunics and hose.
Coif or hood of felt.
Breeches.

Feet

Startups or Peros (*vide* Romans)—high shoes, front laced, with wooden pegged soles.

CHAPTER VII

THE THREE EDWARDS, 1272–1377

THERE were so many wars during the first Edward's reign that clothing took a secondary place in men's minds. After Edward II came to the throne, however, an age

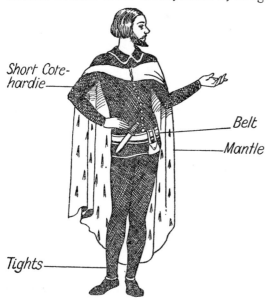

Short Cote-hardie

Belt

Mantle

Tights

MAN—EDWARD III

of great splendour in colour and material began. The art of blending colours made its initial attempts at a more elaborately hued scheme and stamped velvets were introduced, probably from the East. With these came rich brocades in conventional patterns, and shimmering satins which contrasted by reason of their soft and gleaming surfaces.

The old baggy and bulky clothes vanished before a costume which, because it approximated more closely to the shape of the body, became more beautiful, and afforded the tailors greater scope for originality in the cut.

In a revolutionary gesture, man revealed his legs in tights which, among the younger and smarter set, were parti-coloured, the materials being of silk in gay colours.

For colder weather a cloak would be worn, to

which was added a hood with its characteristic trailing strip called a liripipe. The same thin perpendicular effect was achieved by the strip-like tippets attached to the sleeves of the cote-hardie.

Unlike their husbands, the women remained conservative and adhered to the older fashions —surely an early and rare instance of women being behindhand in the modes. Apart from the fact that they shaped the upper part of their gowns to their figures, there is little of a distinctive nature to indicate, except that the male cote-hardie was adapted to the other sex.

The women had a revolution in the matter of their hair which, formerly hidden from sight, was now displayed to the public view.

The sumptuary laws were enacted in 1363

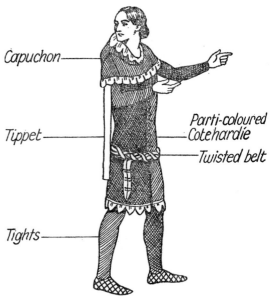

Capuchon

Parti-coloured Cotehardie

Twisted belt

Tippet

Tights

MAN, ABOUT 1350

and were a curious attempt to control personal extravagance. Their enforcement was not altogether a success. (Attention should be paid to them, as in stage work it helps to define the class position of the characters.) Briefly summarized, they allowed the following things to the classes stated.

Royal Family and Very Wealthy Nobles—Ermine and Lettice fur and pearls. (Pearls allowed to others on head-dresses.)

Knights and Rich Ladies—Cloth of gold and silver, jewellery-embroidered habits, linings of miniver and other expensive furs.

Squires and Less Rich Knights—Cloth of silver, silver adorned girdles. Best wool cloth.

Lesser folk—Woollens only; no silk or embroidery or jewellery of gold and silver ornaments.

It is amusing to find that the penalty for breach of these laws was the confiscation of the offending garments.

DRESS (EDWARD I)
MEN

The *Cotehardie* (men) was the new mode. It was a close-fitting garment like a coat. It reached to the knees and was fastened by a waist belt. Its front was slit and fastened with buttons and a row

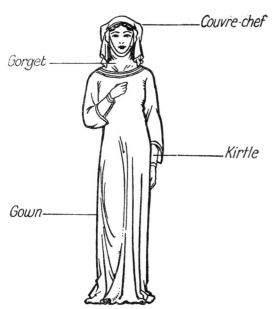

LADY DE COBHAM, 1320 (COBHAM)

of buttons fastened the sleeves from elbow to wrist. The sleeves were closely fitted to the arm and at the elbow a long hanging sleeve fell nearly to the ground. It could be bordered with fur.

The *Surcoat* (men) was the same as before, but heraldic designs appeared upon it in embroidered work.

Tights (men) were worn with the cotehardie, and the effect was quite different from the pre-

A LADY, 1350–60

vious reign, the men wearing a clean-cut sparse costume.

The *Mantle* (men and women) alone remained in generous width and length as of old.

DRESS (EDWARD I)
WOMEN

The *Kirtle* (women) closely fitted the body and was often laced, with tight sleeves buttoned from elbow to wrist. Over it was

The *Loose Gown* (women), of a different colour from the kirtle but with a lining that matched the kirtle. Its sleeves were quite long and loose, and there could be a train. It was confined by

The *Girdle*, which was slung from the hips. The over-gown was pulled through the girdle in front so as to show the kirtle. A two-colour effect was given by the combined frocks—one shade for kirtle, skirt front and sleeves, and gown lining, the other for the gown exterior.

DRESS (EDWARD II AND III)
MEN

The *Cotehardie* (men) was the same, but was parti-coloured vertically.

The *Belt* carried a pouch and dagger.

The *Cape* (men) was either long or short as

Wimple —   — Metal Band

— Cloak

SPANISH TURBAN, 1300 (LINCOLN)

taste dictated. It was edged and collared in fur, and buttoned at the neck.

DRESS (EDWARD II AND III)
WOMEN

The *Full Gown* (women) was the same as before, except that *Tippets* were worn from 1350 to 1380. These were long strips of cloth or fur fastened just above the elbow to the sleeves. Before these came in the sleeves were wide and long.

The *Kirtle* (women) was worn under the gown as before.

The *Cyclas* (women) was used in Edward II's reign only, and was a tight surcoat. It was shorter in front than behind, and had no sleeves.

LEGS

Tights (men), which were parti-coloured to match the cotehardie, gave great prominence to the legs. This bi-coloration was by way of either a single colour to each leg or the two shades were combined on each leg, vertically divided. The shades must alternate with those of the cotehardie, i.e. if the latter is red on the right and green on the left, then the tights must be green on the right and red on the left. It was a fashion that no doubt owed its inspiration to the growing popularity of heraldry. We have already noted that coats of arms began to adorn the surcoat in Edward I's reign.

These parti-coloured tights came in during the reigns of Edward II and Edward III only.

FEET

Dark leather shoes with longer points than before were worn by men and women, the latter's being less sharp. State shoes were embroidered all over. Black cloth boots, like hose, with a sole attached, had straps below the knee. They were also made of silk, leather or velvet, embroidered on the inner side with a band of stitching.

HAIR

The men's hair was long and bushy in Edward I's time. During Edward II's and III's reigns it was still bushy, but was cut round and curled. Faces were clean shaven, but old men wore a beard parted into two curling points.

The women's hair in Edward I's time was parted in the middle and bunched on either side of the face in a bag or net, and was dressed over the ears.

In the time of Edward II and Edward III girls wore two plaits and placed the gorget under them. The women of this date still wore the hair in side nets.

HATS (EDWARD I)

The *Beaver* (men) was a hat with a turned up brim and a tall crown with a somewhat ridiculous feather in front. It was placed on top of

— Liripipe to hood

EARLY CHAPERON

The *Hood* or *Capuchon* (men), which was the same as before, except that

The *Liripipe* (men) was now part of it. This was an exaggeration of the original peak to the hood, and attained a great length. A good general length is sufficient to drop on the shoulder, though it was often so long that it could be wound round the neck like a scarf.

The beaver hat was optional. If worn, it should be in conjunction with the hood.

The *Gorget* (women) is another name for the

chin band, which was a linen band drawn over the head, with another under the chin.

The *Wimple* (women) remained as before but was now worn by the older women. Also it was now dyed yellow.

Caps were endless in variety, a popular one being The *Spanish Turban* (women), in which the forehead band was widened and stiffened, not unlike the modern Russian tiara one sees in pictures of the massacred Russian Royal Family.

HATS (EDWARD III)

The men had the liripipe attached to the hood, as before, but it was longer. It was even longer than floor length, in which case it was knotted to clear the floor, or was wound round the head, with the end tucked in or draped about the shoulders. It was in this case a scarf attached to a hat.

The women wore gorget and wimple of fine lawn. Silk ribbon fillets bound round the brow were popular, as were also the side nets for the hair as before, the nets being made in gold work and jewelled.

PEASANTS

The peasants still remained much the same, but the Sumptuary Laws checked any originality in costume as far as they were concerned, and

SIDE NET CAP

no peasant wore fur. The materials for his dresses were mostly coarse-grained cloth, chiefly brown.

THE ORDER OF THE GARTER

As this distinguished order was created by Edward III in 1348 it may be well to give a brief description of its robes.

These consisted of a mantle, tunic, and hood. The mantle was of dark blue velvet, lined with scarlet, having a large red St. George's Cross on a silver shield on the left shoulder. The tunic was

lined with fur—ermine for the king, and miniver for the knights. It was thickly embroidered with garters in blue and gold, with the motto *Honi soit qui mal y pense* on them. The garter was worn round the left knee only and was in blue silk or cloth, decorated with gold and with golden buckles and tongue-end.

SCALLOPS

To all garments of this period "dagging" was done. This consisted of scalloping or cutting the edges of the clothes into points, semicircles, or irregular pieces resembling leaves.

MAN'S BEAVER HAT

SUMMARY
MEN (EDWARD I)
Dress

Cotehardie—tight knee-length coat. Tight sleeves with strip from elbow to ground attached. Belt.
Surcoat—now heraldic.
Mantle—still long.

Legs

Tights.

Feet

Dark leather shoes, with longer points. Boots, embroidered inner side.

Hair

Long and bushy.

Hats

Beaver with turn up brim, tall crown, feather.
Hood or capuchon with liripipe, with or without beaver hat on top.

WOMEN (EDWARD I)
Dress

Kirtle—close fit, laced, long tight sleeves, buttoned from elbow to wrist.
Loose gown—over the above. Train. Long hanging sleeves. Lined.

Girdle—on hips. Gown pulled up in front to
    show kirtle.
Mantle.

Feet

Shoes less pointed than men's.

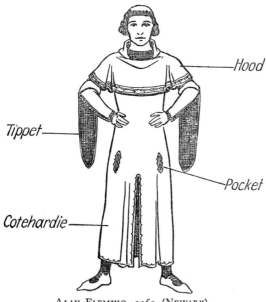

ALAN FLEMING, 1361 (NEWARK)

Hair

Parted middle, over ears in bunches.

Hats

Gorget and fillet—linen band on head and
    under chin.
Wimple—added for older women, coloured
    yellow.
Caps—endless.
Couvre-chef—a veil.
Spanish turban with stiff band on forehead.

MEN (EDWARD II AND III)

Dress

Cotehardie—parti-coloured, with tippets.
Belt at waist with pouch and dagger.

Capes—long or short. Collar and edge furred.
    Buttons at neck.

Legs

Tights now parti-coloured.

Hair

Bushy, cut round, curled. Clean shaven. Old
    men wore biforked beards.

Hats

Liripipe to hood is very long.

WOMEN (EDWARD II AND III)

Dress

Cotehardie—long gored skirt, tight sleeves,
    back laced, hip belt, low neck, not parti-
    coloured.
Super cotehardie—long, loose, sleeveless, large
    armholes.
Full gown—sometimes trained, with tippets
    —long strips—and wide elbow sleeves,
    over a
Kirtle—tight sleeves.
Cyclas—tight sleeveless surcoat, shorter in
    front (Edward II only).

Feet—as before.

Hair

Girls—two braids, gorget under them.
Women—two side bunches netted.

Hats

Gorget and wimple of fine lawn.
Silk ribbon fillets.
Gold side nets.
Couvre-chef—a veil.

PEASANTS

As in previous reigns. Sumptuary laws affect the
    materials and furs used in each class.

CHAPTER VIII

RICHARD OF BORDEAUX, 1377–99

THE pendulum again swings. During the three Edwards men revolted from long trailing skirts and their clothes became curtailed. In Richard II's reign they adopted a sort of compromise, and wore short dresses with trailing sleeves. The clever young king was much in advance of his day in his peace policies, but he loved display of a less harmful sort than war, that is, in pageantry and costume. It became an age of extravagance in dress, in material, cut, and adornment. Dagging was applied to everything. This was the scalloping, or circular-, or leaf-shaped cutting to the edges of the clothes, producing an effect like the mantling that surrounds a shield of arms. Parti-colouring continued, and increased to such an extent that a really smart man never dreamed of wearing two shoes alike. But it was in the headgear of the women that design really attained its height. The simple wimple swelled out; the side hair nets did the like, and we arrive at the beautiful, reticulated head dress, and the "Juliet" caul and the hennin. In the next reign we shall see the full blossoming of these head-dresses into fantastic horn, heart, and steeple shapes.

The standard dresses are the houppelande overcoat and the Zouave-like super cotehardie jacket. Buttons were sewn on in great profusion, and it should be remembered that these were bead shaped, and not the modern flat buttons. Trains were much in vogue, and the ladies' skirts were gored to form a wide, many-folded frock.

DRESS

The *Cotehardie* (men and women) (see summary), was adopted by the women as well as the men and was now jewelled.

The *Tabard* (men) was the heraldic surcoat also already described. Since the arms of the wearer were embroidered upon it, it became a kind of visiting card, since everyone who was anyone understood heraldry.

The *Houppelande* (men and women) was also called a pelican, and was an overcoat worn over the cotehardie. It had a high, bell-shaped collar, standing stiffly up round the neck, and long, full sleeves with dagged edges, cut like surplice sleeves. It was a full-length dress, buttoned down its entire length with many small buttons set closely together. It could also be buttoned for a few inches down the collar, with the rest not

Turban　　*Turban*

HOUPPELANDES

buttoned. One side was slashed from knee to hem. It was lined occasionally with fur, but more often with a contrasting colour, and the sleeves were turned back at the wrist so as to show this lining. The back part often trailed on the floor. The tight-fitting sleeves of the cotehardie showed under the houppelande sleeves where their upper part was cut away. The collar was similarly rolled, in which case the two top buttons were unfastened. Young men wore a houppelande that stopped abruptly just below the waist, the skirt becoming a mere frill, but the sleeves were as long as in the other type. This looked rather odd, the huge sleeves, almost sweeping the floor, being stuck on to a tight little jacket, with tights.

The *Cloak* (men) was fastened on the right shoulder.

The *Baldrick* (men) was a gaily embroidered or chased metal belt, from which hung the *Gipciere*, a purse-pouch suspended by two straps. The belt was narrow. One end fell in front, and

Super Cotehardie — Nebule — Veil — Reticulated Cap — Cotehardie — Houppelande

was often in leather. It also supported a finely chased or carved dagger, or this was worn on a separate ribbon or chain.

Tippets (women) continued in fashion. They were long strips of material reaching from elbow to knee, and they were set in an over sleeve that ended just above the elbow.

Mantles (women) were simple, as before, open in front, and fastened by two silk cords across the chest.

The *Surcoat* or *Super Cotehardie* (women) was worn in this period over the cotehardie. It was fur-lined, sleeveless, with enormous arm-holes and a low neck with cut away sides in front, so that little material remained in the dress. It was usually edged with fur all round, and also round the arm holes. In front, its edges nearly met, and later revealed a narrow front, pointed at the bottom, and adorned with a few buttons. It was a sleeveless waistcoat. This garment came in during the end of Edward III's reign, and continued until the end of Henry IV's reign.

The *Gown* (women) was long and loose, but had the favourite tight sleeves, buttoned at the wrist, and overhanging the back of the hand. It also had a V or a square cut neck.

LEGS

Tights (men) were parti-coloured, each leg being different, or each leg itself was divided into two colours vertically.

FEET

Crakowes (men and women) took their name from the Polish city of Cracow. Like much else in the period, they were exaggerated as much as six to twelve inches long, which were tied to a garter below the knee. To stiffen this projection, they were stuffed or wired at the end. They were laced, buckled, or buttoned, but the women's were rather shorter than the men's. In bad weather they were protected out of doors by the

Poulaines, which were wooden clogs with the same pointed toe pieces. These shoes were so extended that it actually became necessary in the

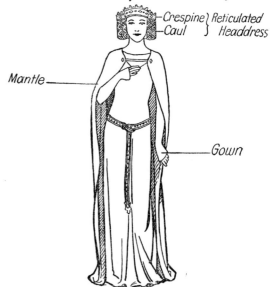

Mantle — Crespine) Reticulated — Caul) Headdress — Gown

LADY BURTON, 1382 (LITTLE CASTERTON)

interests of traffic congestion to pass laws limiting their length!

HAIR

Men wore their hair fairly long, and, since the King's was a pale gold, dyes were used to secure the same shade! Forked beards, with moustaches were worn by older men. The brow was bound with a golden fillet decorated with flowers in enamel—a pretty custom. The women plucked their eyebrows, and shaved the backs of their necks in the manner of our own century. Their hair was stuffed into the two side bags called the Reticulated head-dress. These now became stiff wire cages on either side of the face, joined together by a decorated band called a *Crespine*, which went along the top of the head in front as a forehead band.

The *Dorelet* (women) was a caul of gold net worn all over the head with the hair tucked underneath it. It was of the "Juliet" type.

The *Nebule* (women) was a cylindrical roll of wire net, worn at first on top of the head, later on sides of the face as well. Its date is 1350–1380.

HATS
MEN

The *Turban* (men) was what its name implies. It had a cloth crown with dagged ends, which overlapped the edge slightly.

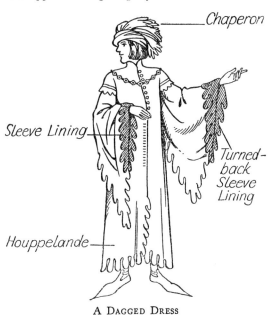

A DAGGED DRESS

The *Cap* (men) round and was brimless, but it was not a skull-cap. It stood up like a fez, and was the favourite for young men, who decorated it with an ostrich feather, at the side.

The *Chaperon* (men) effected the greatest trans-

formation from the original hood shape in which it was still made. The men decided to put the crown of their heads through the face opening, leaving the cape part, which used to cover the shoulders, to form a huge rosette at the side, it was secured in place by twisting the now long

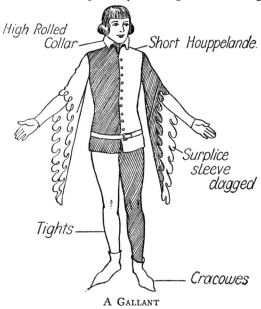

A GALLANT

liripipe round it. The liripipe was also used as a scarf round the neck. It was originally merely the peak of the hood.

HATS
WOMEN

The *Capuchon* (women) was the hood of yore and retained its old shape for women, being a cape, to which was attached a close head-covering, ending in a peak at the back of the head. The head cover was turned up over the head in bad weather, but otherwise it could be worn hanging at the back of the neck. In its original shape, it is still the correct style of academic hood, and is now so worn by many graduates, though the eighteenth-century wigs caused the head opening to widen considerably, with the result commonly seen to-day of a graduate wearing his hood half-way down his back instead of on his shoulders.

The *Fillet* (women) was a narrow strip of linen round the forehead and was worn with

The *Gorget* (women), which was a strip of

linen passed round the throat several times and fastened to the hair above the ears, where it was also kept in place by the fillet.

There was plenty of variety in design, though the essentials were retained; materials were of the richest; velvets, silks, and fine linens, with sweeping trains, and the graceful floating veils of gauze or thicker material. Jewellery was finely wrought, and colourings were vivid. The parti-coloured men's dress formed effective foils to the

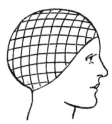

DORELET OR CAUL

women's simpler two-colour schemes, whilst the firm, straight limbs of the young men in their tights contrasted well with the long, heavy folds and wide skirts of their women folk.

PEASANTS

Peasants change little through many centuries. The tunic was loose, long, and belted. It was set off by the hood, which was still worn in its original serviceable shape, and it had not succumbed to the fantastic shape in which it was twisted by the rich people. On top of this Capuchon was also worn during travel out of doors and in bad weather a slouched hat of the "Robin Hood" variety, though many English people went bareheaded at all times. Sober colours and coarse fabrics should be used for peasants' clothes. The fashions had affected their dresses to the extent that the tunic skirt and cape of the hood were now dagged at the edges in scallops, and colour came into the breeches or stockings (called chausses), which were now cheerful and bright. Boots were of black cloth or felt, but could not have lasted any length of time one would think. So much for the men.

As regards the women, the gown was sometimes laced in front and turned up over the knees to show a short coloured underskirt horizontally striped. This idea is still carried out amongst certain fisher women in the North of Scotland.

Instead of the stripes, they could have radiating rays of colour.

Citizens and middle-class wives would wear a sober modification of the noble ladies' dress, but they eschewed the elegant head-dresses in favour of a simple wimple and veil, or a hood hung back, not on top of the head. Aprons were worn, and bodices were plain and tight with long sleeves, also self-fitting. The conical felt hat was sometimes worn on top of the wimple.

Young women did their hair in a pigtail or two braids. They wore straw or felt slouched hats. Plain cotehardies were pulled up over a belt round the hips. Smock-chemises were worn, by poorer people. Coloured stockings and brown leather shoes completed the picture.

SUMMARY
Dress   MEN

Cotehardie, jewelled.

Tabard—an heraldic surcoat.

Houppelande—long full sleeves, high bell-shaped collar, many buttons, very long or very short, side slashed.

Cloak—on right shoulder.

Gipciere—pouch on two straps from belt.

Baldrick—narrow belt, end falls in front.

Dagger, jewelled—on ribbon or chain.

RETICULATED WING CAP, 1380–1400

Legs

Tights.

Feet

Crakowes—shoes, 6 in. long, stuffed or wired points.

Poulaines—wooden clogs with pointed toe.

Hair

Long, often dyed yellow. Moustache. Forked beard.

Fillet on brow in gold and enamel flowers.

Hats

Turban—cloth crown, dagged ends overlap edge.

Cap—round, brimless, with one ostrich feather.

Chaperon—hood with head put through face opening, the cape made into rosette, the liripipe knotted round as scarf or hat band.

Jewels

Huge rings, heavy chains, great elaboration.

WOMEN

Dress

Houppelande—as men.

Tippet—strips from elbow to knee, attached to an oversleeve.

Mantle—as before.

Cotehardie—long gored skirt, long tight sleeves, back laced, hip belt, low neck, parti-coloured.

Surcoat—fur edged and lined, sleeveless, wide armholes, cut away sides, waist length, parti-colour.

Gown—long, loose. Tight sleeves buttoned at wrist. V neck.

Feet

Crakowes—shoes less pointed than the men's. Laced, buckled, or buttoned.

Hair

Back of neck shaved, eyebrows plucked.

Reticulated—netted side bags and crespine (forehead band).

Dorelet—gold net caul.

Nebule—wire cylinder round face.

Hats

Capuchon—a hood as before.

Fillet and gorget—as before. For country folk.

Jewels

Gloves, rings, chains. Great profusion.

PEASANTS
MEN

Dress

Tunic—long, loose, belted. Dagged skirt and cape.

Legs

Chausses, thick, bright coloured.

Feet

Black cloth or felt boots.

Hair

Rough.

Hats

Capuchon.

Slouched hat. "Robin Hood" type.

PEASANTS
WOMEN

Dress

Gown. Sometimes front laced and turned up over knees, long tight sleeves.

Underskirt—striped horizontally. Plain cotehardie.

Cotehardie—plain. Aprons.

Feet

Coloured stockings. Leather shoes.

Hair

No nebule or dorelet. Pigtail or two braids for girls.

Hats

Veil or wimple. Slouch hat of straw or felt.

Conical felt hat over wimple.

CHAPTER IX

THE THREE HENRIES, 1399–1461

RICHARD OF BORDEAUX, sneered at by some historians, was wise beyond his time; he had a fixed policy of peace, and in this he gave his long-suffering people a welcome

KING HENRY IV

period of relief between the sword rattling Edward III and the equally militaristic Henry of Lancaster. During Richard's reign the people had time to cultivate the arts and culture of peace, and their costumes reflected this fact by their brilliance of colour and design, and by the new modes that were introduced. England, thrust back into the gloom of almost perpetual war under the three Henries, had little time to invent new fashions, and even if the women had found time, there were few men at home to admire them. The only new things that the period evolved were the women's hats—and these were certainly wonderfully made. Sugar loaves, horns, hearts, steeples—all were pressed into the service of millinery.

The pendulum which started swinging away from the curtailed styles of the Edwards to the

longer clothes of Richard of Bordeaux, continued to move in the same direction, not having attained the end of its movement nor coming back in the opposite direction. Consequently dress tended to become, on the whole, slightly more solid with the almost constant wearing of the ankle-length Houppelande.

It is rather typical of the difference between the characters of the gay, artistic and clever Richard and the pompous, self-important, humorless Henry IV. The fantastic fashions of the former king reflect his character just as truly as the more sombre styles reveal the man who crushed him.

TURBAN (HENRY VI)

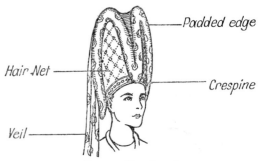

FORKED HAT (1435)

The typical note of the period was the full sleeve which was gathered in at the wrist—and of course the remarkable hats of the ladies.

The story is told (and I believe it can be verified in history) of the fashionable court lady who went a-shopping in Cheapside in one of the largest of these padded and wired-out creations. London stalls were set close together perforce, in the narrow medieval streets, so that their canopies sometimes nearly met. The lady, tempted by the display of goods, ventured further down an alley than was wise—with the result that she got stuck by the horns of her head-dress catching in the canopies—and she was only able to extricate herself after the merchants had completely taken down the offending stall-covers!

Truly, this was the age of hats—as a glance at the Summary will show.

DRESS

The *Cotehardie* (men and women) was becoming old-fashioned for men. It was a garment with a wide gored skirt, long tight sleeves, a hip belt, and it was laced at the back or made loose enough to slip on without lacing (though that

ROUNDLET

HORNED HEAD-DRESS

mode was becoming out of date). It had a low neck and was parti-coloured.

The *Super Cotehardie* (women) was still the vogue, but was now fur-edged as well as fur-lined,

the edging showing all round the garment from neck to waist, and at the back. It was a sleeveless coatee, with wide armholes and a cutaway front.

The *Houppelande* (men and women) could be worn long or short (the latter for young men). It had the same wide sleeves as before, the collar had become even higher, and was rolled over at the top. The main difference was that dagging

CIVILIANS 1400 (SILBROOK)

was going out: it was retained only on the cuff, which was made wide enough to fold into regular pleats within the belt. In the later period the wide open sleeves were displaced by the bag sleeve, which was made full at the top to below the elbow, from where it gradually narrowed to the wrist, where it was gathered into a deep cuff by a button, or put into a simple wrist band.

The *Baldrick* (men) struck another distinctive note. It was a long loop of cloth or leather, hung with small bells all round. It was worn diagonally over the left shoulder, and fell to the right knee at front and back. In Henry VI's reign this gave way to an horizontal belt, which had small bells only across its front. What the effect of a large gathering of fashionables, with these belts on, sounded like can be left to the imagination. Evidently strident voices had to be developed.

But then it was an age when the loudest shouters were the most heard in other respects.

LEGS

Tights (men) were parti-coloured.

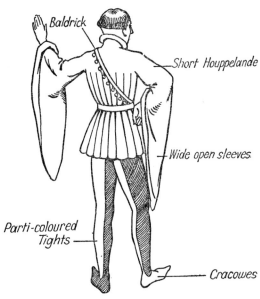

Baldrick

Short Houppelande

Wide open sleeves

Parti-coloured
Tights

Cracowes

A YOUNG MAN (HENRY V)

FEET

Shoes also caught the parti-colour infection, and no decently dressed gallant dreamt of going about with two shoes that matched in colour. They had to agree with the shades of the rest of the costume. The tops were long enough to roll back to show the coloured lining, which had to agree with the general colour scheme. The long points continued until Henry VI's time, when they were replaced by shorter toes, on shoes laced at the sides. For bad weather the wooden clogs called *Poulaines* were still required. No difference from the previous period was made in the women's shoes.

HAIR

The *Hair* (men) was now closely cropped, being completely shaved at the back of the neck and over the ears—a fashion that may still be seen, somewhat modified, to-day. The older men wore pointed, rather Vandyck-like, beards, but these had two curled points instead of the single one we recognize as the true Vandyck. The women's

hair was only seen through the gold net bags or cauls, and often little enough showed then if a heavy veil or other contraption was added. It was not just put into these cauls in any manner; contemporary pictures prove that it was carefully plaited before insertion into the net.

HATS
MEN

Hats were varied. We have the old *Turban* (men), which was extensively worn in the reigns of Henry IV and V. It was a round cloth crown with dagged ends overlapping the edge. It was a large, clumsy looking headgear, and the ragged end, which flapped about on top or at the side, gave an effect not unlike a cock's comb.

The *Roundlet* (men) was the distinctive Henry IV hat. It had a small stiffened rolling brim with a draped crown and a long streamer,

Cropped Hair

Roundlet

Bag Sleeve

ARCHITECT, 1440 (ROUEN)

which was broad, and hung from the crown right down the side of the body. It was so long that it could be looped up and fastened to the skirt by a brooch or clasp, though a more moderate version reached to the shoulder only.

The *Sugar-loaf* (men) was a brimless oval cap and was popular under Henry V, specially for young men; it was a kind of elongated fez, often of white.

The *Hood* (men) was cut as of yore, but the face opening was now edged with fur, which indicated that the inside was also similarly lined. It was, when worn, usually shown over the head, and was not hung on the back of the shoulders.

The *Tall Hat* (men) had a turned up brim, which was cut out into squares.

The *Hood* (men and women) was the same as before, but it was usually worn by country folk and the poorer classes.

HATS
WOMEN

The *Hennin* (women) was a tall sugar-loaf or steeple-shaped cone of buckram, covered with silk or brocade. The end was not yet sharply pointed, but was rounded, and the whole was covered with a floating veil hanging over the back. The weight

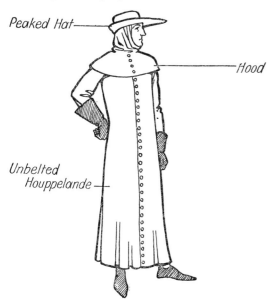

Peaked Hat—

—Hood

Unbelted Houppelande—

HENRY IV PERIOD

of this head-dress, which hung backwards, would have tipped it over but for the *Frontlet*, which was designed to balance it, and was made of a deep band of black velvet, rectangular shaped, covering the top of the head and falling on either side of the face to the shoulders. The Hennin was lined with thin steel or wire netting forming a close-

4—(G.122)·

fitting cap for the head, and in this way it was kept on. Long floating *Veils* of white gauze were worn with all the head-dresses of this period (save the hood) at will, but they were not needed for the horned and heart hats, though they were

Heart-shape Hat—

High-waisted —Gown

HENRY VI PERIOD

usually worn. The veil must accompany the hennin always.

The *Horned* head-dress had many varieties and modifications, but the earliest form consisted of two horns of wire foundation, sticking outwards and upwards from the sides of the head. The beginnings of this style were found in the *Reticulated* head-dress that was made from two cylinders in gold net worn on each side of the face. These cylinders were now elongated to an inordinate length and curved so that they resembled the Viking helmets of many centuries previously. The patterns on these horns were many. They were formed by plaiting and twisting the gold wire or by covering the horns with brocade and silk, and even twisting material round them. Another variation was to retain the *Reticulated* side bags and to place on top of them two side horns of curved wire from which hung the veil, the top of the wire being covered by the edge of the veil, which was brought over as a valance. A more solid effect was given by enlarging the crespine till it became a kind of toque placed over the veil, which was worn over the side bags. The toque was embroidered and jewelled, as were the side bags and the horns when the horns were made of solid material.

The *Crespine* was the metal connecting band over the forehead between the two side bags.

The next step was to alter the shape of the horns and to make them point directly upwards first instead of outwards. This *Forked* the hat and heightened it, and it was accompanied by a modified hennin, in which the round pointed end was cut off, leaving a short roll with a flat end. All were attached to the caul-cap on the head, the flat-ended short hennin pointing out at the back of the head, the cap covering it, and the horns standing above it. A veil was pinned at the front, where it met the centre of the forehead, and was drawn over the ends of the horns and floated down the back of the head, but the veil did not cover the pattern of the horns.

The *Heart* shape hat was immortalized by Sir John Tenniel in his drawings of the Duchess in *Alice in Wonderland*. The hair was padded and stuffed till it attained considerable height; it was placed in nets, and the curved part of the heart shape was covered with the veil.

The *Turban* was an enormously inflated caul, i.e. netted cap, into which the hair was placed. It was nicknamed the "Orange" by the irreverent. These hats lacked the fine simplicity of an earlier period.

SUMMARY
MEN
Dress

Cotehardie.

Houppelande—long or short, long wide sleeves, higher collar, regular pleats, geometrical designs.

Houppelande with bag sleeve—leg of mutton shape, deep cuff or plain wrist band. Dagged cuff.

Cloak.

Baldrick—belt hung with small bells, worn diagonally over left shoulder.

Baldrick—belt with bells across front, worn horizontally (Henry VI).

Legs

Tights—parti-coloured.

Feet

Shoes—long pointed. Top turned back to show lining. Parti-coloured.

Shoes—shorter toes, laced at sides (Henry VI).

Poulaines—wooden clogs.

Hair

Short—cut close, shaved at back and over ears.

Beards—short, Vandyck shaped; but in two curls for older men.

Hats

Roundlet—small round with stiff rolling brim, draped crown, long broad streamer over side (Henry IV).

Turban—cloth crown, dagged ends overlap edge (Henry IV and V).

Sugar-loaf—brimless oval (Henry V).

Hood—fur-edged round face opening.

Tall—turned up brim cut in square scallops.

WOMEN
Dress

Houppelande—as above.

Cotehardie—long gored skirt, back laced, long tight sleeves, hip belt, parti-coloured, low neck.

Super cotehardie—fur lined and edged, sleeveless, wide armholes, cut away sides, waist length.

Mantle—as before, strings across chest.

High-waisted gown—long gored skirt, belt high up, trained, V-neck fur-edged.

Feet

Cracowes—slightly pointed, laced, buckled, or buttoned.

Hair

All concealed under the gold net cap.

Hats

Reticulated—netted side bags or side wings.

Hood—for country folk.

Hennin—sugar loaf, with frontlet and veil.

Horned—at sides with crespine and veil.

Forked—pointless roll back of head with horns upright above head, no frontlet.

Heart—heart-shaped frame and veil.

Turban—inflated caul, no veil or frontlet.

Frontlet—black velvet strip hanging to shoulders either side of face.

YORKIST LADIES, 1450

CHAPTER X

YORKIST, 1461–85

THE years from 1461 to 1485—the brief age of authority of the Yorkist Kings, Edward IV, Edward V, and Richard III, were not years of great change in costume, though they will ever be remembered by reason of the startling codpiece, and also the ladies' high-waisted-gown. Hats remained as original as ever, the principal features being the delightful Butterfly for the women and the endless variety of low-crowned hats for the men.

DRESS
MEN

The *Doublet* (men) was worn to hip length only, but it had been developed by padding on the breast and back, the material being gathered into formal fluted folds and confined by the belt. The collar continued to be high, but was open at the

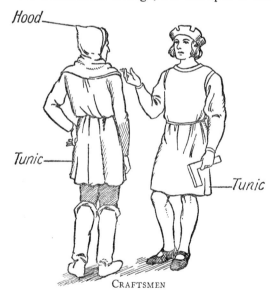

CRAFTSMEN

front. The sleeves were tight, and extended to the wrist, but a hanging sleeve was added at will, with an elbow opening, through which the inner sleeve and arm were thrust, leaving the rest of the outer sleeve to dangle. After 1480 hanging sleeves

became longer, and were often loosely looped together behind the back. At this date slashing came in, and revealed the embroidered shirt at the elbows and shoulders. The shoulders were

KING RICHARD III

artificially raised by padding, and the front of the doublet was opened to show the shirt, and loosely laced across the V.

The *Jerkin* (men) was also hip length. It could be extended to the middle of the thighs, but its sleeves were roomy and loose at the wrist, and were slit down the front seam to form long hanging sleeves. The slashings became much longer and larger, and often extended from the shoulder almost to the wrist, where in the earlier reigns they gave mere glimpses of the shirt.

The *Gown* (men) was the houppelande slightly modified. *Cloaks* (men) were sometimes worn, chiefly by older people.

The *Shirt* (men) came into its own, and was richly embroidered in black and red silk and (later) in gold thread. For the first time it had a definite neck band.

DRESS
WOMEN

The *Houppelande* (women) was modified slightly and became tighter and more shaped to

39

the body. Towards the end of this period it moulded the bust.

The *High-waisted Gown* (women) was the almost universal dress. It had a wide, gored skirt, with a train, and long, tight sleeves coming well over the wrist and hands, where it widened into

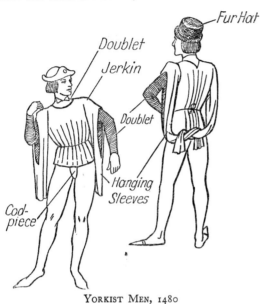

YORKIST MEN, 1480

a square cut cuff. It was trimmed with fur round the skirt bottom and the neck opening, and was finished off with a broad belt. The materials used were beautiful damask and tapestry patterns in brocade and rich silks of conventional design, which are still popular in our church furnishings. The pineapple, pomegranate, vine, and grape, together with leaves that are familiar on English trees, were utilized for these designs.

The principal changes were in the neck opening, which in 1460 was round, and which, in 1480, had become square. In the latter form it was so wide that it almost bared the shoulders and gave that "slipping off" impression which so much intrigued the Early Victorian men.

LEGS

Tights (men) had the codpiece added, though it had not the elaboration of the codpiece of the Tudor period. This codpiece was a stuffed small bag placed at the fork of the tights and fastened up by laced "points" or strings.

FEET

Shoes (men) had the toes stuffed with moss and hay and were the familiar *Poulaines* and *Crakowes*. From 1470 to 1480 the points were of immense length, and finished in a long needle point, which was sometimes pinned back over the shoe for convenience.

Boots were laced on the inner sides and the tops were turned back in a peak behind. Loose fitting thigh boots had the top rolled to show the silk lining.

HAIR

Hair (men) was bobbed in an attractive fashion, but the Bowl crop of Henry V had definitely gone out of favour. The dandy wore his hair long over the forehead, even longer over the neck and nearly to the shoulders. The parting was in the middle.

Hair (women) showed little, but it must not be assumed that because the veil and enormous head gear hid most of it, it was bundled up and stuffed anyhow into the gold net cauls. Contem-

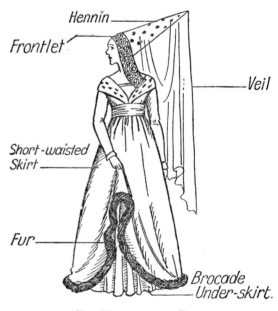

THE HIGH-WAISTED DRESS

porary illustrations show that the hair was carefully braided in square-crossing patterns.

HATS

MEN

Hats (men) were varied. The crowns were high or low; the brims narrow or broad. A conical hat was like a Turk's fez or, when longer, became a sugar loaf shape. The *Bycocket* was pointed and pulled down in front, with a turned-up brim at the back, and was rather like the modern felt Trilby, with the exception that there was no dent in the top of the crown. It was mostly favoured by the sober, who dared not wear the more fashionable small caps. Tall, upright, single ostrich feathers in front or at the back added to the fantasy. Jewelled hat bands and brooches kept the shape together, and maintained the turned-up brim for the wealthy. After 1475 a kind of "smoking cap," like the caps of the Victorians, was worn. It had a deep turn-up all round. The most popular types were the sugar-loaf and the low cap with turn-up.

HATS

WOMEN

Hats (women) were as elaborate as before.

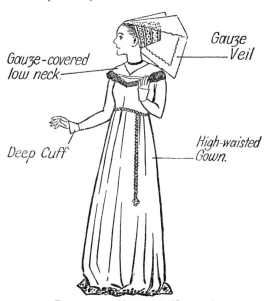

BUTTERFLY HAT, 1478 (OULTON)

A new type was the charming *Butterfly* headdress, which was worn between 1450 and 1480. This was a floating gauze veil stretched

over wires, which were tilted at the back of the head at an angle of 45 degrees. The gold net cap enclosed the hair, and was often placed at the

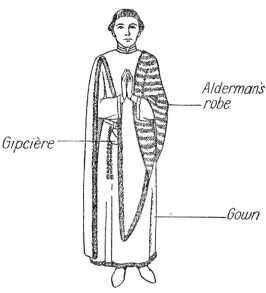

ALDERMAN FIELD, 1474 (LONDON)

extreme back of the head. It revealed the front hair, which was brushed back from the forehead. The frontlet sometimes covered this front hair, but it was made of white gauze instead of black velvet.

Another new type was the *Barbe*, which was worn by older women. It was a veil over the head and sides of the face, with a kind of linen bib worn above or below the chin and covering the upper part of the chest. It was attached to a chin band, and was pleated in formal folds vertically. The whole gave a nun-like appearance. Ladies of the upper class covered the chin; others wore the band under the chin.

It is customary to dress this period in the acutely pointed steeple hats that are so familiar in manuscripts and illuminations, but in England this is not strictly correct. The genuine steeple was extensively worn on the Continent, but it was not popular in England. Perhaps the English women felt that its sharp point emphasized their own angularities. The *Steeple* in our own country was generally rounded off at the end to make an elongated sugar loaf hat without the acute angled point. From all these hats floated the gauze or linen veils that were attached to the front. A small loop of string or material was seen exactly in the centre of the forehead. It rested on the bare skin, and is thought to have been placed there for convenience in pulling on the headdress.

The *Beehive* hat was a truncated sugar loaf with little gradation, and was smaller at the top of the crown. It was covered with a veil, which was tucked in closely to the hat.

Walking sticks began to be fashionable for the men.

THE BARBE

SUMMARY
MEN
Dress

Doublet to 1480—padded, fluted, hip length, high open collar, close and/or hanging sleeves to wrist.

Doublet from 1480—open down breast, loosely laced across, high padded shoulders, shirt shows at slashes of elbow and shoulders.

Jerkin—hip and mid-thigh length, roomy sleeves, loose at wrist, slit down front seam to make long hanging sleeve, looped behind.

Gown—modified houppelande.

Cloaks—rare.

Shirt with neckband—embroidered 1480 onwards.

Legs

Tights and codpiece.

Feet

Immense needle points 1470–80, then fade out.

Stuffed toes.

Puolaines and Crakowes.

Laced rear-peaked boots.   Roll-top thigh boots.

Hair

Long over forehead and nearly to shoulders.

Bobbed.

No bowl crops.

Hats

Crowned—high or low.

Brimmed—narrow or broad.

Conical—fez or long sugar loaf.

Tall upright ostrich feather, front or back.

Bycocket—"Robin Hood" type.

Jewelled hat bands and brooches.

"Smoking caps" with deep turn-up, after 1475.

WOMEN
Dress

Houppelande—tighter and, later, moulded to form.

High waisted gown—neck 1460 round; neck 1480 square, almost bare shoulders. Long tight sleeves, widened at wrist to square cuff. Broad belt, fur trimming.

Feet

Concealed by skirt.

Hair

Concealed under hat, but braided to show through.

Hats

Forked with veil.

Beehive with veil.

Butterfly 1450–80 with veil and/or frontlet.

Hennin 1460–70 or steeple, not sharp pointed, with veil.

Wimple for widows.

Barbe—wimple with linen bib and chin band, vertically pleated.

PEASANTS

As in previous reign.

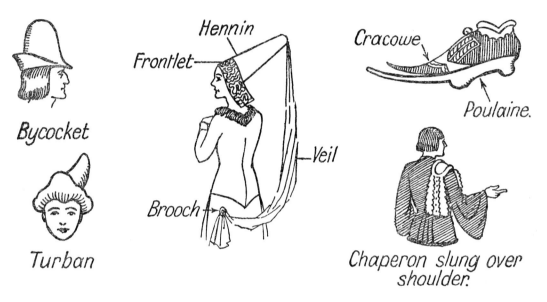

Bycocket

Turban

Frontlet

Hennin

Brooch

Veil

Cracowe

Poulaine.

Chaperon slung over shoulder.

SOME YORKIST HATS AND A SHOE

CHAPTER XI

HENRY VII, 1485–1509

FROM 1485 to 1509, the period of the reign of the new Tudor king, dignity returned to fashion with the long gown and chain and the gable hat, and continued throughout the whole

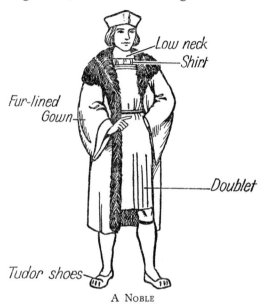

Low neck
Shirt
Fur-lined Gown
Doublet
Tudor shoes

A NOBLE

from Italy and the East, and jewellery became massive and finely wrought, especially in ladies' girdles and pendants and the brooches in men's hats.

The new note was in the increased importance of the white shirt, richly embroidered in black and white thread, and even in colours, and in the stomacher or waistcoat, which was of brocade. The ladies originated the gable hat and abandoned the fantastic wired shapes of the Lancastrian and Yorkist times. Slashings began to appear, somewhat timidly, in Henry VII's reign. On the whole, costuming in this reign was sober and restrained, and thoroughly sound. It was during the reign of his son, who spent his father's savings, and then robbed the Church for more,

Veil
Liripipe
The Gown
Chemise
Tight Bodice
Rolled Cuff
Full Skirt

MERCHANT CLASS

of the Tudor line's rule, with slight returns to the freakish in the more exaggerated modes of Henry the Eighth and Elizabeth, though the general modes retained their dignity. Costume was symbolic of the Tudor monarchs themselves since all (with the exception of the young Edward VI) had greatness in no small measure, and despite the tempestuous outbursts of the royal Blue Beard and the Virgin Queen, they always managed to keep their personal dignity.

It was a period that became increasingly prosperous, for there were no wars, and the nation had time and money with which to develop its civilization. There sprang up a new race of nobles whose claims to peerages, like those of our own day, depended on money instead of on birth and breeding. This position was reflected in the increased gorgeousness of materials and designs for clothes. Rich silks, figured brocades and damasks, stamped velvets and cloth of gold, were imported

that clothing became really extravagant and less dignified and quiet.

DRESS
MEN

The *Linen Shirt* (men) was gathered at the neck into pleats and embroidered with red and black thread. It showed through the slashings of the stomacher and from elbow to wrist if the stomacher had no sleeves.

44

The *Stomacher* (men) was of patterned fabric, rich and elaborate, with its floral design conventionalized and outlined in gold thread. It reached from the chest, where it was square cut at the neck to the waist, where it was laced or tied to the tights.

The *Doublet* (men), worn over the stomacher, was close fitting, and quilted, as in the previous reigns, but was open down the front in a V-shape and loosely laced across, thus showing the stomacher. It had a short hip-covering skirt, or a slightly longer skirt, and its sleeves were slashed at the elbow and hung down from there loosely, again revealing the stomacher (if sleeved) or the shirt sleeves. The doublet sleeves were close from elbow to shoulder.

The *Jerkin* (men) was occasionally worn over the doublet, and had either no sleeves or wide or hanging sleeves. These garments were held to the waist by a narrow *Sash*.

The *Gown* (men) was the characteristic note of

MERCHANT AND WIFE, 1490
(Holme-by-Newark, Notts)

this age, and was long, but the sleeves had become mere cylindrical rolls of cloth with lengthwise arm openings. A broad square cut collar extended down the back and continued along the edges of the front in revers faced with silk or fur.

The *Petti-cote* (men) was a shorter version of the long coat.

DRESS
WOMEN

The *Gown* (women) was long, and made from rich silks with a broad square-cut neck outlined with bands of embroidery. A train was added by the upper classes. The sleeves were close at the top and wide at the elbow and banded, often with

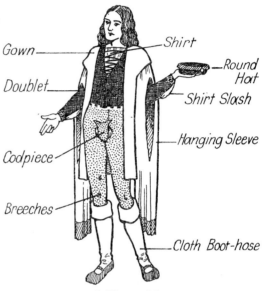

A YOUNG MAN

fur. It was the custom to lift the skirt to show the under dress of rich material, generally figured. The gown was occasionally fur-lined.

The *Chemise* (women) was white and pleated, and showed above the neck opening of the gown.

The *Underdress* was on the same cut as the over-gown, but was of figured damask or woven tapestry or cut velvet, but the pattern was fairly simple as the split opening of the over-gown did not come into fashion until Henry VIII's time, so that until then the under-gown was not permanently displayed.

The *Cloak* (women) was full and ample, and had open sleeves, which were necessary to the bulky lines of the clothes that were worn under it.

LEGS

Tights (men) were of fabric, silk or velvet, cut on the cross. Dandies wore striped tights, which had slashed and puffed knees. A curious mode was to have a different material and colour at the hips, and this was slashed and sometimes attached to the body of the garment by loose lacings. Through all these slashings showed the under-clothes of white, which were slightly pulled through to form little puffs.

FEET

Shoes were of velvet or leather with bulbous

HENRY VII

rounded toes, and were sometimes slashed to show the coloured stockings beneath them.

HAIR

Hair (men) was worn flowing to the shoulders, and was usually parted in the middle. *Hair* (women) was also parted in the middle, but only a small portion was visible in front on the fore-head, as the rest of the head was completely covered by the headdress.

HATS
MEN

Hats (men) were of velvet in two shapes. One had the brim turned up on all sides and the four corners pinched together to form a square cap—an early form of the biretta now worn by the clergy. The other had a broad brim, turned up but without cornering, to which were added feathers turning backwards. This type was worn over a close-fitting cap.

HATS
WOMEN

Hats (women). The *Gable* or Kennel type was the characteristic piece, and was in three sections. The first was a white coif or close-fitting cap, over which was placed a piece of material in silk, velvet, or embroidered cloth, nearly always black. It was stiffened like a roof or tent so that it hung in a point at the top and angles at the sides, and there were strings at the sides with which to tie back the hanging ends from the neck. A stiff band of material em-broidered on its front edge with pearls was added to the whole, to show in front. It, too, was stiffened and bent in the centre and placed over the coif. The coif was first, the pearl band next, and then the black, embroidered veiling.

Another type was the *Franco-Flemish*, which was simpler in outline. Made of dark material, it covered the head and sides of the face with ample folds. It had a bright lining, which was turned back on the top of the head in front to add a note of colour.

Older women wore the pleated barbe of linen with a plain arched linen hood faintly dipping in front on the forehead (the precursor of the Mary Queen of Scots hat). This was put on over a stiffened front, or the material itself was stiffened and hung over the face and outward on the shoulders. The *Barbe* was a kind of pleated bib, covering the chest up to the chin and occasionally extending over the chin.

JEWELLERY

Jewellery (men) was principally shown in the massive and beautiful neck chains that hung, like a modern Mayor's official chain, from each shoulder in a wide curve across breast and back. Pendants were added. These were crosses and other designs with a touch of the Renaissance, such as allegorical figures of cupids, arabesques, and conventionalized natural forms. Rings and belts were also of gold, and all the jewellery was heavy and massive to harmonize with the heavy and massive lines of the clothes worn. A thin, delicate piece of goldsmith's work would have looked tawdry and out of place.

Jewellery (women) was chiefly centred in the long waist chain with a long hanging end reaching three-quarters of the way down the skirt. From it depended a large round pendant. Elaborate crosses with pearl drops at the ends were used as brooches on the breast. Occasionally brooches adorned the men's hats. Rings were large and square.

PEASANTS

Peasants wore much the same type of clothes but in plainer materials and simpler cut. Stockings were of white wool, and slipper-shoes of leather were popular. Outer cloaks were worn by wealthy citizens only. Shirts were of coarse, unbleached linen of a grey-brown shade with turn-down collars, or upstanding collars cut away slightly in front. The main robe was cassock-like and girdled with a belt. Working-class people wore a shorter tunic.

Though they would have been much insulted had they been called peasants, it is convenient here to discuss that merchant class which was becoming so important a factor in the national life. The staple industry of the country (as indeed it was called) was the wool trade. Its merchants could vie with the nobles in the splendour of their homes and the lavish churches which they built and endowed. They delighted in erecting stately tombs for themselves, and in enshrining them in dignified chantry chapels attached to their parish churches. Many details of their costume may be seen on the monumental brasses and tombs in the wool country of the Cotswolds, and the Midlands.

Yet with all their wealth and magnificence, they seem to have been content to dress soberly, at any rate as regards cut, and the cassock-shaped gown seen in our illustrations is typical of these merchants.

What they lacked in the design of their garments, however, they made up in the richness of their materials. In my "Story of Holme-by-Newark Church and its Founder" I give an account of the actual clothes worn by its wool-merchant founder. They are taken from his will of 1491 which is still preserved, and the picture you see of John and Isabella Barton, is a vitalized version of the figures on their tomb in that church.

A silver girdle, to which was attached a leather bag pocket, confined the waist of the tunic beneath this scarlet coat, furred with martin, and this you will see in the colour plate in this chapter. Other coats of his were made of crimson with velvet revers; of violet lined with frieze or with say, and of red furred with mink. His best coat was of camlet, and about his neck hung a massive

ELIZABETH OF YORK

silver chain. When in his Sunday best he must have looked not unlike a modern mayor.

SUMMARY

MEN

Dress

Linen shirt—pleated at neck, embroidered black and white thread, shows through slashed points of

Stomacher—sleeve optional, patterned fabric waistcoat, from chest to waist, where it is laced or tied to tights.

Doublet—over stomacher, close fit, quilted, open in front to show stomacher, short

skirt, close sleeves to elbow. From elbow
to wrist reveals shirt or stomacher sleeves.
Jerkin—hip length, sleeves hanging, or wide,
or none.
Sash—narrow.
Gown—long; sleeves cloth cylinders with
long arm slits, broad square collar with front
revers.
Petti-cote—short version of long coat.

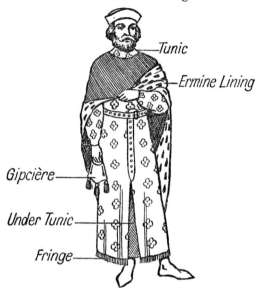

GENTLEMAN, 1450–1500 (ALL SAINTS, YORK)

Legs

Tights—fabric with codpiece, striped, slashed
and puffed knee, hips different colour.

Feet

Shoes—velvet or leather, bun toed, slight
slashings and puffs.
Stockings—coloured.

Hair

Flowing to shoulders. Square cut. Beard rare.

Hats

Turn-up brim, four corners pinched together.
Broad heavy brim with back-turning feathers
over skull cap.

Jewellery

Gold chains with pendants (see also Women).

WOMEN

Dress

Chemise—pleated white, shows above gown.
Gown—long, rich silk, broad square neck outlined with embroidery band, train. Sleeve
close at top, wide at elbow and hand, fur
banded. Tight bodice. Lift to show—
Underdress—costly figured material.
Cloak—full and ample, open sleeves.

Hair

Parted middle and brushed back, only visible
in front.

Hats

Gable—white coif, over which black silk or
velvet stiffened like sloping roof, and stiff
band of material pearl embroidered. Side
strings to tie back from neck.
Franco-Flemish—ample dark veil on head and
shoulders, turned back on top to show gay
lining.
Barbe—pleated linen with plain arched linen
hood, slight front dip, on stiffening over head
and shoulders, with barbe-pleated bib on
chest.

Jewellery

Long belts, with pendants, necklaces, and
rings, massive and finely wrought for both
sexes, and pendants.

PEASANTS

Dress

Outer cloaks for citizens.
Shirts—coarse grey-brown; collar turned down
or up.
Gown—cassock shape; belted.
Short tunic for workmen.

Legs

Stockings—white wool.

Feet

Slipper shoes of leather.

A Tudor Merchant and His Wife

CHAPTER XII

TUDOR, 1509–58

ARRIVING at the Tudor period we come to the reigns of Henry VIII and Mary. The massive form and later gross obesity of King Henry influenced the fashions that were designed to disguise his uncouth shape, but under Mary a return to the normal was made, and the modes became more natural in shape. The enormous wealth hoarded by Henry's father was spent lavishly by his son, who then looted the Church for more. A great deal of this went in clothes and jewellery, and the splendours of the Field of the Cloth of Gold and of the courts of the King and Cardinal were maintained largely for political reasons and the need for impressing Europe with the importance of England.

The chief change was from the long-skirted men of Henry VII to the square shoulders and short skirts of his son, and, with the women, the arrival of the split skirt, which revealed the gorgeous under fabric of the petti-cote.

DRESS

MEN

A larger number of clothes were visible.

The *Shirt* (men) was white and had frills at the wrist and neck, with the breast embroidered

EDWARD VI IN MARIAN CAP

chiefly in red and black or even gold, where it showed. It had sleeves sufficiently large to allow them to be pulled through the slashings of the

outer garments to make the puffed "blistering." Under Queen Mary a Spanish ruff was added.

The *Doublet* (men) was of knee length, with large slit sleeves and a full pleated skirt. The

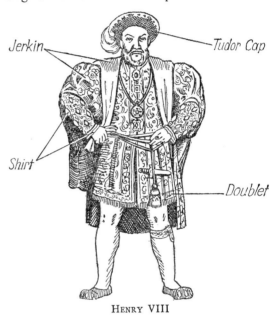

HENRY VIII

shoulders, eked out with padding, were extremely broad. The slits were vertical and regular, their ends being closed with jewelled brooches for the rich. The doublet was fastened down the front to the waist; below was left unfastened. It was fur-lined, and the lining showed at the bottom of the skirt. Under Queen Mary the shape became more self-fitting and padding went out of favour. The skirt had a pleated effect. Over it was worn

The *Jerkin* (men), which was of ankle length for old men; others wore it to just above the knees. It was an overcoat, with a huge wide collar and fur-lined revers down the front. It could be sleeveless; or have a half-sleeve formed of one large puff from shoulder to elbow, or have a hanging sleeve from the elbow.

The *Vest* (men) was worn only when the

doublet was cut low in the chest to display the vest. It was of elaborately embroidered velvet or brocade and was sleeveless.

The *Belt* (men) had become a mere sash.

The *Cape* (men) was circular to just below the waist, and banded with several lines of horizontal braiding at the edge.

QUEEN MARY, 1541 (LONDON)

DRESS
WOMEN

Stays (women) were of leather or bone and with the *Hoop* (women), which was bell-shaped, formed the foundation for the tight and smooth outer garments.

The *Chemise* (women) was embroidered; a good deal of it showed when it covered the chest, as the bodice was low and square.

The *Petticoat* or *Kirtle* (women) was a most important garment, and was of brocaded velvet or silk, with large symmetrical designs of fruit and leaves. It was stretched tightly over the hoop, and its pattern matched the undersleeves of the gown.

The *Gown* (women) was bell-shaped, with a skirt open from waist to hem in an inverted V shape. The waist was gored and the long padded bodice went to a point below the waist line. The square-cut neck was low and showed the bare skin unless the chemise was worn gathered up to the neck. The lined bodice was fastened

at the back, and as its shoulder seams were long the armhole was not in its natural place, but about two inches down the arm, where a distinct line was shown. These sleeves were wide at the elbow and banded with fur or velvet; thus was disclosed the tight undersleeve, which at the elbow became a huge puff or "bishop" sleeve. The undersleeve matched the petticoat. Under Queen Mary the low neck disappeared in favour of a high-cut bodice with an open collar to just below the throat; its edges were turned back, and spread out on either side of the throat and over the back. This alteration was typical of the change from the over-nuptial Henry to the respectable Mary.

The *Partlet* (women) was a fine linen neck-filling, with the older fashioned square-cut neck.

Bands were separate short neck-frills.

LEGS

The *Breeches* (men) were puffed and slashed like the doublet, and had a codpiece, which

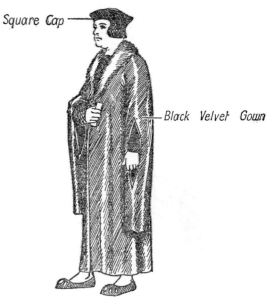

THOMAS CROMWELL, 1537 (LONDON)

showed where the doublet was unfastened. They were worn under the doublet. The codpiece was a padded flap at the fork of the legs. It was tied with ribbons called "points," with the white shirt pulled through at each side to show.

Stockings (men) were for the first time of silk, but of a thicker silk than modern stockings.

FEET

Shoes (men and women) became more natural in shape, though they were still bun toed. They covered the instep and had a series of slits lengthways through which different coloured materials were pulled.

In Mary's reign they were as broad as 7 inches. *Mules* were heelless velvet slippers. *Boots* had a turnover cut out like a battlement below the knee, and another at the calf. *Pinsnets* were women's thin cork-soled shoes.

HAIR

Hair (men) was short. Men were clean shaven or a short fringe of beard, with similar whiskers, was worn. The King's hair was red.

Hair (women) was parted in the middle, or less often braided, but only the front portion was visible. Under Queen Mary it was puffed out instead of being flattened, and more was seen by thrusting back the hat.

HATS
MEN

Hats (men) were the black velvet square caps, familiarized by Sir Thomas More and Holbein.

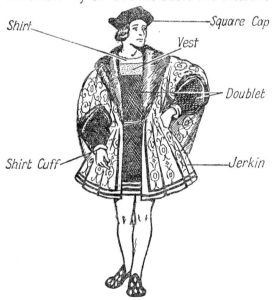

DR. ZELLE (BRUSSELS)

The velvet skull cap and Henry's Tudor cap were also black. The latter was a circle of stiffened velvet gathered into a narrow brim. It is still worn by doctors in the universities. If one side only was turned up, a jewel held the single turn-up. If all sides were turned up, then they were regularly jewelled all round. A long, curling ostrich feather was placed across the front or slightly at the side, and the crown was flat. The Marian cap was gathered into a head band and had no brim.

HATS
WOMEN

Hats (women) were of two kinds—the Gable and the French Hood. Both were elaborate, and consisted of three or four different pieces.

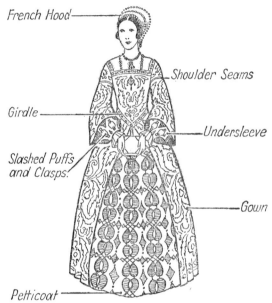

PRINCESS ELIZABETH, 1546 (HAMPTON COURT)

The *Gable Hat* (women) first had a strip of brown or black silk crossed over the forehead and sewn across in stripes. This showed beneath the gable point. Next the stiff white hood, or coif, which was jewelled in front about two or three inches wide (or the jewelled piece was separate) was worn.

Later was worn a long bag of velvet or satin, usually black, which was sewn to the cap, and the whole was covered with a rectangular piece of material long enough to form the gable or sloped roof part on top of the head, with falls on either side of the face. The pendant pieces had strings attached for the purpose of tying the sides back on themselves so that the ends were facing upwards and nearly reaching the first slope of the gable. Subsequently, these ends were permanently sewn upwards in the same position. The strings might also be used to fasten the ends together by passing the ends of the strings under the chin. The material of this piece was velvet, silk, or embroidered fabric. Stiffening was used to maintain the acute angles in position.

The *French Hood* (women) came in under Henry VIII. First was worn a flat frill of gold net or white lawn. Over this and behind it was

PEASANTS

The peasants' clothes were of plain cloth or serge, and, of course, no "blistering" was allowed. Dark blue was a favourite and serviceable colour. Men's shirts were of unbleached linen or calico with narrow collars turned over. Wealthy traders and citizens wore a mantle, which followed the general lines of the jerkin, but was of full length. Over a doublet merchants wore a long gown of sober cut, a square cap, and perhaps a gold or silver chain like a mayor's chain. Breeches were in two puffs to the knee and woollen stockings

Striped Silk — Tied Pendant

White Hood — Velvet Bag

Henry VIII Neck —

THE GABLE HOOD, 1525

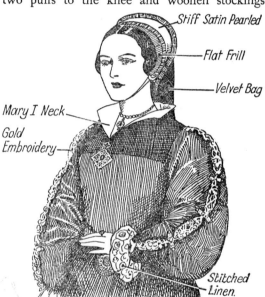

Stiff Satin Pearled

Flat Frill

Velvet Bag

Mary I Neck —

Gold Embroidery —

Stitched Linen.

THE FRENCH HOOD, 1541

a two-inch wide stiff band of velvet or satin, edged with pearls and covering and curling round the ears. The velvet bag was added as before, or a short veil was fastened to the back of the head. This type of hat revealed more of the face. Under Queen Mary the head-dress became less stiff and elaborate, and was a simple black velvet cap set far back on the head with a slight peak over the forehead. A velvet strip hung from the back.

A jewelled *Girdle* (women) surrounded the waist and hung down for a good length in front, finishing with a beautifully designed piece of goldsmith's work in the form of a pendant, ball, or cross. This was large and richly jewelled. From the men's girdles hung short daggers which were for ornament rather than use.

were mostly white. Leather shoes were slipper-shaped, slightly square toed, and without slittings. Low-crowned felt hats with wide brims were used.

For peasant women the gown, with its long and tight bodice and sleeves, back laced, the skirt split to show a plainish petticoat, was the invariable feature. Girls had their skirts pleated into the bodice. Aprons were useful both outside and indoors. Stockings were of bright colours in wool, and felt or leather shoes were worn.

SUMMARY
MEN

Dress

Shirt—white, frilled wrist and neck, embroidered breast, large sleeves. Under Mary a ruff added.

Doublet—knee length, large slit sleeves, full pleated skirt, fur lined, wide shoulders. Under Mary closer fit, and less padding.

Jerkin—long or short fur-lined coat, huge flat collar and revers, sleeveless or one large puff, knee length, open in front.

Vest—sleeveless, embroidered velvet or brocade, worn if doubtlet cut low enough to show it.

Cape—(Mary only) circular to just below waist.

Belt—a sash.

Legs

Breeches—puffed and slashed, codpiece.

Stockings—thick silk.

Feet

Shoes—more natural, cover instep, bun toed. Mules. Boots.

Hair

Short, clean shaven, short fringe beard and whiskers.

Hats

Black velvet square cap.

Velvet skull cap.

Stiff velvet circle in narrow brim, one or all sides turned up, jewel, flat crown, feather across front.

WOMEN

Dress

Stays—bone or leather.

Hoop—bell-shaped.

Chemise—embroidered.

Petticoat—stretched, large pattern, matched undersleeves.

Gown—bell-shape, skirt open in front from waist, gored waist, lined and padded bodice long and pointed. Square, low neck, back laced. Shoulder seams long so armhole is two inches down arm. Sleeves wide at elbow with broad fur or velvet bands. Tight under sleeves of fabric.

(Mary only) bodice cut high, collar open to below throat and spread out each side and at back.

Partlet—(Mary only) linen, filling in neck.

Bands—simple neck-frills.

Feet

As men, and pinsnets.

Hair

Mid parted or braided, seen only in front. Under Mary puffed and more seen.

Hats

Gable—1st strip, brown or black silk; 2nd, stiff white coif or hood jewelled; 3rd, long black velvet or satin bag; 4th, black silk, velvet or embroidered strip.

French hood—1st flat, gold net or lawn frill; 2nd, stiff velvet or satin pearled band; 3rd, velvet bag or short veil on back of head.

Cap—(Mary only) simple black velvet on back of head, peak on forehead, velvet strip hung behind.

PEASANTS
MEN

Dress

Plain cloth or serge, no blisters.

Shirts—unbleached linen or calico, narrow turn-down collars.

Mantle or gown—only for rich citizens.

Legs

Breeches—two puffs to knee.

Stockings—wool, often white.

Feet

Shoes—leather, slipper shaped.

Hats

Low-crowned felt, wide brim.

Flat cloth cap.

PEASANTS
WOMEN

Dress

Coarse serge or cloth, dark blue being mostly worn.

Gown—tight, long bodice, tight sleeves, back laced. Skirt split to show petticoat. Girls had short skirts pleated to bodice.

Petticoat—apron.

Legs

Stockings—gray wool.

Feet

Felt or leather shoes.

CHAPTER XIII

SHAKESPEARE'S ENGLAND, 1558–1625

GLORIANA, outwardly, was nothing but a walking wardrobe—a mass of wires, stays, and struts, to which were fastened the stiff barbaric clothes that almost disguised the

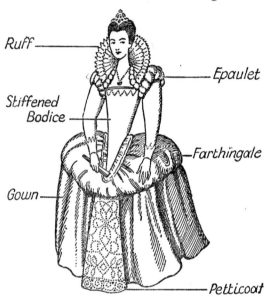

Ruff———

———Epaulet

Stiffened Bodice———

———Farthingale

Gown———

———Petticoat

QUEEN ELIZABETH, 1600

fact that she had a human shape. Her head was covered with a ginger wig; her teeth were black; and the only parts of her skin that she could not cover with materials were effectively concealed under a coat of raddle.

Scots James was no better. He was so terrified of assassination that he invented a suit that was so padded and stuffed that he looked like a large balloon, badly balanced on two sausages, and he also wore a large ruff and a ridiculously small "top hat."

The *tout ensemble* of both these personages was comic, but as they were royal despots, nobody dared to tell them so, and the Court had to follow their examples.

The period was one of adventurous travel, and, as in similar times before, this was reflected in the fashions: the Spanish Cape, the Italian

Doublet, and the Venetian Trunkhose were worn. Women's clothes remained the same, except for the development of the huge ruff and the enormous farthingale, but the men wore the close-fitting doublet and abandoned their over-broad shoulder.

The body sank into insignificance under the attack of the wire and padding industries and man became a mere peg on which to support garments which could hardly be called clothes, but rather a series of draperies concealing the machinery underneath.

The enormous lace ruffs, to judge from existing painted tombs, were often starched or dyed a yellow shade, but white was the usual colour in the portraits of the period.

Here again the style was characteristic of the contemporary ruler. For was it not an age of

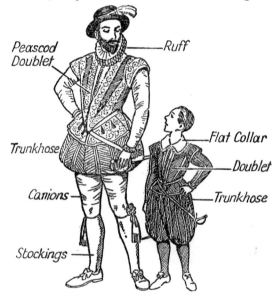

Peascod Doublet———

———Ruff

———Flat Collar

Trunkhose———

———Doublet

Canions———

———Trunkhose

Stockings———

SIR WALTER RALEIGH AND SON, 1602

expansion? In commerce with foreign countries and navigation in distance lands; with explorers and adventurers like Drake, Hawkins and Fro-bisher; in literature too, new thought was developed and new modes of expression came to the surface. The Theatre took a great step forward, when it ceased to be a mere appanage of a nobleman's entourage, and relied on the support of the common people. Shakespeare's was by no means the only literary name; expansion came through the writings of Dekker, Marlowe, Beaumont, and Fletcher, to name but a few Elizabethan and Jacobean playwrights.

Elizabeth, with her thousands of dresses, must have been a constant incentive to every right-minded woman to spend as much as possible of a husband's income on adornment. James Stuart was the reverse of the flamboyant Elizabeth Tudor. Consequently the inflated fashions collapsed and his reign forms a transitional stage into the graceful and reasonable garments of the Martyr King.

ELIZABETHAN DRESS
MEN

The *Spanish Cape* (men) was circular, with a high collar, and was banded along its outer edge with braids.

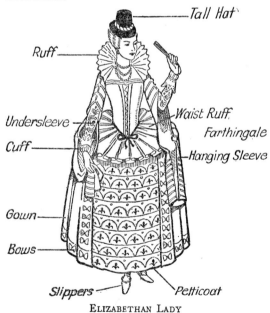

ELIZABETHAN LADY

The *Italian Doublet* closely fitted the body from neck to just below the waist, where it ended in a short frill. It was boned and padded so that the front edge was curved outwards to a point

below the waist, which looked like, and was called, a peascod. The armhole was outlined with a padded crescent-shaped epaulet, and at first the sleeves (which were of a different colour) were

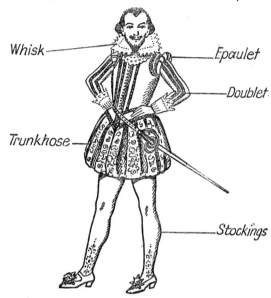

RICHARD SACKVILLE, LORD DORSET, 1616

tight, long, and slashed, but later they were not slashed. The wrist finished with a frill or turned back linen cuff, lace edged, and the sleeve could at option be split to show the under sleeve. The tunic was buttoned down the centre, and could be opened to disclose the vest, in which case it was reversed with a different colour. It had a high collar.

The *Ruff* (men) was starched yellow. It folded into figure eight shape and encircled the neck.

The *Collar* (men) was of white linen turned down or square and wired, but these two latter alternatives to the ruff really became general in James I's time.

ELIZABETHAN DRESS
WOMEN

The women wore a linen *Chemise*, a leather or whalebone *Corset*, and a huge wheel or hoop of whalebone called a *Farthingale*, which was attached just below the waist. Over this several *Petticoats* and two *Gowns* were worn. The cut of the gowns was fuller, but, as in the previous reign, they had hanging sleeves of lawn and cambric, or lace, stuck to the armhole of the under robe, and a deep point to the bodice.

The *Ruff* (women) was of cambric or lawn, plain or lace edged, and if it was very large it had to be underpropped with bones. The enormous upstanding lace collar, wired to stand up at the back of the neck, came in at the close of the reign, about 1580. There was another late variant of the circular ruff. It parted in the middle and formed a semi-circle or a heart-shape on back and shoulders only.

LEGS

The *Trunk Hose* (men) were really breeches, much slashed, puffed, and padded. They were

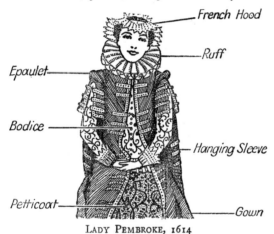

French Hood

Ruff

Epaulet

Bodice

Hanging Sleeve

Petticoat

Gown

LADY PEMBROKE, 1614

almost circular. They ended at mid thigh and were "paned" with decorative vertical bands. With these might be worn *Canions* (men), which were tight shorts to the knee, over which the stocking was taken. They were padded. If the trunk hose and canions were worn they were in one garment and the stockings were separate. If they were not, then the trunk hose were worn with stocking tights, which came farther up the leg, well above the knee.

Stockings (men) were long and came above the knee. If no canions were worn, the stockings came nearly to the fork, and were joined on to the trunk hose breeches.

FEET

Shoes (men) had a high instep, buckled or rosetted, and were made in velvet, leather, and cloth.

James I shoes were square toed. Thigh boots were worn.

Slippers (women) were of velvet or satin, which necessitated the 2 in. to 7 in. thick cork-soled wooden *Chopines* (women) to be added for street wear. Shoes (women) had turned-up toes and high heels.

HAIR

The *Hair* (men) was long and brushed back. They wore a pointed beard and moustache. A dandy wore on his shoulder one love lock which was delicately tied with a ribbon!

Hair (women) was curled and frizzed and dyed golden. It was worn high on the forehead and away from the sides of the face.

HATS

Hats (men) were round or flat with soft crowns and narrow brims and a feather. A gold lace or twisted cord went round the crown. Felt, beaver, sarcenet, and velvet were the materials.

The *French Hood* (women) was much the same as in the previous reign.

The *Tall Hat* (women) was exactly like the men's tall hat—shallow brimmed, high crowned, and with a twist of material round the crown. About 1590 the veil of the French Hood was wired into arches behind the shoulders. Smaller bonnets were also worn.

JAMES I. DRESS
MEN

Breeches (men) became looser and longer, and covered the knee, where they were buttoned or ribbon-tied, though the older circular type of trunk hose continued to be fashionable.

The *Ruff* (men) was succeeded by the *Whisk* (men), a stiff semi-circular collar of lace, square in front, and wired out. The ruff remained popular, but it was not so modish. The remainder of the costume was as before.

JAMES I DRESS
WOMEN

The *Collar* (women) changed from the circular ruff to the wired lace or cambric collar standing up at the back of the neck and attached to the open neck on each side in front. It was dyed different shades, and was circular, except in front, where it was square cut. Another form, a heart shape, was in two circles at the back. This type was popularized by Elizabeth, but it became more general and smaller in James I's reign.

The *Waist Ruff* (women) came in at the close of Elizabeth's reign, and was a box-pleated rectangle, tied round the waist with a bow in front and resting on the horizontal part of the skirt, which was upheld by the farthingale.

The *Petticoat* (women) was of satin, and short enough to disclose the feet in their dainty satin slippers.

The *Gown* (women) had a low-cut square-neck opening, and tight sleeves to the elbow, from which dangled long streamers—relics of the hanging sleeves. The bodice was cylindrical and pointed, all creases being removed by the corset, and the skirt opened in front to reveal the satin petticoat. The undersleeves, which showed from elbow to wrist, were ruffed at the wrist with small frills or were finished with cambric cuffs stitched in coloured and black thread or with lace cuffs—both were of the turn-back type.

Feet

Shoes (men and women) were ribbon rosetted, and the women also wore rosettes of lace.

Hair

Hair (men) was worn half-way down the neck, and was brushed back. It had the almost invariable addition of a short pointed beard and a small

JAMES I's QUEEN

tuft, not joined to the beard, just below the lip, and moustaches were slightly pointed.

Hair (women) was dressed high and backwards from the face.

Hats

The *Tall Crowned Hat* (men and women) was of small black felt with a high crown and small brim, a cord or twisted material round the crown, and a feather starting in front and fastened with a jewel at the side. The men also wore a beaver hat with a white plume erect behind it.

Jewellery

Jewellery: Many necklaces, chiefly pearl, for the women, and gold chains with large rings for

JAMES I's DAUGHTER, QUEEN OF BOHEMIA, C. 1620

men. The folding fan made its appearance for the first time and displaced the flag-type fan.

SUMMARY
Men (Elizabeth)

Dress

Spanish Cape—high collar.

Italian Doublet—close fit, small frill below waist, padded and boned to form curved convex shape pointed downwards. Sleeves differed in colour and split to show undersleeve. Tight, long, slashed sleeve and turn-back cuff, armhole covered by epaulet. High collar, buttoned down centre or open to show vest. Vertical embroidered panels.

Ruff—yellow starched linen, figure eight shape.

Collar—white linen, turned down or square and wired.

Legs

Trunk Hose—round breeches, very full at top, end at mid-thigh; slashed, puffed, padded.

Canions—shorts, padded (1570 on).
Stockings—long to above knee.

Feet

Shoes—high instep, buckled or rosetted, leather, velvet, or cloth. Thigh boots.

Hair

Long, brushed back, pointed beard, moustache slight. Love lock on one shoulder, ribbon tied.

Hats

Round or flat, soft crown, narrow brim, feathered, gold lace or twisted cord round crown. Felt, beaver, sarcenet, or velvet.

Jewellery

Large rings.

WOMEN (ELIZABETH)

Dress

Corset—leather or whalebone.
Farthingale—huge bone wheel below waist.
Petticoats—several.
Chemise—linen.
Two Gowns—hanging sleeves of lawn or cambric to underdress; general style as Henry VIII, long point to bodice.
Ruff—cambric or lawn, plain or lace edged, underpropped if large: (1) circular; (2) semi-circular; (3) upstanding at back, round or heart shaped.

Feet

Slippers—velvet or satin.
Chopines—cork soled over shoes.
Shoes—high heels, turned-up toes.

Hair

Curled, dyed, frizzed, high on forehead and clear of sides of face.

Hats

French Hood—as Mary's reign.
Tall Hat—shallow brim, high crown as men.

Jewels

Chains, pins, scented embroidered gloves, lace or silk handkerchiefs, flag-shaped fans in hand or girdle, masks for street and theatre.

MEN (JAMES I)

Dress

Breeches—loose, cover knees where buttoned or ribbon tied.
Rest, as above, but less slashes and padding.
Whisk—a standing collar vice ruff.

Feet

Shoes—ribbon rosetted.

Hair

Half down neck; pointed beard; lip tuft; moustache; brushed back hair.

Hats

Tall crowned, wide brimmed.
Beaver hats with white plume erect at back.

WOMEN (JAMES I)

Dress

Collar—wired lace or cambric dyed. Fans out behind.
Waist Ruff—box pleat, tied above farthingale.
Farthingale—huge bone wheel below waist.
Petticoat—satin, shows feet.
Gown—low-cut square neck, open cylinder bodice, tight sleeves to elbow; from there streamers, open skirt in front to show petticoat; undersleeves to wrist where ruffed or with cambric or lace cuffs.

Feet

Shoes—lace rosetted.

Hair

High dressed.

Hats

Same as men, high-crowned felt. No caps.

Jewels

Necklaces—many. Folding fan first arrived.

CHARLES I AND HIS QUEEN

CHAPTER XIV

THE MARTYR KING, 1625–49

KING CHARLES THE FIRST was an artist and a saint. He was one of the earliest of our monarchs to live a pure home life, and his devotion to the historic Church cost him his life. He was one of the most cultured men in Europe, and his art collections in London and Windsor for the most part happily remain with us. As the patron of Vandyck and Rubens he has earned undying gratitude. The fashions during his reign became less awkward and more graceful and easy, and the gentlemen knew how to wear their clothes with an air. It was a thoroughly artistic period.

Whatever else men might say of King Charles the First, he was a gentleman and a man of culture. Being so he knew how to wear his clothes with an air and a manner. His cavalier courtiers imitated their monarch and brought the dash of gallant adventure to ennoble the circumstances within which they moved and had their being.

Some of them carried things to extremes, and a royal favourite, the Duke of Buckingham, even irritated Parliament by his extravagances in dress. Unhappily such a case is unlikely to happen to-day. How much gayer life would be if we wore bright colours and clothes of an inspiring shape.

Jacobean stiffness and padding gave way before a looser and more comfortable style of costume. Its effect on the wearer must have been a relief since the clothes approximated closely to the shape of the body without being rigid.

Hair was curled and lace came into great prominence, not only in the flat Vandyck collars but also in the turned back cuffs, and as trimming for babies' bonnets.

Children looked charming miniatures of their elders and the styles suited both young and old equally well.

The influence of Puritanism, with its dour negation of beauty in line and form, had the opposite effect on the well-born, who became in the later period more *degagé*, more studiedly careless and dashing, with a touch of fantasy which was effective because it was carefully restrained within limits.

The women abandoned the absurd Farthingale hoops so the skirt became more natural, though its fullness remained.

Rich satins were worn by men and women alike, and piece-lace was occasionally made into

QUEEN HENRIETTA MARIA (LONDON)

complete dresses over a foundation of contrasting material.

The feather fan added attraction by allowing women something useful to assist in their time-honoured pastime of flirting!

The King was unlucky: he was by no means a fool—indeed he reduced the National Debt by half—but he had the misfortune to live in an age of fanatics, and he fell a victim to religious and political strife caused by a minority of irreconcileables rather than by the mass of popular feeling.

The triumph of Puritanism had a profound effect on clothing fashions, for the world had not at that time arrived at a condition where political changes were not reflected in costume. The Great Rebellion swept away the Cavalier and his dress and an age of severity set in. Man, however, cannot endure for long restrictions on his free will, and after eleven years beauty returned to dress when the King came into his own again.

DRESS
MEN

The *Doublet* (men) was busked with bones and was corset-like. Until 1632 it had a pointed waist,

CHILDREN OF CHARLES I (LONDON)

with four to six vertical slits on the breast and back. The sleeves were close-fitting and plain, but another type had the sleeve close from wrist to elbow, where it widened into a large puff, which was paned to show the linen shirt. Panning was a series of strips of material with gaps vertically cut between. After 1628 the doublet became deeper and less pointed, and was loose fitting with only a slight point in front. The epaulets, which were slight at first, disappeared during the reign. After 1645 the jacket became skimpy and reached to just above the hips, leaving a gap to show the shirt, which was pulled out. It had no waist.

The shortening of the doublet and the practice of leaving the lower half unbuttoned allowed the white shirt to show below it at the waist. In Charles II's reign it became shorter still, and turned into an "Eton jacket." Simultaneously with this curtailment, which occurred about 1645, the breeches changed into full, loose, tubular trousers like modern "shorts." They were edged

with lace or ribbon bows at the waist, the knees, and down the side seams.

"Tassets" was the name given to the small skirts of the doublet.

The *Breeches* (men) were fastened by points, i.e. a row of bows at the waist. Trunk hose remained only for pages, and in State robes.

In 1620 they had a high waist and full knickers to just above the knee. In 1628 they reached to below the knee, and were gartered with a large bow or rosette, and buttoned all down the side. If the lower buttons above the knee were unfastened they disclosed the linen lining. In 1640 they had become full and open, i.e. tubular, and were unconfined at the knee, or they were close at the knee, and finished with ribbons. The waist dropped to just over the hips so that the full shirt bulged out above them and between them and the now short doublet. This was a precursor of the Charles II costume.

The *Jerkin* (men) was sleeveless or had hang-

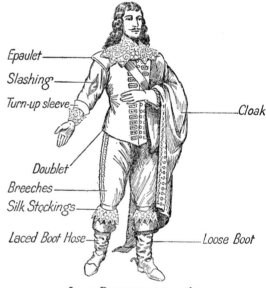

LORD PETERBOROUGH, 1635

ing sleeves. In leather, as the buff coat, it was laced up the front and sometimes had loose sleeves to match, or close stuff sleeves striped with braid or lace horizontally or vertically. It was a military garment.

The *Coat* (men) was cassocked-shaped, and reached to mid-thigh. It had wide sleeves, the cuff being turned up broadly. It was worn during evenings.

The *Cloak* (men) became longer and fuller, and reached at least to the knee, sometimes lower, and was draped over the arm.

The *Gown* (men) was of the type still worn by Chancellors and Lord Mayors, and was worn by older men.

DRESS
WOMEN

The *Bodice* (women) up to 1630 had a deep point and a wasp waist. After that date it was low-necked, with a high waist and skirt tabs like the men's doublets, and was worn over a round pointed stomacher, which matched. The sleeves were at first close to the wrist and followed the men's fashions by developing into large puffs, or they were leg-of-mutton types with slashings. The commonest form was in one puff to below

GENTLEMAN OF 1645

the elbow, and, later, to the elbow only, the bare arm showing in either case.

The *Skirt* (women) was gathered at the waist and hung loosely. It had, at option, the reversed V opening, in which case

The *Petticoat* (women) showed when the skirt opened in a front ∧, but otherwise it did not,

as the fashion of raising the upper skirt to show the under-robe had gone out.

The *Gown* (older women) was close at the throat and fitted the body, after the type of Lady Pembroke—see page 56. The skirt was full.

LEGS

Silk stockings were popular, and the men wore enormous boots, which necessitated *Boot Hose*

KING CHARLES I (LONDON)

(men) of material edged deeply with lace, which fell over the boot top. The more economical wore *Boot Hose Tops*, which had no calves; the boot covered the rest. Garters, finished with a great bow at the side, or large rosettes in coloured ribbon, were prominent.

FEET

Spurred boots were almost *de rigueur*. Their tops were folded down and over. The spur strap passed through a winged leather plaque on the front of the instep. Spurs had large rowels. Some wide-spreading top-boots had their tops so loose that they formed a cup all round. All had square heels. Red heels for evening wear remained the mark of the aristocrat. The wide tops came in about 1640. Shoes had rosettes and were rather square toed, and fairly high heeled. Rosettes were wide, single, double, or treble bows.

HAIR

Men wore their hair off the brow and to one side and level with the jaw till 1628, but afterwards it lengthened and they had a fringe on the brow. The Vandyck pointed beard remained until 1640, but was then displaced by the chin tuft, which began in 1630 and lasted till 1645. Moustaches were brushed upwards like that of "The Laughing Cavalier."

The women wore their hair brushed back off

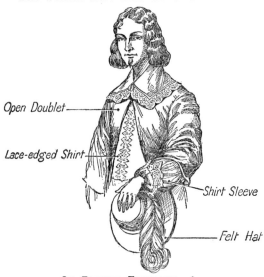

Open Doublet

Lace-edged Shirt

Shirt Sleeve

Felt Hat

SIR RICHARD FANSHAWE, 1644

the face and tied into a bun at the back. On the forehead was a fringe, or kiss curls were worn there. Ringlets appeared and, as the reign proceeded, they were worn longer. At first they were mere bunches at each side of the face, but in the end they became long corkscrew curls. Pearl ropes adorned the head. Jewellery was much less profuse and consequently more tasteful than it was in the previous periods.

HATS

The *Sombrero* (men) of black felt, loose and wide brimmed, with one side turned up, and with a fairly high crown, is well known. One or two ostrich feathers adorned it at one side, or a hat band was formed of the cut ends of ostrich feathers. After 1640 the Puritan type began to be worn, the crown became higher and the brim narrower, and the whole appearance was marred. The *Montero* (men) was a cap used for sport,

and had a loose, adaptable brim, which could be turned either up or down at taste. The women were usually bareheaded, though they occasionally wore a loose gauze veil or a loose hood. The Cavalier hat was used only for riding.

The high felt hat was almost universally worn at the end of Charles I's reign and (robbed of its feather and ribbon) by the Puritans.

LINEN

Cleanliness was a feature of the Carolean Court. In consequence linen played an important part. Lovely lace collars were wired into various shapes. The old whisk was succeeded by the *Falling Ruff* (men), which was the old ruff lying down instead of standing up. This became the *Falling Band* (men), which was a collar of the same shape but without the gathers of the ruff. Both hung from the throat to the shoulders, the band being wider and deeper. After 1640 they shrank in size. Cuffs were deep and turned up over the doublet sleeve. The sword was suspended by a broad waist sash, worn horizontally, or from the *Baldrick*, or sword belt, hung diagonally over the right shoulder.

Up to 1635 the women wore the *fan-shaped* wired-up ruffs, as before. Older women still wore the *cart-wheel ruff* of the reigns of Elizabeth and James I. After 1630 the *broad falling collar*, like the men's, came in, and, like theirs, it was made of linen or lace. Later, the broad falling collar with the *upstanding fan collar* was worn. From 1635 the low neck was covered with a neckerchief folded diagonally, and by 1650 the neck line had become horizontal and presented that appearance of the bodice falling off altogether which was so much loved by the Early Victorians.

SUMMARY
MEN
Dress

Doublet—pointed waist, busked. Vertical slits front and back. Close sleeves or close wrist to elbow, then wide puff, paned below to show shirt. Looser and less pointed later. Epaulets disappeared gradually. Skirt shortened to hips later.

Breeches—row of bows at waist. In 1620 high waist and knickers above knee. In 1628 knickers below knee. In 1640 "shorts," open and fuller.

Jerkin—sleeveless or hanging sleeves. Leather front laced. Loose sleeves, matching or striped, optional.

Coat—loose, cassock-like to mid-thigh with wide sleeve and broad turn-up cuff for evening wear.

Cloak—full to knee or lower.

Gown—like Chancellor's for older men.

Shirt—linen. When doublet shortened to hips, the shirt showed in bulge there.

Legs

Silk stockings. Boot hose, edged lace deeply.
Boot hose tops, without calf.
Garters—great bow below knee or rosette.

Feet

Spurred boots, top folded down.
Wide spreading top-boots, high square heels.
Red heels for dress wear. Rosetted shoes.

Hair

Off brow one side, level with jaw. Later, lengthened with a fringe. Van Dyck beard to 1640. Chin tuft 1630–40. Moustache brushed up.

Hats

Sombrero—high crown, wide brim cocked. Ostrich feathers or feather hat band.
High conical crown, narrow brim later.
Montero—cap with reversible brim for sport.
Fur cap—close fitting.

Linen

The whisk collar to 1630.
Falling ruff.
Falling band.
Deep turn-up cuffs.

Sash broad over waist, or shoulder belt-baldrick for sword.

WOMEN

Dress

Bodice—deep pointed wasp waist, and stomacher.

After 1630 low neck, high waist; skirt tabs like doublet, and round stomacher to match.

Sleeves—close to wrist or puffed, as men, or leg-of-mutton, slashed. Later, one puff to below elbow, then to above elbow unslashed. Bare arm.

Skirt—waist gathered, opening optional, hung loose.

Petticoat—showed at opening of skirt. Often unseen.

Gowns—older women, close throat, fitted body, full skirt.

Feet

Satin shoes rosetted.
Leather riding boots as men.

Hair

Off face to bun at back. Head fringe or kiss curls. Ringlets. Corkscrew curls. Pearls.

Hats

Mostly bare heads. Loose gauze veil. Loose hood. Cavalier hat for riding.

Linen

Fan-shape wired ruffs as before to 1635.
Cart-wheel ruff for older women.
Broad falling collar. Falling collar and/or upstanding collar.
Square kerchief over neck opening.
Horizontal opening after 1650.

CHAPTER XV

PURITANISM, 1649–60

PURITANISM has gained more credit than is its due, owing to the extremely inaccurate historians of the Victorian era who had a habit of making their history fit their politics. What is regarded by the man in the street as the

Tall Felt Hat

Plain Collar

Black Cloak

Doublet

Breeches

Garter

age of liberty and freedom was, in reality, quite the reverse.

England was under the domination of a crude, brutal, and unrefined man—that of the Dictator Cromwell. The effect was that everyone had to conform to the standard pattern. Dress, as a result, became harsh and plain, like its exponents, and it lacked all grace of colour, shape, and design.

The modes, stripped of every atom of charm, remained the same as at the end of the reign of the Martyr King, but the extreme of Puritan dress was affected chiefly by the more fanatical types such as the "Roundheads." Others avoided the strictly cropped head, and the favoured few of Cromwell's entourage wore what they liked. A General Harrison, though he was a Puritan, at a reception appeared in scarlet trimmed with silver lace and ribbons. This was

exceptional. Most men wore their hair fairly long and brushed in any style.

All ribbons, lace, and embroideries were abandoned. Materials were of muddy brown, funeral black, and other shades that were reminiscent of dirt and mud.

DRESS

MEN

The *Doublet* (men), robbed of its point and shape, became a badly fitting sack.

The *Breeches* (men) were quite plain, and had no decorated bands up the sides. They were gathered into a band at the knee.

The *Shirt* (men) did not show except where the deep, plain, white linen cuff was turned up over the sleeves of the doublet or jerkin.

The *Coat* (men) was like a cassock, and fell to

High Hat

Linen Collar

the middle of the thigh. It had fairly wide sleeves to enable it to go over the inner sleeves of the rest of the costume.

The *Gown* (men) was still worn by the older

men, and was much the same as that of a modern lord mayor's, except that it had no bands of metal lace or other decoration.

DRESS
WOMEN

The *Bodice* (women) had a square-cut, fairly low, neck, but not as low as in Royalist times. It had a straight waistband, and the pointed shapes were abandoned. The square tabs into which the skirt of the bodice was cut in the preceding reign were discontinued, save, oddly enough, for one solitary tab, which, like a tail, hung on in the middle of the back. The sleeves were plain and close fitting, though sleeves of elbow length were worn by the more "abandoned" women—chiefly working class.

The *Skirt* (women) was plain. It was gathered into the waist by a band and was somewhat loose in cut. The ∧ opening, which used to reveal the petticoat in the King's time, was considered indelicate.

The *Apron* (women) was of plain linen of the usual type.

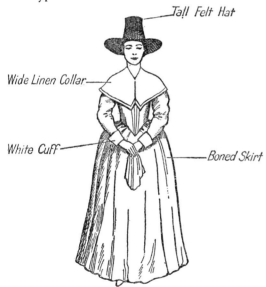

The *Gown* (women) was the older women's garment and was made as previously.

The period gives no assistance to the artist who has to design its costumes, but if pearl and oyster greys or pleasant cinnamon browns are contrasted with the large spaces of white linen

in apron, kerchief, collar, and cuffs, a suitable effect can be obtained.

LEGS

The men wore plain black cloth or wool stockings of thick material, and women rosettes to their shoes. Red heels were abolished.

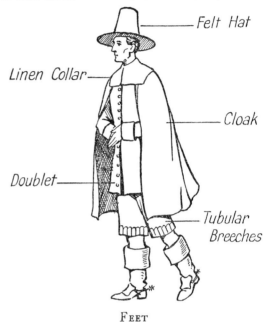

FEET

Very wide tops of black leather or brown were put on the thigh boots, and shoes with plain metal buckles—perhaps even silver—were worn. They were much like modern court shoes with square buckles about half an inch in breadth.

HAIR

Close-cropped hair was the mark of the extremely righteous and of the fanatic, but the bulk of the men refused to comply with this custom and wore their hair fairly long to about the top of the nape of the neck. It was parted in the middle and was roughly brushed. Faces were clean shaven. The women dressed their hair straightly and plainly, and hid most of it under the white linen caps. No curls or pearls helped to make the hair more beautiful.

HATS

The hat *par excellence* was the comic black felt with a high crown and a narrow brim. Older men wore close-fitting skull-shaped caps. The women wore the linen coif or skull-cap, rather more of a mob-cap cut than the men's, and over this the Puritan high-crowned men's hat. Black silk hoods were popular; sometimes they were attached to a full-length cape over the shoulders.

Halberd

Comb Morion

Corslet

Breeches

Ribbon Garters

No jewellery of any kind was worn. Market baskets in wicker, oval in shape, with circular handles, are effective properties, and tall plain walking sticks with, perhaps, a plain silver knob may be used by the men.

People affected dour and severe expressions to denote the lack of humour and graciousness of their outlook. This should be observed in stage work of this period.

Women for the most part still went about bareheaded, though the Puritans considered this immodest. Hats should, therefore, be worn in representations of the early part of this period though not towards its end. Lace caps were also worn by the more daring and the more conservative, and it is probable that country folk still wore what they possessed, no matter whether it was "Royalist" in style or not. The use of the tall hat worn over the lace or linen cap can be seen in remote parts of Wales to this very day.

LINEN

It was an age of linen.

Plain square-cut collars like immense Eton

collars were worn by men and women alike. They were of the falling band type of the previous reign, but lay flatter on the body. Deep linen cuffs were turned back over the wrists. No lace was used. The square white kerchief was folded diagonally, as before, over the breast and shoulders, and gave a V opening effect to the neck. The collars were wide at first, but towards the close of the revolutionary period they shrank in size.

THE TRANSITION TO MONARCHY

The Puritan regime originated no new styles of dress, but merely modified the modes of Royalist days. Everything was sobered down—there was no lace, there were no ribbons or feathers; plain linen instead of fine lace, straight lines instead of curves were the vogue. The ruff was generally abandoned, although it was in its simpler form of a falling band lace collar.

At the same time, the governing faction wore what they liked. I have instanced the case of the Puritan General Harrison. Another similar case

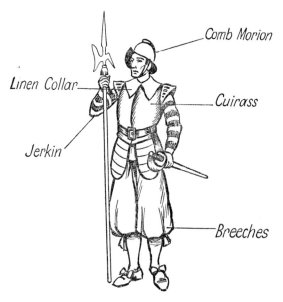

Comb Morion

Linen Collar

Cuirass

Jerkin

Breeches

was that of the Protector Cromwell's daughter, who, according to her portrait in the National Portrait Gallery, London, in 1658, was dressed in the height of the French fashion. The date of this painting should be borne in mind. After the execution of the king the Puritan Party was in the ascendancy, and the Roundhead fashions were dominant. After some years of Oliver's iron rule the nation (which had never approved of the King's martyrdom) made its feelings felt more strongly, and a definite move towards the restoration of the monarchy began. Elizabeth Cromwell's portrait was painted only two years before the King came into his own again: men were looking towards France, where resided the Queen Mother, and their thoughts were reflected in their clothes. Presbyterian fashions fell into definite dislike and disuse, and were replaced by clothes common to the rest of the Royalist States of Europe, in herald of the approaching dawn of liberty, which was to break into day with the return of the Merry Monarch.

SUMMARY

Men

Dress
Doublet—plain and fairly loose fitting.
Breeches—plain, no decoration, band at knee.
Shirt—not showing, save at turn-up cuff.
Jerkin—for soldiers and artisans.
Coat—loose, cassock-like to mid-thigh, fairly wide sleeve, turn-up cuff.
Cloak—plain, not very full, to mid-thigh.
Gown—for older men like a mayor's.

Legs
Cloth stockings or woollen.

Feet
Thigh boots—wide tops.
Shoes with plain silver or metal buckles.

Hair
Close cropped.
Clean shaven.
Long to back of head and mid-parted.

Hats
Broad brim, high crown, black felt.
Caps for old men.

Linen
Plain linen collars, falling band type, square cut.
Deep linen cuffs, turned back over sleeve.

Women

Dress
Bodice—square, lowish neck, straight waistband, no square tabs, save one in centre of back.
Sleeves—plain and close fitting.
Skirt—waist gathered, no ∧ opening.
Petticoat—unseen.
Apron—plain linen.
Gowns—for older women.

Legs
Shoe rosettes permitted.

Hair
Straight dressed, no curls or pearls.

Hats
Black silk hoods, sometimes attached to
Full-length capes.
Linen coifs or caps.
Black felt broad brim and high crown. Can be worn with or without coif.

Linen
Wide collars, square cut, no lace.
Later collars shrank in size.
Kerchief square, folded diagonally over neck opening.
Broad linen cuffs.

Jewellery
None.

CHAPTER XVI

RESTORATION, 1660–89

RESTORATION of the monarchy meant also restoration of artistry in dress, and the general relief at the cessation of the Republican Autocracy caused expansion in

EARLY RESTORATION MAN

design and gaiety in colour. The period divided itself sharply into two sections of men's costume. In the beginning it continued the "Eton Jacket" style, where it left off under Charles I, but instead of the "Shorts" came the kilt-like petticoat breeches. This ended with the importation of the "Persian Vest," a long, heavily braided cassock-like coat, which was worn during the rest of Charles II's reign and that of his brother. The period covers 1660 to 1689.

DRESS

MEN

The Doublet (men) became short, like an Eton jacket, and was left open in front. It had short sleeves to just below the elbow, where they were finished with a deep fringe of looped ribbon.

The sleeve had a front opening till 1665, but afterwards was turned up from the elbow in a close-buttoned cuff. It followed therefore that—

The *Shirt* (men) showed greatly. It was puffed out over the waist and through the sleeve slits. Ribbon-tied till 1680, it had deep lace ruffles at the wrists, and a ruche or frill at the breast-opening, towards the close of its popularity.

The *Collar* (men) continued as the Falling Band till 1670, but afterwards became a mere bib on the breast with the corners rounded. At the end of this period the collar as such ceased to be worn, and the *Neckcloth*, which was a scarf tied at the throat to form a cravat with falling ends, lace edged, took its place.

The *Cassock Coat* (men) was worn over the short doublet in the early part of the period, but

A FAMILY, 1688

was replaced by the similar Tunic Coat when the Eton jacket went out.

The *Vest* or *Waistcoat* (men), as it was soon called, accompanied the tunic from 1664. It was long-sleeved, and reached to the fork.

68

The *Tunic* or *Coat* (men) from 1664 was a cassock-like coat reaching to mid-thigh. In 1670 it reached to below the knee, and it had elbow sleeves finished with broad turned-up cuffs. It was slit up each side and at the back. These slits, as well as the front, were trimmed heavily in the frogging manner with dummy buttons and buttonholes. The resultant horizontal effect on a long coat was the distinguishing mark of the bulk of the Restoration period.

Cloaks (men) were used for travelling, but were not used continuously with day dress as they were in the previous reign. The hat and cloak romance had vanished.

Petticoat Breeches (men) were at first much like kilts, and in the sixties they had ribbon loops at the waist, hem, and sides. In the seventies, they reached only to mid-thigh, and after then they were replaced by full breeches gartered at the knee. Breeches became narrower in the

LATE RESTORATION MAN

eighties. In the nineties they were plain and tight-fitting, and strapped below the knee with a buckle or six buttons. They were made either of black velvet or material of a colour that matched the rest of the suit.

6—(G.122)

DRESS
WOMEN

The *Bodice* (women) took the shape of the corset under it, the shoulders being bare. The

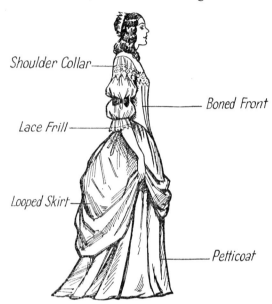

EARLY RESTORATION LADY. c. 1660 (BERLIN)

less daring veiled this expanse of skin with a scarf, or pulled up the chemise to fill the hiatus. The bodice was either laced at the back or fastened in front, generally the former. It had elbow sleeves, sometimes slashed in front, and a row of bows adorned the front of the bodice. The sleeves were puffed till 1670, and then became loose and tubular in shape. Throughout the period they were often of shoulder length only. The end of the sleeve was finished with a row of ribbon loops. Instead of the former deep collar, the lace edging to the neck became a mere border.

The *Skirt* (women) had a front ʌ, which was tied back by bows or clasps right along. Another mode was to pull back the skirt and to fasten it at the back. This disclosed the differently coloured lining, which the former method did not.

The *Petticoat* (women), which showed prominently, was decorated with embroidery or other patterns.

Gowns (women) in 1680 incorporated the bodice and skirt in a one-piece garment.

LEGS

Boot Hose and *Boot Hose Tops* have previously been described.

Stirrup Hose widened above the knee, and were fastened to the petticoat breeches by ribbon points. Often a second pair was worn over them. Their wide tops dropped over the garters and below the knee, and were finished with a deep, full flounce of lace or linen. A separate valance of linen or lace was popular between 1660 and

Semi-classical mode

NELL GWYNN

1670. These knee frills went with the petticoat breeches kilt costume, but not with the later cassock-coat costume. After 1680, with the advent of coat and vest, the knee ribbons vanished and the stockings were rolled over the breeches. After 1690 there was no rolling, but the stocking was drawn above the knee.

FEET

The *Jack Boot* (men) had a square-shaped cuff-like top above the knee and a square toe. These high boots were characteristic of the age. From 1670 they were laced up the front.

Spatter Dashes (men) were, as their appro-

priate name denotes, leggings worn with shoes from 1690 onwards.

Shoes of black, with prominent upstanding tongues, came in in 1680, but red heels were worn for evening dress occasions only. Particularly to be noted is the disappearance of rosettes, their place being taken by a stiff butterfly bow on the shoe. Shoe buckles were also worn from 1680.

In the sixties the women wore high-heeled *Louis Shoes* with taper toes, which were made of satin, needlework, or brocade, the instep being finished with a buckle or a bow.

Mules (women) were slippers with high heels and cut-away sides, so that only the toe and instep were covered over.

Buskins (women), worn for riding, were made of leather or satin.

HAIR

The *men* were clean-shaven, though here and there the chin tuft still lingered amongst the older men who had not changed. The moustache became a mere thread from the nostrils to the corners of the lips—a fashion popularized by Charles II. The great novelty was the introduction of the *Periwig* (men), which fashion the King brought over after his European travels. It was, of course, worn purely as an artificial covering, and there was no attempt to make it look like natural hair. The head was shaved to accommodate the erection, which was quite graceful. In its early stages it was an irregular mass of curly hair reaching to the shoulders, but later it became formalized into rather stiff corkscrew curls and was a more solid looking mass. This change took place in the seventies.

Three distinct changes marked the *Women*. In the sixties their hair was puffed above the ears and wires held it well away from the cheeks at each side. By the seventies the wires had been dropped, and the side curls were quite close to the face. Ten years later a centre parting heralded the approach of the Queen Anne styles.

HATS
MEN

In the beginning of this period the steeple crowned felt hat remained, but a new variety was introduced with a flat crown and wide brims,

CHARLES II AND HIS QUEEN

something like a Harrow or Boater hat of to-day. It was stiffened. Plumes and ribbon decoration remained popular until the 'eighties.

HATS
WOMEN

The women still went about bare-headed, but when they needed a covering they wore a loose silk hood or a simple kerchief (countrywomen almost always wore one or other of these types when they wanted hats). For riding purposes men's hats were worn, or rather hats similar to the men's—wide-brimmed felt with a feather or ribbon bunch trimmings.

SUMMARY
MEN

Dress

Doublet—Short Eton, open front, short sleeves to below elbow with deep fringe looped ribbons. Front opening to sleeve till 1665; after that sleeve turned up at elbow in close buttoned cuff.

Shirt—early, bulged at waist and showing front. Ribbon tied to 1680. Deep wrist ruffles. Ruche or frill at opening.

Collar—falling band square cut to 1670. Then breast bib with round corners. Then neckcloth.

Cassock coat—worn over short doublet.

Vest or waistcoat—1664 on. Long-sleeved to fork. Over it was

Tunic or Coat—long cassock coat to mid-thigh; 1670 to below knee with elbow sleeves and broad turn-up cuff. Slit up to hip each side and back. Dummy button trimmed.

Cloak—mainly travelling.

Petticoat breeches—kilt-like. In 1660 ribbon loops at waist, hem, and sides; 1670 to mid-thigh. Afterwards full breeches, knee-gartered. Narrower in 1680. In 1690 plain tight strapped below knee, with buckle or buttons. Black velvet or match suit.

Legs

Boot hose and boot hose tops till 1680.

Stirrup hose—widened at knee. Fastened to Petti-breeches by points. Often two pairs worn. Wide tops drooped over garters in flounce below knee.

Lace or linen valance 1660–70. After 1680

no knee ribbon and stocking rolled over breech. After 1690's no roll and stocking was drawn above knee.

Feet

Jack boot—square cuff top above knee. Square toe. 1670 onwards laced.

Spatter dashes.—leggings worn with shoes 1690 onwards.

Black shoes with upstanding tongues to 1680 (red heels for dress). No rosettes, but butterfly ribbon bows. Shoe buckles 1680 onwards.

Hair

Clean-shaven. Thread moustache.

Periwig. Irregular in 1660's; corkscrew formal in 1670's.

Hats

Steeple crown in 1660's.

Low flat crown (Boater), 1665–75. Plumes and ribbons to 1680.

WOMEN

Dress

Bodice—corset, bare shoulders, or scar for chemise covers, back laced or front fastened. Bows in front. Elbow sleeves, some front slashed. Puffs to 1670, then loose tubes. Elbow fringe of ribbon loops. Often shoulder length sleeves. Lace border to low neck.

Skirt—front ∧ tied back by bows or clasps or fastened behind to show lining.

Petticoat.

Gowns—one-piece version of above in 1680. Deep collars for older folk.

Feet

High Louis heels, taper toes, satin, brocade, or needlework. Instep buckle or bow.

Mules—high heel, only toe and instep covered.

Buskins—for riding. Tall. Satin or leather.

Hair

1660. Puffed above ears. Corkscrews wired away from cheeks.

1670. Side curls close to face. Mop of curls over head or forehead.

1680. Centre parting.

Hats

Bare mostly.

Kerchiefs. Loose hoods.

For riding—men's hats.

CHAPTER XVII

DUTCH WILLIAM, AND AFTER, 1689–1727

DUTCH fashions affected English modes when William of Orange took over, in right of his wife, the throne vacated by her father, James II. They modified our clothes

GENTLEMAN WITH MUFF

by making them more precise in cut, with carefully pressed seams and stiffly arranged folds, instead of the more natural shapes into which materials had hitherto fallen: the domination of the tailor over the seamstress and of the triumph of formalism over Nature began.

A distinction may be drawn between the broad outlines of the clothes of the gentry and those of the commons—

GENTRY	COMMONS
Wide sleeves	Closer sleeves
Coat knee length	Coat below knee
Cocked hat	Uncocked hat

William III's reign was from 1689 to 1702, Anne ruled from then till 1714, and George I till 1727.

DRESS (WILLIAM III)
MEN

The style for men at the latter part of the Restoration period remained in force. Skirts were made wider, sleeve cuffs broader, and the wig fuller, and the petticoat breeches gave place to tighter-fitting varieties, which reached below the knee. The flat "boater" hat became a cocked hat by turning up two of its sides, and buckles replaced rosettes and bows on the shoes.

The snuff box began to be seen. It does not reach its zenith until the time of the middle Georges.

Both *coat* and *waistcoat* (men) were richly embroidered, and the button-holes were elaborately frogged. Waistcoats were made of Calimanco, which was a material of wool or linen weave, faced on one side with satin, on which a rich design was worked.

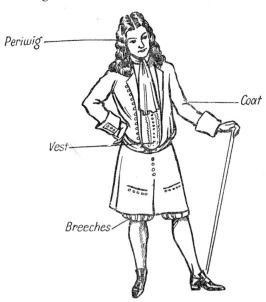

GENTLEMAN, 1680

DRESS (WILLIAM III)
WOMEN

The full *sleeve* (women) was replaced by a tighter sleeve, ending in a cuff above the elbow. Beneath this appeared the under sleeve of lace or lawn, with a ruffle springing from the gather at the forearm.

The waist-line was straight, not pointed, and often concealed by small decorative aprons. In Anne's time more flounces and frills were developed, and the skirt became bell-shaped by the addition of the circular hoop.

Flowered materials and sprigged designs came in about this time, and for riding purposes the women adopted men's dress styles, including their hats, wigs, and coats.

The age favoured well-fed, rounded appearances, and to assist Nature, when she was not naturally inclined to mould the face into the desired shape, artificial aids, called "plumpers," were supplied and worn. This fashion accounts for the universally well-fed appearance of the ladies in portraits of the Queen Anne period. The fashion for wide skirts had a reflex action on the furniture of the day: wide-seated chairs came in. Getting through doorways was not easily managed, as houses, unlike furniture, were

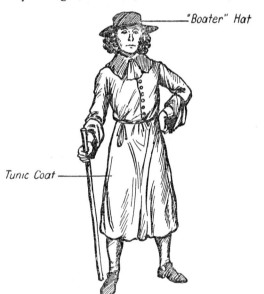

A WORKING MAN, 1688–1711

less readily adaptable to current modes. To pass through a doorway a lady had to depress her hoop by folding it in front or lifting it at the sides. When sitting down she had also to be careful. The back part of the hoop had to be "sat upon"

from the bottom so that it doubled up under the person.

HAIR

The men devised fresh head-wear. This took the form of the *Ramillies wig*, which was a powdered, brushed-back peruke, with the hair

LOUIS XIV, 1694

puffed out at the sides, and at the back a long queue, fastened with black bows at its top and bottom. During the reigns of both William and Anne no real changes in clothes occurred, but there were these changes in the hair of the men and the hats of both sexes. If they indicate that in those days the head was esteemed more than the body, it is a good sign, but it is difficult to be convinced of the truth of so flattering an explanation.

The wig became larger, higher, and fuller, and its cost was so high that stealing it was profitable, though risky; indeed men had their wigs snatched off their own heads in the street.

Women, too, wore the same styles, but thought of a fresh hair-dressing. This was a high wired erection, placed on the top of the head, and giving considerable extra height to the wearer when the hair was carried over it.

HATS

The *Commode* (women) was an erection of wired lace placed upon the top of the head in tiers, three or four in all, rising above each other. They diminished in width as they rose, and at the sides had long lappets of lace, which fell over the shoulders.

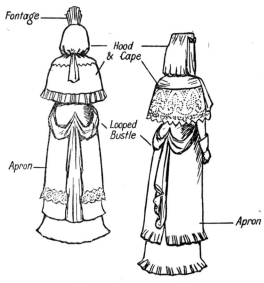

LADIES OUTDOORS, 1696

DRESS (GEORGE I)
MEN

George I's reign brought scarcely any change in fashion. The full periwig had been displaced by the Ramillies and other shorter wigs powdered white, but they were still a modern Justice's full-bottomed wig in that they had front lappets over each shoulder, finishing with a tied loop of hair. The coats were flared even fuller than before and worn buttoned only at the waist. This caused the upper part to bulge outwards. Shoe buckles were larger.

DRESS (GEORGE I)
WOMEN

The principal change in women's dress was the disappearance of the stiff front "V" of the bodice in favour of a bodice that was close fitting and boned, but had a scarcely perceptible dip in the front of the waist-line, which was thus nearly straight. The "V" having gone, the bodice was

the same colour and material all round. The commode or fontage was replaced by the mob cap.

SUMMARY
MEN

Dress

Collar—neck-cloth or cravat. Brussels lace. Ends passed through waistcoat button-holes. Very long. Geneva bands, smaller than above.

Tunic or coat—as before, but open to show waistcoat, skirts were wider, cuffs broader. In Anne's reign skirt shortened; cuff revers were still larger, and lace ruffles; skirt wired out in wide flare.

Waistcoat—as before, but with pockets in Anne's reign.

Breeches—petticoat breeches replaced by tighter ones to below knee.

Cloak—winter and travel.

Muffs—small round.

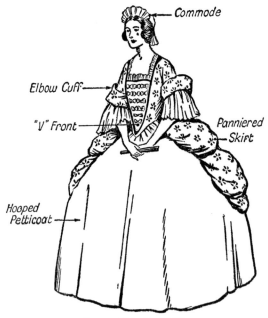

LADY. QUEEN ANNE

Legs

Stockings drawn over breeches, sometimes to mid-thigh. In Anne's reign they were still above the knee, but gartered below it, and mainly blue or red.

Feet

Buckles instead of rosettes to shoes. In Anne's reign red heels, small buckles, and square toes.

Hair

Periwig—higher and fuller than before.
No moustache or beard.
Ramillies wig—Anne's reign. White, brushed back, and puffed at sides. Long pigtail, plaited. Black bow top and bottom of queue.

Hats

Felt "boater," but with two sides turned up. Ribbon bows. Often carried under arm. In Anne's reign three turn-ups and laced with gold or silver galoon; sometimes feather edge.

Jewellery

Snuff boxes. Amber- or gold-topped canes. Masks.

LADY. GEORGE I

WOMEN

Dress

Bodice—higher neck, tight sleeve. Cuff above elbow. Lace or lawn ruffles below. Long gloves. Round neck opening wide. Stiff "V" front, laced across. Under George I no "V."
Skirt—front "V" showed petticoat. Looped round body in front, and hung in loose folds behind as panniers.

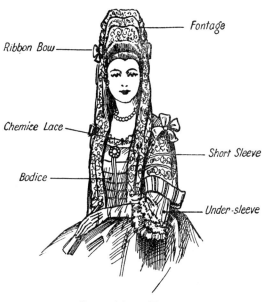

QUEEN MARY II, 1694

Petticoat—in Anne's reign widened and touched the ground; frilled.
Hoop—bell-shaped; 1710 on, widening till 1740.
Cape—short black, deep frill.
Apron—small black silk.

Hair

Brushed up on wire frame to give height. In Anne's reign less high and more natural.

Hats

Hood—usually without commode.
Lace shawl or
Commode or fontage—upright lace in tiers, pleated. Long lappets over shoulders. In Anne's reign became lower and gradually displaced by
Mob caps—lace or linen, frilled.

CHAPTER XVIII

GEORGE II, 1727–60

GEORGE II's reign lasted from 1727 to 1760 and was distinguished by the cult of the "pastoral," which caused a rage for the imitation shepherds and shepherdesses that

Bag Wig

No Collar

Wide Revers

Shirt

Chapeau Bras

SIR BENJAMIN KEENE, K.B., 1730–50

are familiar to us in Dresden china. It was a prettily dressed period almost all the time. The ladies' skirts were braided, quilted in diagonals, and richly embroidered, and the *motifs* included flowers, fruit, and even animals. The men's coats and waistcoats were marvels of beautiful embroidery and delightfully coloured silks and satins, garnished with gold and silver threads and sequins. Ribbed silks were worn, and the effect of men allowing themselves to wear cheerful and bright colours, with artistic designs upon them, was seen almost for the last time. Modern dress for men has sunk to a dreadful, drab uniformity, which has neither shape nor shade.

Powder and patches summarize the epoch, and the patches (which were worn high up on the cheek or near the eyes) were made in an extra-

ordinary range of subjects. Even coaches and horses and the cabriolet were popular. The commoner variety was the simple dot. Slender canes of elegant wood and massive round gold knobs were carried by the men, and the periwig was put away for ever.

No longer can it be said that people all dressed alike: the new fashions gave scope for originality in treatment, and the personality of the wearer was reflected in his clothes.

There was plenty of time on hand, and the art of manners reached a high point of elegance. The swing of a gold knobbed cane, the flirt of a fan, or the carriage of a coat became a study and a science. The heavy wigs forced their wearers to

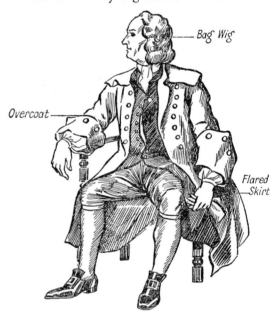

Bag Wig

Overcoat

Flared Skirt

CAPTAIN CORAM, 1740

maintain an upright carriage and modern slouching was scarcely heard of. Young ladies were trained by the use of the back board; chairs were upright and thinly upholstered; men were expected to carry themselves like men. The tailor thus had an adequate frame on which to display his goods and a well-thought-out design was rewarded by the appreciation of its wearer and a recommendation to his friends.

It is the age of the flowered waistcoat, and is perhaps of all periods, the most attractive for men's costumes. The waistcoats, being longer than now, and having large flap pockets, gave space and scope for embroidery. They were made in almost every conceivable shade, in silks, satins, velvets, and brocades. The edges were richly trimmed, chiefly with fairly natural flower and leaf forms, into which a quantity of gold braid and "lace" was introduced. Cut velvets formed the flowers and several shades of these were introduced into the same garment. Gold and silver sequins were sewn on in profusion and added sparkle to an already dazzling effect.

This embroidery was placed on the edges of both coat and waistcoat, on the pocket flaps of both, and upon the wide cuff-revers.

In the early part of the reign the men presented the same appearance as in that of George I.

Mr. and Miss Lloyd, 1752-59

They wore the widely flared skirted coat, with its long row of buttons down one edge, only one or two being brought into actual use in order to produce a bulging effect above the waist, where the coat fell outwards. About 1750 the coat shrank into a more closely fitting style, and was slightly cut away at the sides, and the waistcoat became shorter. Great elegance was given to both by the trimming of their vertical edges. Velvets as well as silks and satins were fashionable.

A change also came over the women's frocks. In the beginning of the reign women wore widely

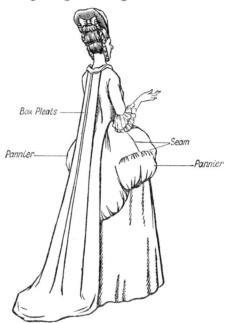

Watteau Pleated Sacque, 1760

belled hoops, but in the 'forties, owing to their increasing inconvenience, they were suppressed in front, the sides only being left belled out in panniers. This style also failing to give sufficient ease, the panniers themselves were abolished; they had almost gone by the end of the reign.

Dress
Men

The *Collar* (men) was in the form of a neck-cloth or cravat with lace ends. Plain ones were also worn, their ends being tucked under the waistcoat.

The *Coat* (men) was widely flared and was sometimes wired out. It had small buttons right down its edge, and was buttoned there with only one or two buttons. There was no collar, or occasionally a small turn-over collar was attached. The cuff revers were wide and reached nearly to the elbow; the sleeve reached nearly to the wrist, where the shirt showed in a puff, frilled or lace-edged.

The *Waistcoat* (men) was long and pocketed, and the pockets were decorated round their edges. It had as many small buttons, closely set, as the coat, and reached nearly to the knees.

Breeches (men) were fairly tight, and reached

LADY CHATHAM, 1750

to the knee, where they were gathered into a plain band, which was buckled or buttoned.

Muffs (men) were worn in the street. They were small and round, and made of fur.

DRESS
WOMEN

The *Hoop* (women) was the foundation of women's dress and ranged over various shapes. In 1735 it was bell-shaped and large. In 1745 the front part of the hoop was narrowed so that the skirt touched the body, but the side parts were as wide as ever and formed panniers.

Over the hoop was placed the *Petticoat*, and over this the sacque and over-skirt. Two alternatives were allowed. A bodice and over-skirt to match could be worn, in which case there was no " V " opening in front to disclose a contrasting skirt, or the sacque could be worn over the bodice and skirt, in which case a " V " was formed by the sacque, thus disclosing the bodice and skirt, which (themselves matching) contrasted with the sacque. The *Sacque* (women) was a long, loose gown of considerable fullness to allow it to go over the hoop. It hung from the shoulders and was close-sleeved to the elbows, where frills showed. It was heavily gathered (later box pleated) at the back, so that long folds of material swept down from the neck to the ground. These gathers allowed the material to widen out at the waist-line to cover the panniers. The sacque did not meet in front, but parted at the sides to disclose the under-garment. Its front edge was trimmed with sewing or metal lace or ribbon. A small frill appeared round the neck, which was slightly low.

The *Bodice* (women) was boned and had a square low neck lace-frilled. There might be a slight point at the waist, but the general impression given was that of a straight waist.

Skirts (women) were all rather shorter than previously.

Aprons (women) were much worn for ornament. They were made of silks and satins. They might be plain or tucked, and they were circular in cut.

LEGS

A fashion set in for white stockings, which soon displaced the coloured stockings previously worn. They were considered to be highly immoral at the time! The gentlemen pulled them over the breeches, where they were fastened by garters, over which they were rolled, so that the garters did not show.

FEET

The men wore square buckles of silver on their shoes, which had upstanding, square-ended tongues and low heels. The women had high heels and pointed toes to their shoes. Riding boots fitted more closely to the leg but were still loose over the knee.

HAIR

The periwig disappeared in favour of the bag wig. This was a white-powdered wig, with its side pieces brought round in front and tied with bows of ribbon. They were long enough to rest on the collar part of the coat. About 1750 these front pieces were curtailed, and their place was taken by tight formal side curls in horizontal rows —say three. Both forms had a queue. The latter was tied with a black ribbon, which was brought round the neck to the front, where it was made into a large bow fastened with a diamond brooch called a solitaire.

The women did not wear wigs, but dressed their own hair smoothly and closely to the head and confined it in the mob cap. The wide skirts contrasted with the small head.

HATS
MEN

The *Chapeau Bras* (men) was a small three-cornered felt hat, sometimes edged with braid or with feather trimming of the fringe type, such as is still seen on the hats of Sheriffs and Mayors. The feathers were ostrich fronds. Though this

KEVENHULLER HAT

hat was worn upon the head, as a hat is intended to be worn, it was also often— more often than n o t — carried under the arm, hence its name.

The *Kevenhuller* (men) was a three-cornered hat that had high turn-up brims with a peak coming in front. It appeared in 1740, and was always banded along the edges with gold braid or other material. It was as shown in the accompanying illustration.

When no wig was worn the shaven head was protected by a turban, but this was only indoor *négligé*.

HATS
WOMEN

The ladies looked charming in a variety of styles, of which the *Mob Cap* was the favourite. Made of linen or lace, it had a small frill, and

Turban

ROUBILIAC, *c.* 1740

was tied with ribbons, cherry and pale or royal blue being the colours most favoured. When made capaciously, they came down the sides of the face and were tied under the chin. The commode entirely disappeared.

Hoods were also worn in black silk or colours.

Tiny *Straw Hats* with wide brims gave a dairymaid effect. They were tied under the chin with streamer ribbons, and the underneath parts of the wide brims were decorated with artificial flowers.

SUMMARY
MEN

Dress

Collar—neck-cloth or cravat. Lace ends, or plain with ends tucked under waistcoat.

Coat—small buttons right down side. Mid-calf length. Fastened only at waist, bulging above and below. Little or no collar rever. Very wide cuff revers nearly to elbow. Flared wired skirt. After 1750 flares cease, and sleeve nearly to wrist.

Waistcoat—long, pocketed, many buttons. Nearly to knees.

Breeches—fairly tight knee-length, where banded.

Muffs—small round.

Shirt—loose sleeves frilled.

Legs

Stockings rolled over breeches. Mainly white.

Feet

Square buckled shoes.

Hair

White bag wig. Queue fastened by black satin tie, joined in front with bow and diamond-brooched. Side lappets till 1750, then side curls.

Hats

Chapeau Bras—very small tricorne, carried under arm.

Kevenhuller—very high cocked tricorne, banded on edge. About 1750.

Turban—without wig.

WOMEN

Dress

Hoop—1735, bell-shaped; 1745, suppressed in front; 1755, smaller all round; 1760, almost gone.

Sacque—long, loose gown, open in front, hangs from shoulder to ground loosely. Gathered in folds over hoop. Panniers.

Petticoat—over the hoop. Shows in front in early period.

Bodice—square open neck, laced frilled. Boned body. Slight point at waist.

Over skirt—panniered at sides. Shorter than before.

The "V" effect may be given by the sacque or the bodice at option.

Aprons—plain or tucked, long or knee-length.

Legs

White stockings.

Feet

Shoes—high heels, pointed toes.

Hair

Smooth and close to head.

Hats

Mob cap with frill. Lace. Also, if fuller, tied under chin.

Lappets—two lace streamers falling from top of head to shoulders.

Straw hats—very small and flat. Flowers under brim. Streamers. Hoods.

At Court, 1760

CHAPTER XIX

THE MAN OF FASHION, 1760–1820

ELABORATION has set in to such an extent that much of my space will be occupied by a carefully tabulated summary, The period dates from 1760 to 1820—the long reign of Farmer George III.

It was an age of solid prosperity and this was reflected in the grave and substantial houses no less than in the rather heavy, massive cut of clothes and the rich, thick, heavily embroidered materials of which they were made. Poor old Farmer George with his enormous family was himself no arbiter of fashion. The heartlessness and ingratitude of his children, headed by the intolerable Frederick, Prince of Wales, and his equally worthless son, "Prince Florizel," gave the poor old King enough to think about and little time for the niceties of dress.

While the cut of men's clothes became more restrained, the fabrics and colours were just as gay as before. Crimson velvet, white satin, and coloured cloths, embroidered and laced with gold or silver, with buttons to match, still were at the service of the man of fashion, who must have found life very pleasant in Bath or in London and even occasionally, and then under protest, at his country seat in the wilds of "uncivilized England."

In the early part the fashionable young man, called a Macaroni, achieved fantastic results by exaggeration. His wig towered high above him, and on top of it was sometimes perched a tiny tricorne hat that had to be raised by his sword or cane. He wore two fobs to his waistcoat, carried a jewelled snuff box, a gold-knobbed amber cane with a tassel, and a diamond-hilted sword. His coat was tight and short like his vest, and his breeches were well moulded to his form.

Dress
Men

The *Coat* (men) tended to change from the square cut ends to a cut away, which became much like our Morning Coat. The collar got higher and higher, the cuff rever went out of

fashion, and double breasted (D.B. in Summary) coats came in about 1780. The stiffened flares of coat and vest disappeared, and the vest lost its long skirts in 1780. *Overcoats* had at first flat, wide collars, sometimes double, and these developed into the double and treble collared capes that are familiar in coaching pictures. The

White Wig

Chapeau Bras

CAPTAIN WADE, 1771, BY GAINSBOROUGH

Shirt had at first a double frill down its front opening, and this, in 1800, became a stiff pouter pigeon single frill, or a white bow neck cloth finished off the shirt.

The sleeves at first remained as before with ruffled lace edges at the wrist. About 1790 the lace disappeared in favour of a small plain linen frill which, in its turn, practically disappeared in 1800 owing to the coat sleeve being narrowed and lengthened with the passing of cuff revers.

For indoor wear a dressing-gown-like coat, called a nightdress, was worn with a turban to cover the head when it was relieved from the hot and heavy wig.

The *Sword* was discouraged and by the eighties had ceased to be worn.

DRESS
WOMEN

Women's dress changed little save in the shape of the hoop, which gradually lessened till it went out in 1790, when a complete change was made by the one-piece dress, which heralded the

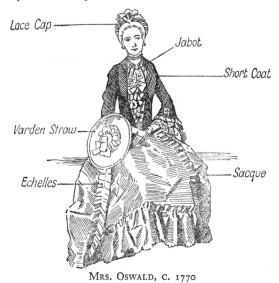

MRS. OSWALD, C. 1770

approaching Empire style with its armpit waist. Apart from Caps, head coverings were unpopular until the nineties, when Straws in many shapes were popular, ceding place to huge Turbans in 1800.

Though the bodices were cut low, the hiatus was bridged by fichus and scarves. The *Polonese* (women) was a Sacque which instead of having straight front edges, curved these away to the back. Echelle trimming to both garments, consisting of a row of tiny bows down the front edge, was widely popular.

LEGS

Stockings (men) were at first coloured, as before; in 1780 white ones came in, and continued until 1800 when black ones were the mode.

FEET

Top Boots (men) were used for riding only until 1780 when they were adopted for walking as well. In 1790 the *Hessian Boot* (men) was introduced. It was a short, close-fitting boot, which came up to the knee, and was finished with a tassel in front. Pumps were used in ballrooms.

HAIR

Wigs (men) remained, but with modifications, and in 1790 went out in favour of natural hair, which was worn long, curly, and brushed back like Nelson's. In 1800 it was shorter but curled all over.

Hair (women) was piled high on the head in an oval shape eked out by wire frames in the seventies; but in the 'eighties and 'nineties it lost its height and widened out with masses of curls on top and long locks of curled hair behind or pulled over the front of the shoulders. In 1800 it became ugly and clumsy, with a front curled fringe, a heavy chignon, and long ringlets at the rear.

HATS
MEN

The Tricorne is the same as the Chapeau Bras described in Chapter XVIII. The Bicorne, as

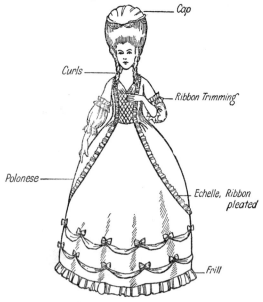

ECHELLED POLONESE, 1776

its name indicates, had only two corners, its edges being turned up like a modern admiral's dress hat: by 1780 it could be worn either long ways or short ways; by 1800 only the latter position was *en règle*. The Kevenhuller hat is illustrated in the previous chapter. The Nivernois was a ridiculously small Chapeau Bras affected by the Macaronis who even went to the length of perching them on top of their high wigs where they must have had considerable difficulty in keeping them on! The wide Quaker hat needs no explanation if you refer to the picture so well known in connexion with porridge. The tall Beaver hat began to be worn in 1780 and has continued in use to the present day, its shape varying slightly in accordance with the dictates of those who sell hats, who (owing to the longevity of a tall hat) have been compelled in self defence to invent a way in which this hat becomes out-of-date even if not outworn. The varying outlines of the tall Beaver are noted in the summary to this chapter.

HATS
WOMEN

Hats (women) were diverse from 1790. The wide Gainsborough straw was familiar, also the Dolly Varden milkmaid straw with flatter brims. In 1800 hideous Turbans and coal scuttle straws were worn. The latter had huge peaks in front

STREET SCENE, 1778

and little back part, and presented a lop-sided view, little of the face being visible.

These 1790 straw hats are familiar through the portraits of Gainsborough. They had wide brims turned up at one side and down on the other and were trimmed with large ostrich feathers

as in the well-known pictures of the Duchess of Devonshire and Mrs. Siddons.

The Dolly Varden hat is seen in our picture of a street scene. Its characteristic notes are the tilting forward over the nose and up at the back

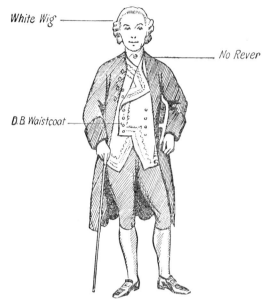

LORD KILMOREY, BY GAINSBOROUGH

and its almost entire absence of crown. It was trimmed with bows of ribbon and flowers.

The Turbans of 1800 can be seen in the illustrations to authentic editions of Thackeray's novels relating to the decade. They were large and rather top heavy and lent themselves to an osprey-like decoration such as wheat ears, stiff feathers, and other upstanding ornaments.

The *Buffon* (women) was a fichu, puffed out pouter-wise on the chest, and gathered in at the waist. It gave a goitre-like effect to the throat.

CHILDREN

Children were charming and the costume maker has ample material for ideas in the numerous family group paintings by Romney, Gainsborough, and Reynolds. Though they dressed in the main like their elders, it was only about now that specific styles for children were designed. Little boys wore pantaloons and knickers but rarely grown-up breeches, while the open necked shirt with its wide flat collar, later to become frilled, was also popular. A linen mob cap, mittens, a wide sashed frock and perhaps a shawl

the style, though it was of course painted in Queen Victoria's reign.

Mob Cap

Hooded Cloak

LADY CAROLINE HOWARD AS A CHILD, 1779

or a scarf are typical of the styles adopted by little girls. Sir John Millais's "Cherry Ripe" shows

Beaver Hat

Flat Square Collar

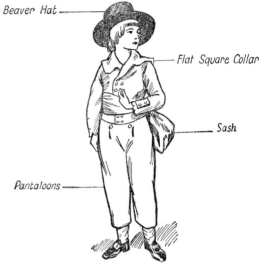

Sash

Pantaloons

LORD ALTHORP AS A BOY, 1786

SUMMARY
MEN

	1770	1780	1790	1800
DRESS				
COAT . .	Curved tails. Close sleeve. Small cuff. Small or no collar rever. Less pocket flap. Very short for beaus.	Cut away. Short square back collar, or D.B. with large lapels, and square tails. Big cuff, not to wrist, showed shirt sleeve.	High collar to ears. Cuff to wrist showed only shirt frill.	Tight sleeves. Cutaway. D.B.
VEST . .	Sleeved. Skirts unstiffened. Buttoned at waist only. (Others not fastened.)	Short skirtless square cut or D.B. with large pointed lapels outside coat. Buttoned all down.	Same.	Striped.
OVERCOAT .	Large cuff. Flat wide collar (often double collar).	Capes instead of collar.		
SHIRT . .	Double frill *jabot* showed through unfastened vest.			Pouter frill or white bow. High cheek collar.
BREECHES .	Hardly seen under long vest and coat.	Skin tight for riding. Bunch of ribbon or buckle at knee.	Breeches or tight pantaloons (trousers) buttoned below calf.	Black pantaloons and breeches.
NIGHTDRESS	A *négligé* indoor dressing gown coat.	Same.		
LEGS				
STOCKINGS .	Gold and silver clocks for State. Black silk usual. Rolled over knee.	White. Under breeches at knee.	White.	Black.
FEET				
SHOES . .	Small oval buckle. Red heel. Rosettes.	Large square buckle or strings. No red heels save for Court.		Pumps.
SPATTERDASHES	Long gaiters.		Short spats.	
TOP BOOTS	For riding.	For walking also.		Heavy turnover.
HESSIANS .			Short close-fitting boot to knee, where tasselled.	Same.
HAIR				
RAMILLIES	Wig as before.	Single broad roll all round.		
PIGTAIL .	Spiral black ribbon case behind.			
WHITE .	Two horizontal side curls very high for beau.			
NATURAL .		Powdered.	Long curly, brushed back.	Short curly all over.
HATS				
TRICORNE .	Laced. Braided. Feather fringed.	No feather fringe.		
BICORNE .	Rare.	Common. Worn long or short ways.	Same.	Worn short ways.
KEVENHULLER	High front peak as before.	Same.	Same.	
NIVERNOIS .	Tiny tricorne for beau.			
WIDE QUAKER		Common.		
TALL BEAVER		Tapering crown.	Straight crown.	Like modern "Topper."
NIGHT CAP	For *négligé* in absence of wig.	Same.		
LINEN				
CRAVAT .	Falling ends.	Plain folded stock or *jabot* of lace.	Choker knotted in front. Very high.	Same.

SUMMARY (*continued*)
MEN

	1770	1780	1790	1800
SLEEVES .	Ruffled lace shirt.	Same.	Small frill.	Unseen.
WIG RIBBON	Loose on shoulders and pinned under throat. Black.			
WHITE BOW	Muslin in huge front bat's-wing bow for beau.			
JEWELS .	Sword losing favour.	No sword.	Same.	Same.
	Tasselled canes, knobbed.	Same.	Same.	Same, plainer.
	Muffs. Snuff boxes.	Same.	Same.	No muffs. Fobs.

WOMEN

	1770	1780	1790	1800
DRESS				
BODICE .	Open laced or not.	Long, close sleeve.		Tight one-piece dress
	Corset shape. Stomacher.			Tight elbow sleeve.
	Echelle—front bows.			Armpit waist. Wider skirts.
	Elbow sleeve flounced. Bell sleeve.			Square neck. V neck bare to shoulders. Fairly wide.
SKIRT . .	Ankle length. Front open. Full gather at hips. Bustle starts. Three frills.	Trains optional.		
OVERCOATS		Short.		Long, fur edged.
PETTICOAT		Quilted.	Quilted.	Very thin and tight.
HOOP . .	Two side hoops.	Bustle, not hoop.	Bustle disappeared.	
SACQUE .	Open to ground or to waist. Pleated edges. Rear box pleat. Three bustles on hoop.	Pleats sewn flat, down to waist.		
POLONESE .	Sacque with front curving away to back.			
RIDING .	As men.			Hooded, fur edged.
CLOAKS .	Armholed.	Same.		
CAPES . .	Long ends in front.	Same.		
FEET				
SHOES . .	High heels for evening.	Round toes.	Flat, heelless.	Same.
	Generally lower.		Satin. Tiny front bow.	
	Ribbon ties, rosettes, buckles.		Ballet shoe with sandal ribbons.	
HAIR . .	High, egg shape, Chignon and nape ringlets.	Broad and flat. Full curls on crown and very long hair behind.	Broad and less high. Same.	Curled. Front fringe. Chignon and long rear ringlets.
HATS . .	Lace or linen caps with long lappets at rear, very large, frilled edges.	Same.	Gainsborough. Dolly Varden straw. Turbans.	Coal scuttle. Straws feathered. Beaver "Topper" Long ostrich plumed Turbans.
	Mobs. Dairymaid straws.	Calash—large hooped hood.	Same.	
LINEN . .	Fichus and scarves.	Same.	Buffon fichu till 1795; afterwards broad frilled collars.	Lace scarves.
	Narrow lace frill above bodice.	Same.		
	Deep sleeve ruffles.			
	Long gloves, mittens, muffs.	Same.	Same.	Same.

CHAPTER XX

EMPIRE AND THE DANDIES, 1820–37

REVOLUTION affected the fashions by a sudden reversion to Classical modes. Instead of the balloon effect, women adopted sylph-like outlines. To so great an extent were these desired, that petticoats became things of the past, and in order to imitate Greek and Roman statues frocks were damped before they were put on. Men were unable to vie with this classicism, but the tight craze influenced them to the extent that they damped their pantaloons before putting them on and then dried them, thus making them skin tight.

Great simplicity went with woman's charming costume. White was extensively worn, and embroidery and trimming ceased. The dress depended on charm of outline and purity of line. Naturally, the fashion was difficult for all but the

A SPORTSMAN, 1814

youngest figures, and it lasted only from 1802 to 1813. The drawings of Kate Greenaway have made it familiar.

With the passing of this fashion came the reign of the Dandies, who were the spiritual descen-

dants of the Macaronis of the 1770's. Unlike them, however, they were not merely youths, but men of substance, headed by no less a personage than the Prince Regent who, no matter

A LADY OF 1826

how despicable his character, largely aided the habit of cleanliness in dress and person, initiated by his one-time friend, Beau Brummell.

Beau Brummell was really a great man, and to regard him merely as a fashion plate would be to misjudge him. He laid immense importance on two much-needed principles. The first was cleanliness and fine linen; the second was avoidance of ostentation in dress. To Brummel is due the changed custom, and to the Prince the fact that it was adopted. The royal circle was naturally filled with men who had plenty of time to spend on dressing, and the modes they affected had such a strong influence on tailoring that never again have Englishmen taken their styles from France, as had up to then been the case.

Count d'Orsay was the disciple of the Dandies, and at the same time shares with Disraeli the honourable place in history of being the last of the *genus*.

Picture him walking down Kensington Gore to Lady Blessington's famous Salon. He wears a blue or black waistcoat splendidly embroidered

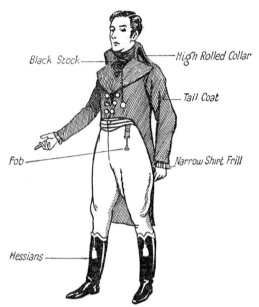

Black Stock

High Rolled Collar

Tail Coat

Fob

Narrow Shirt Frill

Hessians

EMPIRE PERIOD MAN
(From a photograph of the Author)

with gold flowers, and has a number of gold chains about his neck, his watch fobs showing at his waist. To support him, he carries a black stick with a white tassel and cord to give it a flourish. On occasion he even wears the older high red heels. Disraeli's coat is of black velvet, his trousers of purple with gold braid down the outer seams. Long lace ruffles are at his wrists, and his white gloves are covered with gold and diamond rings worn outside them. It was an age when publicity could still be gained by the individual without the aid of a Press agent. As such, it was at least genuine! Disraeli was, of course, bizarre and hardly typical; D'Orsay was a more representative type; Byron was a figure of mystery and romance, and his collar made him world famous, no less than the originality and daring of his poems and his life.

The note of the period was the absence of colour from the men's clothes: blacks and dark blues and browns held sway and the gorgeous rainbow riot of George III's long reign faded away.

The ladies, after tiring of the Empire fashions, swelled out again, though without the rarely beautiful hoop. Both skirts and sleeves took on more fullness, and hair was charmingly dressed and adorned with many ribbon bows. A similar remark applies to the men's hair which was curled all over the head in imitation of Prince Florizel, who had a fine head of natural hair. Later, he adopted a brown wig, which continued the illusion of perpetual youth that was so necessary in the Royal Juan.

Towards the end of the period the Gigot or leg-of-mutton sleeve was invented, and with the near approach of Victoria to the throne this was divided into several puffs by bands down the arm. The style was called "François Premier,"

Greek Mode

Tight Half-Sleeve

High Waist

EMPIRE PERIOD WOMAN

as it was a revival of the male sleeve of that reign.

Rather hideous turbans surmounted the head, and Thackeray made great play with them in his own drawings and writings. There were many caricatures in this period, notably the somewhat coarse ones by Gilray, and they can be taken as guides with the caution that the exaggeration on which caricature depends must be modified.

EMPIRE MEN, 1802-13
DRESS

The *Coat* had broad swallow-tails, and was cut away squarely above the waist with a double breast adorned with large brass or gilt buttons. For evening wear even finer buttons of crystal silver and gold were used. It had a high collar and a tight sleeve coming well down to the back of the hand, where peeped out a narrow band of linen. Blue, dark brown, and bottle green were the usual shades.

The *Vest* was short and square cut, with small lapels, no longer overlapping the coat. Beau Brummell laid down the rule that buff or light shades were correct for the morning, and white alone was permissible at night. The waistcoat was singly-breasted.

Pantaloons were trousers, tight, and reaching

GEORGE IV WOMAN

to the middle of the calf. They were buttoned at the side, where the calf narrows into the ankle. Their sides were braided in semi-military fashion, and black was essential at night, though lighter shades were worn at other times.

Breeches were made of buckskin and were alternative to pantaloons.

LEGS

Striped silk stockings were worn in the evenings; unstriped silk or cotton ones in the day time.

FEET

The distinction should be noted that topboots

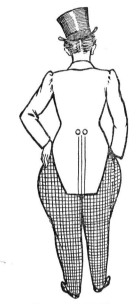

GEORGE IV MAN

were worn with breeches, but Hessians with pantaloons.

EMPIRE WOMEN, 1802-13
DRESS

The *Empire Gown* had short tight sleeves reaching only half-way down the upper arm, and finished with long gloves, which were coloured to match the shoes; its armpit waist was girdled by a narrow ribbon with long ends fringed. The neck was cut low, and scarves were worn. The skirt was smooth in front without gathers, the necessary fullness to enable the wearer to move being given by gathers at the back. It was laced up the back, and designed to reveal the natural outlines as much as possible. It was, therefore, made of the thinnest of materials—muslin and lawn—and its whiteness was unrelieved by any trimming or embroidery. A petticoat might be worn, but as this hid the limbs it was often abandoned. For out of doors a *Pelisse* of thin silk was allowed, but it afforded little warmth to an already too thin costume. It had sleeves, and was a short mantle. Parasols, gloves, reticules, and scarves completed the toilette.

HAIR

The *Hair* was worn in Classical fashion, piled high on the head in a tapering cone bound round with ribbons.

HATS

Turbans of velvet, silk, crepe, and muslin attained voluminous proportions, and were made rather ridiculous by the large single ostrich feather, which curled outwards over the face, or at the side, but chiefly in front.

REGENCY AND LATER MEN, 1813–37
DRESS

The same *Coat* was worn, but its colours were blue, grey, and buff. The collar became higher and the lapels broader, whilst the sleeve had a small puff at the top. In Sailor William's time, velvet collars and cuffs were added, and in 1825 appeared the *Frock Coat* in dark blue or brown, with a high rolled collar and fur edging along the bottom.

The *Vest* was the same, but was striped, or checks were made by appliqueing on thin silk strands in yellow.

LEGS

Breeches ceased to be worn for everyday use during the reign of William IV, and *Trousers* took their place. They were strapped under the instep and braided at the sides at option. *Pantaloons* continued in use. *Peg-top Trousers* were not beautiful, and gave scope to the fun makers. They were full at the waist, and tapered to the ankle, where they were tight. Vertical striped materials, as well as plainer ones, were used for them.

LINEN

The *Stock*, of fine linen, was lightly starched and put on over the throat, wound round the neck once or twice in careful creases, and then tied over in cravat fashion in front, where it was pinned or otherwise steadied. Black silk was also worn for it.

The *Shirt* was frilled and starched in front,

and had a high collar, which was carefully turned over the stock. The Byron collar showed the neck without the stock, but was not common. Under William IV overcoats were made with long capes reaching to the waist.

HAIR

The *Hair* was brushed out at the sides, and faces were clean shaven.

HATS

Tall high square *Beaver Hats*, in various shades of black, grey, and biscuit, were worn. They were furry, not smooth like a modern top hat. They curved inwards in the middle of the crown, and the brim was rolled at the sides rather more than it is to-day.

REGENCY AND LATER WOMEN, 1813–37

The *Bodice* had its waist shifted lower to the normal waist-line, where it had a rather broad belt of the same material as the costume. The waist was also pointed a little. The shoulder seam dropped to below its proper place, thus baring the shoulders, while the sleeve filled out into a "Bishop" type. Diagonal pleats and tucks were given to the bodice. With William IV came the leg-of-mutton sleeve, wide from shoulder to elbow, from which it became tight to the wrist. Soon after its appearance it was divided into double puffs by a ribbon tied on half way, and just before the close (about 1835) of the period it was further divided into several puffs in a similar way to give an imitation of the style of François Ier, of France, from whom the fashion took its name. The dropping of the seams off the shoulder forced the bodice to slip and bare the shoulders. To prevent it from falling off the bare shoulders yokes were introduced. These were made of muslin at first, but this proving to be not sufficiently substantial, yokes of the same material as the dress were made.

It was an age of crude, strong colouring, and magentas, gamboges, violets, resedas, and emeralds dazzled the eyes of the traveller in Regent Street and Carlton House Terrace.

Like the bodice, the *Skirt* became fuller and wider at the bottom, and it was shortened to ankle length under William IV. To aid in this fattening process, the *Petticoat* was restored to favour, and was stiffened or made of thick material in order to hold out the skirt.

The foundation of the bodice was a *Corset*, over which it was loosely draped.

The *Pelisse* did not remain unaffected by the general enlargement. It cast off its thin silks, and was wadded or quilted to present a stiffer and more ungainly appearance.

FEET

Shoes remained small, but were more practical than formerly; the old velvets went out in favour of leather and black glazed material. The type for indoors was that of the ballet shoe, tied with ribbons crossed in front and fastened behind.

HAIR

Hair was rather charming. It was parted in the centre and neatly brushed down there to flourish into clusters of curls at the sides and over the forehead. Several formal ribbon bows were added at the top.

HATS

Hats were in straw, with large brims, adorned with feathers, and worn at the back of the head like the bonnets. Ribbons and flowers were impartially used on both hats and bonnets. The latter had flowers under the brim and ribbons across the top to tie below the chin in a bow and falling ends. The Coal-scuttle hat was made on a foundation covered in silk, or of straw. At first the angle of the poke rose sharply, but later the angle ceased and the slope from back to front was by a gradual rise.

SUMMARY

MEN, EMPIRE

Dress

    Coat—cut away, square tails. Double-breasted high collar. Tight sleeve. Blue, dark brown, bottle green.

    Vest—short. Small lapels. Morning, buff or light; evening, white. Single-breasted.

    Pantaloons — calf-length trousers. Tight. Buttoned below calf. Braided sides. Black for evening.

    Or Breeches—buckskin.

    Stock—linen.

Legs

    Striped silk stockings for evening.

Feet

    Hessians—short close-fitting boot to knee, where tasselled. Worn with pantaloons.

    Top Boots—worn with breeches.

    Shoes—black, worn with pantaloons.

A BOY

Hair

    Frizzed out at sides. Clean-shaven.

Hats

    Opera for evening.

    Beaver for day. Tall square.

WOMEN, EMPIRE

Dress

    Empire Gown—white muslin or lawn. No decoration. Armpit waist. Low bodice. Skirt not full in front, slight gathers behind. Back laced. Sleeve tight to upper arm. Waist ribbon.

    Petticoat—none, or extremely thin.

    Pelisse—sleeved mantle, thin silk, for outdoors.

    Gloves—long to above elbow. Coloured to match shoes. Reticule—handbag.

    Scarves.

Feet

    Slippers—low-heeled, velvet.

Hair

    Classical, piled high and wound round with ribbon bands.

Hats

Wide straw. Turbans of velvet, silk, crepe, muslin.

Dress   MEN, REGENCY AND LATER

Coat—buff, blue, grey. High collar, broad lapels. Cut-away tails. Double-breasted. Long sleeve, puffed at top. High waist. Brass buttons. For William IV, velvet collars and cuffs. 1825 onwards, frock coat, dark blue or brown. Fur bottom band. High roll fur collar.

SHOE, 1800

Vest—as before, striped or checked.

Pantaloons—as before.

Breeches—as before (except for riding), not worn under William IV.

Trousers—strapped under instep, 1830 onwards.

Peg-tops—trousers full at waist, tight at ankle.

Stock—linen or black silk neckcloth. Tied as cravat.

Shirt—frilled. High collar turned over stock.

Overcoat—under William IV long capes to waist.

Fob—watch pendant.

Feet

As before.

Hair

Short. Full at sides, brushed over to eyes. Side whiskers. Bushy in front. Under William IV centre parted occasionally.

Hats

High beaver.

Dress   WOMEN, REGENCY AND LATER

Bodice—short pointed waist. Shoulder seam drops. Larger sleeve, diagonal pleats and tucks. Evening, bare shoulders. Under William IV, leg-of-mutton sleeve to elbow, tight to wrist, or double puffs. Later, many puffs. Muslin yokes, later matching dress. Normal waist-line. Belt. Yokes first of muslin, of material towards close.

Skirt—round and full. Ankle length under William IV.

Petticoat—stiff to hold out skirt.

Corset.

Pelisse—wadded and thicker.

Feet

Shoes—stouter, leather, black glaze.

Hair

Centre parting. Curl clusters forehead and sides. Ribbon bows.

Hats

Straw—large brim, large feathers, ribbons, flowers.

Bonnet—coal-scuttle, straw or silk covered. Sharp angle first, later less acute. Trimmed under front.

CHAPTER XXI

THE CRINOLINE, 1850–60

THE pageant of clothes has ended. Gone are the lovely colours and resplendent materials which men delighted to wear; gone also are the gracefully formed fashions of

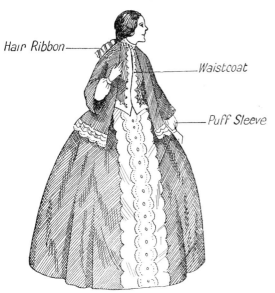

ZOUAVE JACKET, 1854

the women; the era of the machine has come and England has given itself over to a wave of materialism no less in thought than in fact.

The Victorian Era was the ugliest period of the centuries; art sank to its lowest ebb; meaningless ornament was applied as a veneer instead of growing out of the necessities of the object it was supposed to adorn. The result was an overloading of an already poor design. The decade of wax flowers, antimacassars, red plush and yellow fringe and of Highland Cattle paintings could not be expected to produce anything more inspiring in its costumes, nor did it.

Colours were crude, patterns were startling, bonnets were frankly hideous.

The disappearance of the higher forms of culture made unnecessary any attraction or beauty in dress, for women ceased to be the central

figures in an artistic salon and considered their sole *métier* to be that of the cultivation of the domestic circle.

The lover of dress meets a period of gloom and little delight can be derived from the costumes of this chapter, or indeed of those to the end of the century.

Until the invention of the steel-ringed crinoline it was necessary—in order to make the skirt swell to the desired balloon-like proportions—to wear petticoats which had to be padded with horsehair to prevent them dropping into their natural folds. A skirt had to be about ten yards round at the bottom, and a tulle dress of four skirts, ruched, took 1,100 yards of material. Thin gauze-like materials were worn and were cheap. Each frock had many flounces. In 1850 the number was

THE FLOUNCED SKIRT, 1856

from 15 to 25. The Empress Eugenie once wore at a State function a white satin frock that had 103 flounces of tulle! The effect of these flounces in the filmiest materials was rather charming, but a frock could be worn only once if it was made of tulle, as it depended entirely on its freshness for its effect.

The popular materials were *crêpe de Chine* organdie muslins, tarlatan, and satin. Empress Eugenie, from patriotic motives, tried to popu-

THE WIDE SKIRT, 1857

larize the heavy Lyons silks, but they were a trial as they much increased the already heavy weight of material that had to be carried. It was necessary owing to the number of the skirts to walk in a special way to secure a graceful effect, and a short glide was found to be the best.

The flounces were made of lace, muslin, and tarlatan over silk of the same colour. These flounces matched the frock or contrasted with it.

DRESS

MEN

The men began to look very much as they look to-day. The frock coat costume was much worn; also a lounge suit, which had the lower front corners of the coat rounded off and a small opening at the neck instead of the modern long revers. The lounge suit could be made in light colours. A popular material was one with a plaid effect: it had horizontal and vertical, rather widely placed stripes. With the lounge suit was worn a bowler or a top hat. The latter should be used with the frock coat. The trousers were

often of plaid and the coat and vest were plain—or a dark coat was worn with light trousers. For evening dress a tail coat, with a low-cut vest showing much starched shirt (which had a small frill) and a huge white bow tie, was correct. The cravat was worn for day wear, but the large bow tie made of wide material was more popular. The lounge coat might be left open. "Swells" often had their waistcoats and coats cut low, and their coats with wide revers to show plenty of shirt, the latter fastened with two pearl buttons.

DRESS

WOMEN

The *Skirt* was wide and had many flounces, but, later, the hoop was lowered so that the dress fitted at the hips, and the flounces were superseded by a single frill at the hem of the skirt. This was towards the end of the sixties. From 1860 onwards the skirt was often drawn up in four places to display underneath the petticoat, which became more decorative.

After my lady had put on her lace-trimmed

THE BELL SLEEVE, 1858

Drawers, she got into her *Under Petticoat*, which was lined and corded with horsehair, and had a straw plait in the hem to make it stand out. The *Petticoats* had then to be managed. Several of these were sewn into one band for convenience:

they must have been difficult to wash. The order of the petticoats was—

1st. A flannel one.
2nd. A horsehair padded one 3½ yards wide.
3rd. One of Indian calico stiffened with cords.
4th. A wheel of thick plaited horsehair.
5th. A starched muslin one with three flounces.
6th. A starched muslin one.
7th. Another of the same kind.
8th. The *Frock*.

The *Bodice* (women), fairly roomy and balloon-like, was gathered in at the waist into a band. The sleeves were narrow at the shoulder, but swelled out in a large open bell at the elbow. It had many flounces, and to it was attached the under sleeve, of white thin material, which was balloon-shaped and gathered at the wrist into a frill. The neck was open a little, and adorned with a narrow lace collar or a bertha of ribbon, ruches, or embroidery. Checks and stripes were in vogue, and the colours tended to be rather "strong."

A curiously masculine effect was given when

OUTDOOR LOOPED DRESS, 1860

for indoor wear about the house the short coat was introduced from Russian sources. It soon developed into the *Zouave Jacket* (women), which was worn with a *Waistcoat* (women).

This Zouave jacket was really a bodice open in the front and worn over a contrasting waist-coat, which showed there. It was braided and embroidered and decorated with large buttons— the larger the more daring—and the vest had to be as "stunning" as possible. The Zouave had long sleeves, which were cut open to the elbow.

THE REDUCED FIGURE, 1868

Owing to the wide sleeves it was impossible to get into a cloak or overcoat. Shawls and mantillas were consequently adopted. The former were square and of cashmere or shot silk, which was always a lovely shade. They were heavily fringed and embroidered by hand in coloured silks.

Small muffs were carried, and the evening frock had a low neck which made it appear to be slipping off the shoulders.

HAIR

MEN

Profusion of hair marked the period. Beards, side whiskers, and heads were frizzed out and curly. An Imperial could be worn, but it was not common till towards the end of the period when the Emperor Napoleon III was imitated.

HAIR
WOMEN

Women smoothly parted their hair in the middle, drew it tightly across the head into a net bag behind, and allowed side clusters to appear to frame the face. At night a wreath of artificial flowers—roses mainly—in circular shape was worn, rather off the head, or it might have a point at the front to form a wreath of the type associated with classical victors.

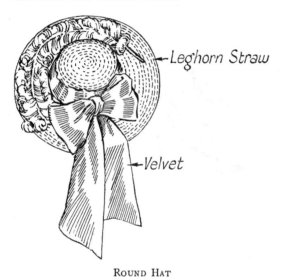

ROUND HAT

HATS
MEN

The silk top hat was worn on all occasions, with lounge suits or frock coats. At evening the opera hat was indispensable to the smart man. The bowler hat, though rather different from that of to-day, first made its appearance. It was worn on informal occasions, had a short straight brim, a bell-shaped fairly low crown, with a knob on the top. A straw boater, exactly in the modern shape, was also worn by bus drivers, etc. Workmen wore a curious round fur cap, square in outline, and the carpenter's square paper cap was often seen. The top hat might be black, white, or grey, but black was mostly used. It could be smooth or furry, and was tall and narrow in the crown. Another type had a larger crown, which curved inwards at its middle and out again at the top, but it was somewhat foreign. Mourn-

ing bands of felt were put on when required, and their widths varied with the depth of woe it was felt proper to indicate.

HATS
WOMEN

The *Poke Bonnet* was extensively worn, but shared its popularity with the much-reviled *Round Hat* or *Leghorn*. Both were made of straw. The bonnet was a coal-scuttle shape, with broad ribbons passing from the top down the sides and tied under the chin, from which the broad ends hung for a considerable length. The under part of the brim, which framed the face, was trimmed with flowers, and the outer crown was also adorned with these or with ribbons and laces. It was correct to wear the bonnet as much off the head as possible, a lot of the smoothly bandolined mid-parted hair being seen. Under the bonnet matrons wore a white cap of lace or material trimmed with ribbon. The round hat

POKE BONNET

was simple and large. It caught the wind very much, and strings by which it could be held down in a gale were attached in front. It could be turned up at each side. The customary trimming was a single ostrich feather curled round the crown, or a broad band of ribbon with two tails behind. (John Leech's pictures in *Punch* throw a flood of light on the costumes of this period.)

JEWELLERY

Heavy gold jewellery, in the form of watch-chains, looped into both waistcoat pockets, began to be worn by the men. Fobs were also used. The women had necklets and rings, also the chatelaine, which was a buckle-hook fastened to the waist at the left side. It had several short chains, to which were attached articles of everyday use, such as scissors, buttonhooks, paper-knives, etc.

SUMMARY
MEN

Dress

Coat—frock or light or plaid, with rounded edges and high neck.

Vest—short, opened high. Single breasted, braid edged.

Tie—bow or Ascot cravat. Black stock rare.

Legs

Trousers—tight, checked, striped, dark with light coat.

Feet

Boots—elastic sided. Low heels. Black.

Hair

Beard—side whiskers. Moustache, Imperial. Thick bushy hair.

Hats

Silk topper—white, grey, or black. High. Straw boater.

Bowler—bell-shaped crown, tight-rolled brim. Black, white, fawn. Knob on top.

Jewellery

Heavy gold watch-chains. Fobs.

WOMEN

Dress

Bodice—balloon-like Pagoda sleeve, narrow shoulder, and large open bell at elbow. Many-flounced. Open neck. Lace collar or bertha of ribbon, ruches, embroidery. For evening, low neck to shoulders.

Undersleeve—white light material from elbow, getting larger till 1860, when it was steel hooped.

Blouses—white, attached to skirt by ribbon braces and sashes.

Zouave—bodice open in front over contrasting vest. Long sleeves cut open to elbow.

Vest—worn with Zouave coat. Cut like a man's.

Shawls—square cashmere, *crêpe de Chine*, embroidered in silk and heavily fringed. No cloaks were possible.

Mantilla—velvet, lace, taffeta.

Skirt—wide, many-flounced. Later it fitted at the hips when hoop lowered and no flounces. From 1860 skirt was drawn up in four places to show petticoat.

Petticoats—seven worn, horsehair stuffed and padded to give width until crinoline of steel wire replaced stuffing and then fewer petticoats were worn. From 1860 onwards the outer petticoat was coloured.

Drawers—long, trimmed with lace.

Flounces—many. Lace-trimmed, scalloped, gauffered, plaited, fringed, looped, festooned.

Feet

Boots—elastic sides. Black cloth, looped tags back and front. Laced ankle boots.

Slippers—no heels.

Hair

Mid-parted. Smooth on top, bun at back, side clusters. Girls wore long braids wound about ears. Wreaths for evening.

Hats

Poke bonnet—straw, ribbon tied under chin. Flower trimmed.

Leghorns—large round hats of straw, ostrich feathered.

Caps—worn under bonnet by elders, white lace, ribbon trimmed.

CHAPTER XXII

GROSVENOR GALLERY, 1870–80

AESTHETICISM, though it was much ridiculed, was really a step in the right direction, for it laid emphasis on a beauty that had wellnigh been forgotten amidst the

François Premier Sleeve

Greek-style Hair

Puff Sleeve

AESTHETIC REVIVALS, 1877

horrors of mid-Victorian prosperity. Its leader and chief apostle was the brilliant author and playwright, Oscar Wilde, whose epigrams and good birth took him easily into the front rank of Society and brought him hosts of imitators. The author of *Lady Windermere's Fan* achieved enormous success with his plays and has attained immortality as the Poet in Gilbert and Sullivan's skit on the craze—*Patience*—quite apart from the intrinsic merit of his own works. The period is the Eighteen Seventies.

The "Greenery-Yallery, Grosvenor-Gallery, Aesthetic Young Man" was so termed because of the breakaway from the current crude colouring and patterning of dress materials in the seventies in favour of sage greens, yellows, cinnamons, and peacock blues. It was a revolt from the cult of the primary colour.

With this was coupled a search for beauty in the blue-and-white porcelain of Japan, the many-hued shades of the peacock, the light oval Oriental hand fan, and a general thirst for the antique in furniture and fittings with a recall to the work of the Old Masters of Italian painting. All this was to the good. Yet being confined to the thinkers, artists, and an inner circle of high society, it did not affect the great mass of the people to any extent. Its importance to the student of dress is in the fact that it was the first herald of a new dawn of real beauty and a much-needed harking back to the antique. It finds its permanent place in theatrical and social history with the large output of plays in the seventies that need to be dressed sympathetically.

The hallmarks of the true devotee (it affected women's clothes more than men's) were the

"GROSVENOR GALLERY," 1882

puffed sleeve, the low neck, and the absence of the bustle.

This revolt, although it did not greatly influence the masses, being confined to the comparatively small circle popularly labelled "Chelsea," deserves due recognition as a turning point in the story of costume. Though its effect was not immediately felt in dress, it had a profound influence on the other arts. William Morris, that Victorian prophet and genius, no less than the pre-Raphaelite Brotherhood—Rossetti, Burne-Jones, Ford Madox Brown, and the rest—reflected the same spirit of revolt. They turned from the popular brown paintings of their day (even grass and sky was coloured thus) to the clear freshness and vital nature of the earlier centuries of painting. They declared war on the worship of the machine, and showed men the dignity of hand craftsmanship, and the beauty which could be found in non-materialistic things.

The Aesthetic Revolt has, then, an honoured place in our history and, regarded for itself alone, it did achieve beauty of costume because it returned to the natural shape of the human body.

That it did not have more influence is a wonder, when we look at the alternative which the fashionable world accepted. The man-woman made her first appearance in the horrific ensemble

BALL DRESS, 1877

of a bowler-hat and ankle length, ulstered male overcoat with patch pockets. The womanly woman ruined her health by squeezing into a wasp-waist. Her corsage was made so tight and

rigid that the natural lines were concealed, while, not content with this abortion, she developed a freakish erection at the back which might have given a Chinaman the impression that the English body was something quite different from that of the rest of the world.

The bustle had a curious history and its rise,

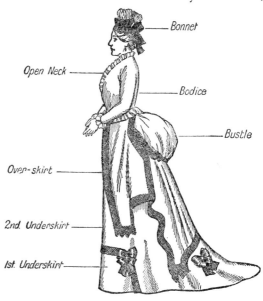

DAY DRESS, 1873

development and fall is, in miniature, an example of the development of one costume into another, as set out in the Appendix.

The sleeve might form a huge puff at the shoulder, from whence it descended in the normal tight sleeve to the wrist: this style was common to the decade. Again, a revival of the French *François Premier* sleeve, with its many puffs right down the whole length of the sleeve, gathered in with narrow velvet ribbons, was popular. It had previously been worn at the beginning of Queen Victoria's reign, and you will see her wearing such a sleeve in the well-known painting of her first council meeting. Two puffs to the elbow and then a straight sleeve were also worn. The neck (which normally was high cut) was, with the Aesthetes, a low one, edged with a narrow frill. This V opening might be cut still lower down the bodice, the opening being filled in with gathered muslin, but still baring an adequate portion of the chest.

In the hair, too, the Aesthetes showed commendable courage. They broke away from the hideous chignon, and took up ancient classical Greek modes. In these the hair was piled fairly high at the back of the head in an upward pointing cone, strung round at intervals with braids of ribbon. On the forehead a natural wave replaced the frizz of the "Philistine" (a Philistine

AN 1877 SWELL

was one who did not favour the craze). Even loose long hair was worn by the daring, or it might be piled high on the head, brushed back, and finished in a knot in the style of Madame Pompadour.

The men folk could not do much to vie with this fashion, but it was a refreshing sign of their own revolt from the mid-Victorian Paterfamilias that they preferred the slender man to the bulbous portly frame that their contemporaries thought "manly."

Punch gives us many pictures of the Aesthetes, and his "Maudles," "Postlethwaites," and "Cimabue Browns" are, despite his ridicule, a class with which one feels in sympathy.

Care should be taken with the settings to include "bric-à-brac." Japanese and Chinese porcelains, huge bowls, oval paper or silk fans with bamboo handles, china elephants, and peacock feathers are typical. Good pictures should

be used, for the pre-Raphaelites were the exponents of Aesthetic principles. The women of Rossetti, Burne-Jones, William Morris, and Holman Hunt are all of this type, and to Morris is due a great debt for his strenuous advocacy of the necessity to lay emphasis on craftsmanship, and his abhorrence of the machines that were slowly killing art in the home.

Apart from the aesthetes were the rank and file of the decade, and some account of the costume of the seventies must be given.

DRESS
MEN

Men were dressed in the frock coat, tight trousers, and top hat. A certain latitude was allowed in the country and amongst the lower orders. This took the form of lounge suits and different hats.

The *Frock Coat* (men) had thin lapels, often covered with velvet. It was single or double-breasted, and was usually worn fully buttoned. To leave the coat unfastened was not good style. It was given grace of shape by well defining the waist.

The *Lounge Coat* (men) had either cut-away or square corners, and was short. Extremists had the skirts flared, but gentlemen did not. The two buttons, which originally held the sword-belt in place, were still stitched on to the lounge coat, as well (of course) as on the frock coat.

The *Waistcoat* (men) was made with a narrow V opening and cut high, though there were instances where the opposite was the case, and the vest was cut extremely low.

The *Tie* was cravat-like, and was made broad, but it was tied in a sailor knot or pulled through a gold tie ring.

LEGS

Trousers (men) were narrow, but not skin tight. Bell bottoms were introduced. Trousers were generally light in shade and almost always checked or plaided. The check was not a series of small squares as to-day; the material was crossed with thin stripes.

DRESS
WOMEN

The *Bodice* (women) was tightly stretched over a corset and of hour-glass shape. If one could possibly squeeze into a 19-in. waist one was in the height of fashion. For evening wear no sleeves were worn, a string of material or ribbon finishing off the armhole. For day wear long tight sleeves reached to the wrist, where they were finished with a narrow frill. The neck, which was low for evening wear, was high during the day and gathered into a frill or a plain band at the top.

The *Skirt* (women) fell to the ground, where it swept up the dust. A long train was added at night, and a short train during the daytime. The skirt followed the natural figure, and was tight-fitting over the hips. At about the knees it widened into a wide skirt, finished with a broad flounce, or with two or three flounces at the hem.

The *Overskirt* (women) was generally made up with the skirt, but appeared like a separate garment, especially when made of contrasting material. It hung down to just below the knees in front, was slightly drawn up at the sides, and loosely folded at the back over a bustle, the wire frame of which held out the skirt. The wired bustle went out in 1877 but left a slight bunch behind.

Overcoats (women) were of different types. One just like a man's was worn. It was of ground length, with a broad waist belt and large buttons, and it had a short hood at the back, lined with silk. It was generally double-breasted, but could be single-breasted, and could also be worn of three-quarter length. Plaids were popular.

A *Short Coat* (women) with a flared skirt at the waist and broad lapels with broad velvet collar and cuffs and a double-breasted fastening was more favoured by matrons. More stately matrons wore a three-quarter length velvet or fur coat with a broad fur-edging all round and also on the cuffs.

Hair

Men's hair was brushed outwards and upwards from every possible portion of the façade. Long beards, side whiskers, middle or side partings— and the wonderful Dundreary moustache—added to their range of choice. The Dundreary moustache was a "dragoon" type, like two large capital S's.

Women adopted the hideous chignon, which

was made as large as possible and tucked into a thick fish net at the back. The hair was brushed away from the face and was rather flat on the crown, with a fringe over the forehead, giving an untidy frizzy effect. Round the chignon (which was a wire cage inserted under the hair) were coiled masses of hair in thick plaits, and ribbons or lace caps, with trimmings, were almost

THE MAN-WOMAN, 1877

compulsory for all right-thinking females over the age of 21 years.

Hats

Men wore almost everywhere and always the top hat, which was higher and narrower than it is to-day. It had a narrow front and rear brim, larger at the sides, but deeply curved round. The line of the side of the hat was also semi-circular, not straight. In the country, bowler, cloth, and straw hats were worn (tradesmen wore these, though the majority wore the topper). The topper was not then a class distinction as it is now. The bowler was almost like our own, but had a higher bell crown and the brim was shaped like the top hat brim.

Women did their best to look charming in small toques trimmed with ribbons and feathers. They had low bell-shaped crowns and short brims.

SUMMARY
MEN
Dress

Overcoat—heavy to ankles. Broad belt. Short hood at back. D.B.

Frock coat—thin lapels. S.B. or D.B. Velvet collar. Waisted.

Lounge coats—cut away or square corners. Short. Two buttons at back. Slightly flounced skirts.

Waistcoat—cut high at neck.

Legs

Trousers—narrow. Checked. Bell bottoms sometimes. Light colour.

Feet

Boots—side elastic insets or buttoned at side. Low heels. Laced shoes occasionally.

Hair

Dundreary moustache. Side whiskers. Long beards. Mid or side parting, well brushed-out thick hair.

Hats

Top hat—black, white, fawn. Silk or beaver. Well curved brim, narrow front and back.

Cloth—bowler shape.

Bowler—informal. High bell crown, narrow, well-curled brim.

Straw—seaside and country use only.

WOMEN
Dress

Bodice—hour-glass corset shape. Twenty-inch waist. Tight, long sleeves. Frill or band fits neck.

Skirt—ground length. Train. Natural outline. Close fitting to half way, then widened. Hem flounce.

Overskirt—apron fashion in front carried up at sides. At back fell in loose folds on bustle. Bustle lessened, 1877.

Overcoat—as men, in plaid. Ground or three-quarter length. Velvet three-quarter length. Broad fur edge and cuff.

Short coat—flared skirt at waist. D.B. Broad lapels. Broad velvet cuff and collar.

Feet

Boots—elastic insets. Shoes.

Hair

Brushed back off face. Chignon in rear. Heavy plaits coiled. Lace caps for all married women. Mid-parted and loose, not covering nape. Forehead fringe.

Hats

Toques—feather or ribbon trimmed. Bell-shaped crown. Short brim.

AESTHETIC MODES

Followed the current fashion with modifications and more natural outline to skirts without bustle. Large puffed sleeves and fairly low necks, frilled or filled in with muslin were typical.

Hair was worn long and loose at back, or dressed in Greek classical style and banded with ribbon. The sacque of Anne's reign was also adopted. Oval Japanese fans were carried. Much sunflower trimming. Peacock feathers. Japanese ornaments. Massive bead necklaces. The François Premier sleeve.

CHAPTER XXIII

NOAH'S ARK, 1880–90

DURING the Eighties of the last century the all-prevailing bustle ceased to dominate the female figure. It dwindled until it became a mere sash and bow at the back, and in this form it was rather more tolerable than

Hour-Glass Bodice

High Draped Bustle

EVENING GOWN, 1882

it was at the height of its development in the previous decade. The Seventies were possibly the most hideous years for women's dress in any age and any land.

The period now under review has been immortalized by the charming drawings of George du Maurier, the talented father of a talented son—Sir Gerald du Maurier. A true artist, George du Maurier managed to make his ladies look pleasant—and when you know his period you will realize how great an artist he must have been—or what an imaginative touch he conveyed with his pencil.

My Lady still looked like an hour-glass, and much damage to health must have been caused by the tight lacing that was required in order to make nature fit the prevailing modes. Man's

hirsute features and potato-bag contours, caused by his shapeless coats and trousers, were a fitting foil to the extraordinary appearance of his womenfolk.

The bustle was worn until the Eighties. The

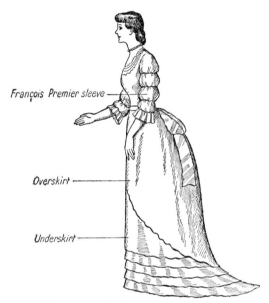

François Premier sleeve

Overskirt

Underskirt

YOUNG GIRL'S EVENING FROCK, 1882

fashionable modified it, and it dwindled into the form of a huge bow and sash at the back without the wire cage that used to stuff out the form into a most unnatural shape.

The overskirt was drawn higher than before. In the Seventies it was about three-quarter length or half-length; in the Eighties it was only quarter-length and, being parted immediately and carried round to the back, was scarcely seen in front.

To the Eighties must be given the credit of perfecting the wasp waist and creating the Noah's Ark figure. Numerous little buttons in vertical rows completed the illusion. The Great Flood idea was reflected in the houses of severe brick with the plainest of doors and windows, and no grace of outline or beauty of design.

It was a prurient and prudish age. Bathing gowns were flounced and frilled and covered the body.

Man continued much as before. His features, covered by masses of bushy hair that bristled out in side whiskers, long beards, and tremendous moustaches, were rarely seen. His trousers were

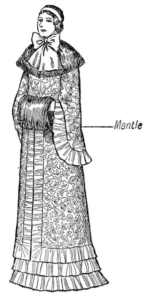

A Matron, 1882

a couple of creased and crumpled objects that might be described as tubes. Similar tubes, though more shapely, covered his head. He wore his hat in the House of Parliament and in the club, and he carried it into ladies' drawing-rooms when he called for afternoon tea, and he took his opera hat into their ballrooms at night. Even in bed he wore a night cap!

Sir John Tenniel has immortalized the period in *Alice in Wonderland* where the queens, with their enormous netted chignons and their many-ruched skirts, are typical of the Age of Hideousness of the Seventies and the early Eighties.

Dress
Men

Man looked best in his long, waisted, *Overcoat*, of three-quarter or longer length, with its broader revers and its side pockets with flaps.

The *Frock Coat* or *Tail Coat* was worn by nearly everyone.

His *Trousers*, coming right down to the instep, were narrow and fairly tight.

His *Lounge Suit* was baggy and creased. It had no waist. The corners were rounded or squarely cut, and the rever was fairly deep.

His *Waistcoat* was cut high to show at the neck only a small V, through which appeared an enormously wide and massive tie of sailor knot variety, or a cravat of dark silk.

His *Collars* varied. The really smart man wore a single choker collar, which gave him a clerical appearance. Most men wore a double collar with long pointed ends that were tucked under the coat, like those worn by butlers, and the bow tie when worn with this had its ends tucked under the collar. Evening dress was almost identical with our own, except for the tighter trousers, and dinner jackets, which came in in 1880, were not worn very much. A velvet smoking jacket could be used instead for informal evening wear.

A Young Matron, 1882

White waistcoats were worn by the smart; others wore black.

The modern differentiation between the tail coat and the frock coat, the former being more formal than the latter, had not been made, and either was worn.

The *Norfolk Jacket* appeared about 1885 for sports wear, and was made in tweeds, with two box pleats vertically down back and front to give play to the arms. A belt to match was attached to the coat by loops.

DRESS
WOMEN

The *Bodice* (women) was corset-shaped, with a V point in front below the waist. As every crease had to be banished the waist was cut in sections, and the lining was shaped exactly to match, the two being stitched together, and the various sections then united so that no wrinkles or puckers were possible. The sleeves were usually tight and fitted smoothly without wrinkles into the armholes. At the elbow they were frilled. For day wear the sleeve was prolonged to the wrist and frilled there. A single shoulder puff, or the many-puffed *François Premier* sleeve, was also worn. The high neck was frilled, and the square yoked bodice was filled in with other material of a lighter type or to match the

A BUSINESS MAN, 1882

main fabric. Ruchings and frills were applied. Low necks were customary for evenings.

The *Skirt* (women) fitted well at the hips, and was kept close to the figure to the knees, from which it widened, and for evenings it was trained. It was elaborately decorated, sometimes with rows of ruchings, sometimes with several frills at the hem or even over the whole of the skirt.

The *Overskirt* (women) continued to be in bustle form, but it was not too exaggerated in shape. It was parted immediately below the point of the bodice, carried round to the back, and there draped in a bunch over the bustle, from whence it trailed downwards over the back of the skirt. It was occasionally fastened with large

FOR SHOPPING, 1882

bows. In this way the overskirt only covered the hips in front. A more graceful type was the overskirt that hung down in front to about half way, and was carried to the back, which it almost covered. At the back of the waist a huge bow sash was tied. Its ends hung right down nearly to the ground. The effect was less rigid.

The *Coat* (women) gave the real Noah's Ark effect. It was creaseless and well defined in its curves, and adorned with numerous small buttons in one or two vertical rows. It had side pockets, and was about half-length. Fairly large muffs were worn, but they were circular in shape or nearly so. Sealskin was fashionable for these short coats, and sealskin or bearskin capes coming well over the shoulders, where they finished, were also worn.

HAIR

The "Kaiser" moustache with upcurling ends but rather thinner, also the "Bismarck" variety, where the ends drooped downwards, were worn. Young men were clean shaven, though many wore large beards, as did practically every older man. Side whiskers and bushy hair untidily brushed were in the mode.

Women's hair was not beautiful. Dressed low on the crown and carried well down the nape of the neck in plaited braids, it looked as though it had been flattened by a heavy hat. A small frizzy fringe covered the forehead. Mid-partings were often worn. There was a tendency to puff out the hair more at the sides; previously it had severely pulled-in sides and plastered effects.

HATS

Men wore the ubiquitous *topper*, either high or low. If low, it was not a "John Bull" hat but tapered upwards. For the country, sport, and informal wear *cloth hats* of tweed were worn, especially for travelling. *Bowlers* with low bell crowns and curled brims were in the main worn by the lower classes only, though they, too, wore the topper.

Bonnets were of straw or of material for matrons. They were trimmed with lace, bows, ribbons, and, rather rarely, with flowers. Low bell-crowned *Hats*, with widish brims turned up, were popular, and were trimmed with ostrich feathers curled round the hatband. Young girls wore *Picture Hats* made in soft materials, with low crowns and wide brims, rather flimsily shaped and adorned with ribbon bands or flowers.

SUMMARY
MEN
Dress

Overcoat—long. Waisted. Broader revers. Side pockets with flaps.

Frock coat or Tail coat—waisted.

Lounge coat—loose and baggy. Rounded or square corners. Fairly deep rever. Waistcoat square ended. Norfolk jacket box pleated.

Legs

Trousers—tight.

Feet

Boots—narrow points or square ends. Cloth or elastic sides.

Hair

Beards. Side whiskers. Clean shaven. Kaiser moustache. *Ad lib* generally.

Hats

Topper—tall or low.

Cloth—in checked tweed.

Bowler—low bell crown. Curled brim.

Linen

Collar—high single choker. Turn down double with points (butler).

Cravat—dark silk with tie-pin.

Sailor knot tie, with tie-ring. Very broad.

WOMEN
Dress

Bodice—corset shaped, creaseless. Pointed in front at waist. Tight sleeves to elbow, where frilled. *François Premier* sleeves. High neck frilled. Square corsage filled muslin or lace. Low neck evening. Single puff sleeves.

Skirt—many frilled or ruched in horizontals. Train at night only.

Overskirt—huge bow, with long ends at back. Short overskirt parted in front carried over hips to back. Bustles.

Coat—tight-fitting corset shape. Many buttons down front in single or double lines vertically. Side pockets. Capes, shoulders only.

Muffs—moderately large. Round.

Hair

Low in front with fringe. Long loose knot at nape. Mid-parting. Slight side puffs.

Hats

Bonnets—of fabric or material. Flowers rare.

Hats—bell crown low. Widish brim turned up. Feather-trimmed round band.

Picture hats—wide brims, low crowns. Soft material. Ribbon band and flowers.

CHAPTER XXIV

THE NINETIES, 1890–1900

THE NINETIES, while they were hideous, were an improvement on the previous decade, since the bustle had vanished.

A curious feature was that the women appeared to be aged almost at once. A married woman could be known by the difference in her clothes from those of the single woman. It must be said that from the artistic standpoint the clothes worn by married women had, generally speaking, no redeeming features.

As soon as a girl was married she was expected to abandon hats in favour of matronly bonnets and toques; she enveloped herself in that most appalling garment, the Victorian stiff mantle. She decorated herself with jet beads and guipure braid and at once added thirty years to her age.

The *ingénue* during her short butterfly existence, managed to look charming, but she had no influence on her mother's costume. Those were the days when parents really did rule, and the opinion of a young woman was neither sought nor tendered.

As for the men! The less said about their costume the better.

It must have been the triumph of a mathematical education, when tubes (symbolic of mechanical and scientific progress) fittingly dictated the shape of his clothes and revealed a mind which could only think in terms of material progress.

However, towards the middle of this decade a change for the better came about. Colours and materials improved and the evening gowns were delightful. Two ball frocks of my mother's stand out vividly in my mind though I was only a baby at the time they were worn. One was of deep primrose yellow ribbed silk. The yoke and skirt were trimmed with bunches of violets, and a diagonal sash of fine white lace was taken across the bodice and round the waist. This mode of draping with lace the tightly moulded bodice removed its hard and stiff appearance. The other was in a delicate shade of apple green silk with vertical silver-green stripes woven into the mate-rial. The yoke and corsage were adorned with most delicate pearl embroidery in a conventional design, while the widely puffed sleeves were masked with filmy white lace which also covered the square neck opening.

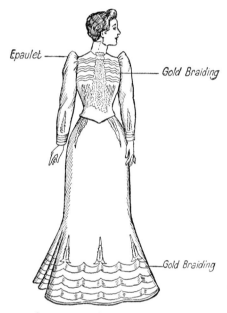

QUEEN MARY'S DAY DRESS, 1893

The use of spotted nets and muslins about 1905 turned the previous modes into the right lines by importing lightness and in substantially and finally removing the harder lines of the Eighties.

The late Victorians were so busy piling up money out of trade, extending their vast Empire, and generally dictating to the whole of Europe through their indomitable leader, the Queen, that they had little time to think about dress. The men remained uniformly undistinguished and ungainly in their costume, which changed but little from that of the previous decade.

In this history of costume it will be noticed that, whereas until George IV each reign embraced a single style, or at most two styles, of dress, when we come to the nineteenth century the changes are so rapid that I am compelled to treat them in periods of ten years at a time. This is in the main due to the decline in the wearing capacities of dress materials, and the poorness of the dyes used. Cheapness became desired everywhere, with the result that materials

A BALL DRESS, 1893

were made without regard to their lasting qualities, and the aniline dyes, freshly discovered, tended to rot the materials. In consequence, clothes wore out more rapidly, necessitating fresh ones, and there was no reason why the opportunity should not be taken to have a complete change in style.

CHILDREN

Children, until the later Georges, were miniature replicas of their parents; then they really blossomed in the rather comic fancy dress into which the late Victorians put them. The "Little Lord Fauntleroy" costume was popularized through the sickly sentiment of Mrs. Burnett's story. The child went about in a kind of travesty of a Charles the First dress, without its natural manliness. Short velvet knickers and a velvet coat, open in front, disclosed a white silk shirt-blouse, with a broad collar of lace or of silk, frilled. The shirt had a vertical frill down the front, where it was buttoned. Stockings and

rosetted shoes were added, and the final touch was given by a huge coloured silk sash ending in a large bow in front at the side. Long ringletted hair made these children (mainly in the richer classes) the butt of their more robustly clad poorer contemporaries. Victorian children had to do as they were told, but when they finally rebelled there was much lamentation at the loss of the long hair that went with this dress.

Little boys were also got up in other fancy dresses, such as the sailor suit, complete with wide brimmed round straw hat, which was a replica of the uniform worn by Her Majesty's seamen. Another creation (in England) was the more natural Scottish costume, which had the merit of picturesqueness without femininity. The Highland dress of kilt, sporran, cut-away coat,

DAY DRESS, 1892

and Glengarry bonnet is too well known to need detailed description.

To-day children are dressed sensibly in shorts and open necks, which allow the sunlight to get at them with beneficial results.

DRESS
MEN

The dinner jacket was the only really new feature, and is said to have been invented at Monte

Carlo because the tail coat caused strain when worn for long hours at a stretch at the gaming tables. Until the death of Edward VII it was never worn for formal evening parties. It was confined to the domestic hearth, where it replaced the black velvet smoking jacket of similar, though looser, cut.

The other innovation was brown boots, which gradually were allowed for street wear, black previously being *de rigueur*.

On the whole, English costume, until we come to Victoria's Reign, was beautiful, serviceable, and artistic. Men's clothes were equally so for a rather shorter time, until George IV struck a death blow by his persistent habit of wearing black.

Queen Victoria's death marks the end of an epoch, and it is significant of her essential greatness that the farther we get away from her times, the greater grows her reputation. One thing she did not achieve—beauty in dress, and this may partly have been due to the indifferent attitude

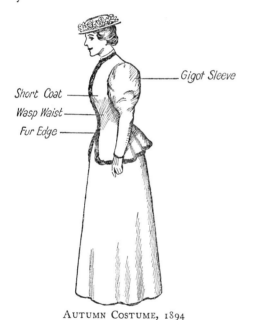

Short Coat —

Wasp Waist —

Fur Edge —

— Gigot Sleeve

AUTUMN COSTUME, 1894

that she herself displayed towards her own costume.

In our own times men have begun to revolt against the cloak of drabness and uniformity that has paralysed all attempts to make their costume pleasing ever since the time of the Prince Regent.

No longer are blacks and browns essential, but blues, greens, and purples may be worn for suits, and the "extras" are even gayer. Sweaters and pullovers of knitted wool are worn in every conceivable colour, and fresh, clear tones in the primary colours everywhere please the eye. This colour revival had previously extended to the ties

Gigot Sleeve —

AFTERNOON FROCK, 1897

and silk handkerchiefs, which still are the vogue, though there is room for improvement in getting brighter colours for the actual suiting materials.

DRESS
WOMEN

The bustle finally vanished in 1891, when the *Skirt* was made to fit closely at the hips, billowing out in a bell shape by means of many gores. Called an umbrella skirt, it was trimmed with guipure and braids of elaborate patterns, placed vertically at intervals down the skirt, and the same trimming was put horizontally on the bodice and skirt hem to match. In the 1900's spotted nets and muslins were worn over coloured silks, and looked very well.

The *Bodice* retained the Noah's Ark bust and fitted tightly by means of gores and pleats. It had a high collar, sometimes edged with a small frill. It was hooked at the back or the front, and, if the latter, the fastenings were concealed with lace falls, which might also encircle the neck.

Sleeves (women) varied. At first they were close-fitting to the wrist, and at the shoulders had peaked epaulets, formed by a puff in the material. These developed into the leg of mutton sleeves with huge shoulder puffs narrowing into a sleeve tight to the wrist. This was a revival of Georgian modes, and occurred in 1893. Finally, about 1895, the tight sleeve was abandoned in favour of one that was full right down and took the name of Bishop's sleeve owing to its likeness to the wide sleeves of the episcopal rochet.

Since the bodice fitted tightly and was brought down in front in a slight peak, no *Belts* were required until its shape changed in 1908, when the gap between bodice and skirt was covered by a sash or fairly broad belt. A masculine version came in with a shirt-blouse, stiff linen collar, and man's straw boater hat, worn with a tweed skirt.

For outer coverings, the popular coat was half-length and flounced out behind by means of gores. It was edged with a narrow band of fur at the neck and wrists, and buttoned down the centre with large bone buttons. Sealskin coats of the same cut were desired by women, but costly full-length fur coats were worn only by the very wealthy. Longer overcoats were also worn, but they were less popular except for older people.

For *Evening Dress* (women) the same styles, slightly modified, were current. For instance, the arms were bare, and covered by long white kid gloves to just above the elbow. The sleeve retained only its large shoulder puff, or even none at all but a single ribbon strap. Short trains were added to the skirts, which were gathered in flat pleats at the back to provide the necessary fullness for them. Necks were low and circular or square cut, with or without a lace frill. Artificial seed pearl trimming sometimes attained beautiful effects in narrow borders.

HAIR

Hair (women) was brushed back from the face in a puff called Pompadour after the famous friend of Louis XV. It was twisted into a top-knot at the back of the head, slightly towards the crown.

HATS

Hats were of straw, with medium-sized brims, trimmed with a feather or with wired upstanding bows. Bonnets were extensively worn. Thick spotted net *Veils*, worn with either hats or bonnets, covered the face, but towards the middle of the Edwardian reign veils went out.

SUMMARY
MEN
Dress

Norfolk jacket—as before, till 1914.
Frock coat—as before.
Lounge coat—as before.
Overcoat—as before.
Vest—straight bottom, S.B.
Ties—loose long-ended bows over collar; small bows under collar flaps; sailor knots.

Evening Dress

Velvet jacket—informal.
Dinner jacket—informal till 1911, with black tie and vest.
Tail coat—with white tie, black or white vest.
Collars—butterfly wing replaced high single; double turnover; "Butler's" low, points under coat.

Legs

Trousers—narrow; mostly pin striped; black.

Feet

Boots—brown worn in street; black usual.

Hair

As you please.

Hats

Topper—fairly tall.
Bowler—low crown.

WOMEN
Dress

Bodice—rather tight Noah's Ark shape bust, high collar. Guipure and braid trimmed horizontally. Front or back hooked. Lace falls in front. 1908 high waisted. Berthas. Sashes. Lace plastrons and *motifs*.
Skirt—fitted hips closely. Many gores to make bell shape till 1908. Rows of braid at bottom. Spotted nets over silks.

Sleeves—large. At first small epaulets. 1893 leg of mutton. 1895 Bishop, with different colour and made to bodice.

Jackets—half-length, below waist. Fur-edged neck and wrists. Buttoned (front, gored).

Belt—none till 1908.

Evening Dress

Large puff sleeves at shoulders. Bare arms; short trains; low necks; panels inserted down front. Lace frill to neck. Skirt gathered in flat pleats at back.

Hair

Pompadour with topknot.

Hats

Straw; medium brim. Trimmed wired bows or feathers.

Bonnets.

Veils—thick spotted.

CHILDREN

Lord Fauntleroy

Velvet jackets and short trousers. Wide hanging sash-belt. Wide lace collar. An imitation of Charles I period. White silk shirt. Rosetted sleeves.

Sailors

Miniature able-bodied seamen.

Scotsmen

Miniature Highlanders. Kilts, sporran, velvet cut-away coat, silver buttoned. Stockings. Bare knees. Glengarry bonnet.

CHAPTER XXV

EDWARD VII, 1901–10

KING EDWARD VII'S reign, coming at the end of the long era of Victorian might, was like the unnatural brightness which precedes a storm. Prosperity continued and was

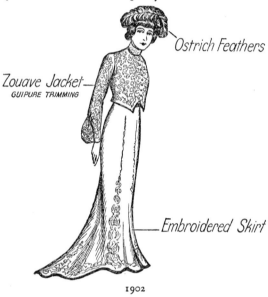

Ostrich Feathers

Zouave Jacket
GUIPURE TRIMMING

Embroidered Skirt

1902

increased through the peace policies of the King and the immense international popularity he enjoyed as the result of his frequent visits to the Continent.

The death of Queen Victoria, who had immured herself within the walls of Windsor, Osborne, or Balmoral for forty years, and was scarcely ever seen by her subjects, brought about the re-emergence of the monarch as the visible head of the nation.

King Edward had great social gifts, coupled with a love of ceremonial and a knowledge of its general utility. This reacted on society, and his reign was marked by great brilliance in social circles. Consequently, costume revived, since there were far more occasions when it could be displayed to advantage.

The influence of the superlatively lovely Queen Alexandra was another contributory factor, and

she definitely set two fashions: the first was her own style of tightly curled, unparted hair; the second was the collar of pearls and diamonds which she almost constantly wore, and which also ensured the maintenance of the high-necked modes for day dresses.

Men's dress changed but little, if at all, save for the introduction of the Norfolk Jacket by the King when Prince of Wales, and which remained in use until the end of his reign.

The women pursued their usual course of change, and the accentuated lines of the Nineties were modified into more graceful shapes without any really striking new fashions. Towards the end of the reign the Hobble skirt produced a slimmer outline, which was set off by the great increase in the width of the hats. Dress remained

Straw Toque
(CORD TRIMMED)

Fichu

Dust Coat

1904

much more formal than in our own times, and no woman would dream of appearing in public without gloves, nor any man without his hat.

Perhaps the most marked difference between

the Edwardian man and the post-War man, lay in the universally worn stiff collar of white linen, and the avoidance of any other colour for suits than black, brown, or grey. Frock coats and silk hats were *de rigueur* for all public functions. Another detail of the same kind was in the colour of the women's shoes. In the daytime brown or black was universal, and variegated leathers and coloured fabrics had not come in. For evenings satin shoes of one colour could be worn to match the dress, but again, variegated brocades and tinsels were not in fashion.

Both men and women carried themselves with greater dignity than they do to-day, and in this they were helped by the style and manner of wearing their clothes.

Dress
Men

There was not much change in the men's clothes and the only innovations were those popularized by the King when Prince of Wales—the Norfolk Jacket which came in about 1885, and

Osprey

Tailed Muff

1909

the Homburg Hat. Change was brought about by the increasing use of the lounge suit for many occasions where the frock coat would have been considered essential in Queen Victoria's reign.

Another change was in the curtailed Dinner Jacket for evening wear. This is thought to have originated at the gaming tables of Monte Carlo, where the use of the long-tailed coat when sitting for long hours at play, became tiring, and the tails were cut off. It should be noted that rigid rules as to the two permissible kinds of evening dress

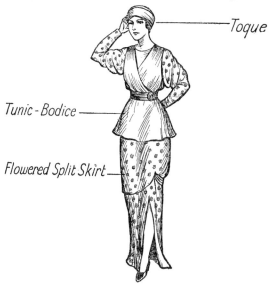

Toque

Tunic-Bodice

Flowered Split Skirt

1912

are still in force. With the tail coat may be worn a white waistcoat and tie if desired, but with the dinner jacket both must be of black always.

Collars at the commencement of the reign were single, but later they became double, or single with the ends turned out in wings. Stiff white linen was universal for all occasions, even when playing tennis or boating. The vogue of the open neck had not begun. For sports a *Flannel Shirt* might be worn but the collar was always attached and closely buttoned up. *Caps* were rounder and smaller than now, and the peaks were shorter. They were used only on very informal occasions.

Dress
Women

For day wear the women wore one and two piece suits. The former arrived in 1908, the latter three years later. Skirts were of ground length, and to prevent wear on the roads the edges were bound with fringed braid inside. The

One Piece Dress had long box pleats vertically and a profusion of buttons decorated it. It was finished with a small lace collar at the neck and had elbow sleeves, from which could protrude half sleeves of lace or material.

The *Two Piece Dress* was cut on similar lines without the pleats. The *Zouave jacket* covered a silk blouse of white or light colour. Face and habit cloths of very smooth felt-like surface were popular, and the edges of the jacket would be decorated with masses of coloured and gilt braid, disposed in serpentine or conventional patterns.

Bertha Cape

Spotted Net

Broad Sash

Lace Motifs

Velvet Ribbon

EVENING DRESS, 1908

Contrasted cloths were appliqued on for decoration.

The *Hobble Skirt* was a development of the one piece dress worn from 1908 to 1911, but owing to its increasing tightness it eventually became impossible to move about and the sides were slit. This was considered somewhat daring, and shortly afterwards the mode died out.

Evening Dresses showed much variety. The corsage was tight and boned, with a V opening in front and at the rear, the latter being less deep than the former. On this foundation the small waists and corsages were draped with lace to soften the effect, and the neck was finished with a draped lace Bertha collar or one of considerable depth in velvet—the latter frequently being square. Short puff sleeves remained from the previous decade.

Evening Skirts sometimes had a panel of contrasting material down the front. A short train was gathered into the waist band, and the skirt remained bell-shaped till 1908, then first grew straight and later narrowed to the hobble fashion. All were of ground length.

Waist Belts were almost always worn from 1908, save with the one piece dress, and were made from narrow ribbon with a wide-ended bow at the back.

Some evening skirts were of spotted muslin net over a colour, e.g. black over white. The Bertha collar might have velvet ruched bands with lace motifs cut out and inset therein. A broad belt of satin with a long streamer tail behind, floated over the slight train.

LEGS

Trousers dropped their bell bottoms and became tightly tubular and of almost the same width the whole way up. *Knickers* were worn with the Norfolk Jacket, chiefly for cycling, which became popular. The Knickers were gathered into a band at the knee.

FEET

Apart from the fact that brown shoes crept in for less informal occasions, there was little change for men, but even in this reign it was not considered the thing to wear brown shoes in town.

The women achieved some alleviation from the everlasting black and brown leather, by the adoption of coloured satin evening shoes. These, however, were of one colour and there were none of the modern suede, crocodile, reptile, and brocaded fabric and velvet types now worn.

HAIR

Whilst *Beards* remained popular with men, there was an increasing use of the full shave. The women parted their hair in the middle, and puffed it out at the sides, ending all with a largish bun at the nape of the neck, which was fastened off with a black *glacé* silk bow. The old Pompadour style brushed upwards and off the forehead was also popular. The Queen's style of tightly curled hair without a parting was frequently seen, especially in Court circles.

HATS

Men's *Caps* were rounder and had smaller peaks than present-day styles. The new style was that of the felt Homburg Hat, which was also made in Austrian Velour.

1905

Two main types of *Women's Hats* were worn. One was the flattish wide low crown with large brim, trimmed with a wing on each side in front, or with bunches of lace or tulle, ribbons, flowers, or large flat black velvet bows. The other had a high crown with a broad upturned brim and was generally decorated with a smart wired lace bunch at one side.

1910

Bonnets, worn by older women, were trimmed with jet beads, artificial flowers, feathers, or ospreys, but the last of these (owing to the cruelty inseparable from their collection) were strongly discountenanced and ultimately were rejected. All hats were of straw, for the felt hat had not arrived for women.

CHILDREN

Children's fashions are best expressed by the word "frilly," for frills finished off both girls' and little boys' clothes. Sailor suits were popular for small boys and in a modified form for girls also. Etons were considered indispensable for the well-dressed boy on Sundays and other formal occasions.

The girls' one piece frock was a simple affair with puffed, or long sleeves (the latter finishing in a wrist band). Lace collars or square yokes and belts were optional alternatives.

Babies wore white flannel and sometimes colours such as navy blue. White swansdown edged the garments.

SUMMARY
MEN
Dress

Overcoat—belted or plain. D.B. or S.B.
Frock coat—silk lapels. S.B. or D.B. waisted.

Paradise Feathers

Stiff Silk Frill

1911

Lounge coat—small revers. Straighter and less waisted than now.
Sweaters—white wool for sports.
Norfolk jacket—tweed for shooting.
Evening dress—tailcoat with white waistcoat and tie. Dinner jacket with black waistcoat and tie.
Collars—stiff white linen. Single high, replaced by double and wing collars.

Legs

Trousers—narrow, checked or striped, close at ankle.
Knickers—narrow band below knee buttoned. For cycling and sport with Norfolk jacket.
Breeches—for riding or shooting.

Feet

Boots—buttoned or side elastics or laced. Brown for informal use.

Shoes—laced. Black mainly, brown occasionally.

Hair

Beards—common. Clean shaven also. Moustaches. Parting *ad lib.*

Hats

Top hat—black, white, grey, fawn. Silk or beaver. The colours for races, country, etc.

Bowler—formal and informal use. Fairly high crown and narrow curled brim. Black, brown, grey.

Straw boater—seaside, river, and country use. Not wide brim.

Homburg—Velour or felt in colours: grey, brown, green, black. Dented on top, brim curled up all round. Self coloured band.

Cloth—bowler shape without top dent. Also with dent in Homburg shape.

Straw—in various shapes imitating the other types. Not very popular.

Caps—cloth. Small and round.

WOMEN

Dress

Blouse and skirt—silk or cotton blouse. Tweed skirt.

Zouave jacket.

Evening-bodice—small swathed waist. Draped lace corsage. Short puff sleeves. Tight corsage under Bertha or deep velvet collar, V back and front. Neck low in front, less so behind.

Evening skirt—front panel to contrast optional. Short train from waist band. Ground level. Bell shape to 1908.

Hobble skirt—1912. Very tight at ankles, later split at sides for walking.

Waist belt, 1908—velvet or satin or matching material. Broad. For evenings had long streamers behind.

One piece dress, 1909—long vertical box pleats, cassock-button trimmed down front. Small collar of lace. Elbow sleeves. Day wear.

Two piece dress—similar skirt but blouse overhung waist not attached to belt. Zouave

fashion. Much braiding. 1912. Day wear.

Ruffles—lace and velvet.

Long gloves.

Muffs and furs to match. Muffs small at first and round. Later larger and square. Fur necklets.

Fur coats—waist length. Full length worn only by the rich. Sealskin, sable, musquash, ermine, but little else.

Legs

Stockings show by 1912 with hobble skirt. Mostly black. Wool or cotton. Silk for the rich only.

Feet

Shoes or boots—black or brown exclusively for day. For evening plain silver or gold. Later plain coloured satin to match frock but no pattern or embroidery.

Hair

Mid parted. Side puffs. Small neck bun.

Silver or metal semicircular hair bands across front hair.

Tiaras—with full dress.

Black, *glacé* silk, wide-ended bow at bun.

Tight curled, no parting, Queen Alexandra type.

Pompadour—upwards and backwards brushed.

Hats

Large brim, wide low crown. Straw with wings or flowers or flat bows.

Broad upturned brim, high crown. Straw with wired lace bunch at side or feathers or ribbon.

Ostrich plumes, Ospreys, tulle trimmings.

Bonnets for older women.

CHILDREN
BOYS

Dress

Shorts—flannel. Grey or coloured.

Knickers—with knee band.

Blouses—to match shorts. Wide collars of silk, etc. Striped zephyrs and printed linens. Lace collars occasionally.

Jerseys—wool, grey, brown, blue. Turned down collar of same.

Eton suits—with topper, bowler, or straw hat.

Straw hats. Top hats—as for adults. School caps with peak.

Norfolk suits.

Dress   GIRLS

One piece frock—flounced. Frilled sleeves. Sash with bow at back. Puffed sleeves. Long sleeves with wrist band. Lace collar and edgings. Square yoke or wide collar. Belt optional.

Short monkey jacket—S.B. for street wear.

Sailor fashions—taped square collar and triple braided skirts.

Tam-o'-shanters. Straw hats.

Babies—capes and bonnets fur edged.

CHAPTER XXVI

THE END OF AN EPOCH, 1910–20

TWENTIETH-century fashions were no longer set by a few people. They seemed to grow and change with a life of their own, becoming ever less formal and more comfortable. There were several revolutions in women's clothes, while men's fashion changed very little, only the details varying—the precise shape of a lapel or the number of buttons on a

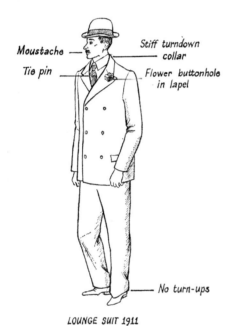

Moustache
Tie pin

Stiff turndown collar
Flower buttonhole in lapel

No turn-ups

LOUNGE SUIT 1911

jacket, for instance. These alterations were so slight, and men's clothes usually so long-lasting, that fashion changes as such are almost impossible to date with any degree of precision.

DRESS

MEN

The *Frock Coat* and *Swallow-tailed Morning Coat* were still worn on formal occasions and by professional men, while the lounge suit was creeping into fashion.

A white, stiff-fronted *Shirt* and white *Waistcoat* were *de rigueur* on formal occasions.

A stiff white *Collar* was worn by day, often above a discreetly striped shirt; it could be a single, doubled over or wing collar. The soft turndown collar worn informally by young men grew constantly more popular.

Two types of *Tie* were worn; a small, neat bow, and the knot with long hanging ends. A tie pin might be worn with the latter.

Waistcoats sometimes matched the suit and sometimes provided a quiet contrast. They were still cut high, to show above the buttoned coat, and slips were often worn with them. These were pieces of white cloth attached inside at the top of the waistcoat, which provided a smart white edging to it. The bottom button was usually left undone.

Overcoats were long—often to the lower calf —full, and double breasted. They might have fur collars and sometimes cuffs. During the First World War overcoats got shorter and were more often single breasted.

A striped *Blazer* was worn with white flannel trousers for informal summer wear out of town. For sporting activities generally there were plus-four suits, as well as Norfolk jackets and knickerbockers. V-necked pullovers and cardigans began to be worn, too.

DRESS

WOMEN

At the beginning of this period the rich curves of preceding years went out of fashion and a wand-like, slender line came in. Clothes were straight with a fairly high waist, or else followed an unbroken princess line. During the War years fashion changed completely, following the natural figure; afterwards the straight line returned. The longest skirts of this period cleared the ground; evening dresses often had trains. Dresses for formal occasions or evening were of soft, fine materials on a firm foundation.

The *Tailored Two-piece Suit*, worn with a blouse, became ever more popular, and the *Blouse-and-Skirt* was also an acceptable day dress. The exceedingly high neckline which had approached the ears sank to the base of the throat in 1911.

Skirts were straight but not narrow. There was much "Grecian" drapery, and a favourite style was a draped crossover to the waist, front and back, with a smooth triangle of material to fill the V. This gave a shallow décolleté at the back too. A soft, full tunic, sometimes slit up to the waist at the side, often went with this dress. In 1912 Paris successfully introduced skirts drawn in so tightly at the ankles (the hobble skirt) that they had to be slit to enable the wearer to walk. Some of these skirts were full at the hips, producing a peg-top effect. Evening dresses were similar, sometimes with a very full tunic over the tight skirt (the pagoda line).

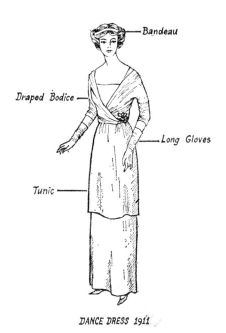

DANCE DRESS 1911

Brilliant colours were fashionable at this time, and V-necks began to be worn in the street by day.

A shorter (above the ankles) full skirt was worn for sport, and knitted coats something like cardigans were sometimes seen. Top coats, belted or unbelted, could be any length. By the time the War began they had a single fastening, near the left hip.

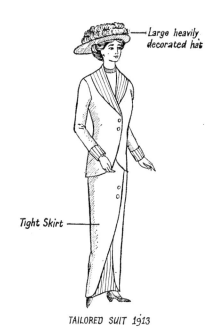

TAILORED SUIT 1913

By 1915 styles had changed completely. There was a natural unconstricted waistline, and full skirts with hems up to the mid-calf. Necklines were lower for daytime; V-necks with turnover collars were thought smart. (From this date the V-neck was never out of fashion.) Afternoon dresses were still fussy, with three-tiered skirts for instance, but their hems too were above the ankle. Top coats were loose and their skirts often shorter and fuller than those of the dress below.

As the War ended fashion forgot the styles that belonged to it, and straight clothes with an unfitted waistline became smart. A belt might mark the position of the waist without drawing in the dress. The chemise dress began to appear. By 1920 skirts were long, though day dresses have never again been so long as to touch the ground.

LEGS

MEN

Trousers were narrow and long, creasing into small folds above the instep. They were turned up at the bottom during active occupations such as tennis. The lower and lower middle classes wore turn-ups regularly however, and in time they were worn by everyone. Only evening trousers have never been cuffed in this way.

A vertical crease down the front also became popular.

LEGS

WOMEN

The new styles showed a good deal of leg one way and another, so *Stockings* became more important. There was a great choice of colour (even bronze, to match bronze shoes) but black was the most popular. Some had lace insertions in front.

Some women wore buttoned gaiters above their shoes.

FEET

MEN

Boots were worn more than shoes—buttoned, laced, cloth-topped. *Spats* were fashionable

Socks might be black, navy blue, grey, or heather mixture (to wear with tweeds). During the War the colour range broadened to include brown and fawn. They had clocks woven into them.

FEET

WOMEN

At first *Boots*, often with a cloth or suede top, were worn out of doors.

Shoes, being always visible, became more important. High heels were fashionable, shaped to curve under the foot. Toes were first pointed, then round, but points came back during the War. They were laced, buttoned, buckled; there were plain court shoes and shoes with straps that were sometimes quite elaborate, twining up above the ankle, and sometimes just ankle straps. Evening shoes might be coloured to match the gown.

HAIR

MEN

Hair was short. There were *Moustaches* of all kinds, and some older men wore beards. Young men were most frequently clean shaven. There was an Army Regulation that officers must wear moustaches, but the compromises of young men hankering after the cleanshaven fashion became so absurd—they were said to sport a "cricket eleven" rather than a moustache—that in 1917 the Regulation was changed.

HAIR

WOMEN

At the beginning of this period hair was puffed up and out and given extra volume by a process known then as "ratting" and fifty years later as "back-combing." It entailed tangling it, then smoothing over the more or less solid mass. Bandeaux and combs were used for ornaments.

Before the War started a simpler, neater style came in, with the hair dressed closer to the head. The waving process known as "Marcelling" had been invented and women could be seen with their hair in a series of smooth ridges. Girls in their teens fastened their hair with large bows of wide ribbon.

By the end of the War some advanced women had bobbed their hair.

HATS

MEN

Several kinds of hats were worn still—*Toppers*, *Bowlers* and the *Soft Homburg*. In summer hard *Straw Hats* and *Panamas* were seen, particularly in the country.

HATS

WOMEN

A large *Hat*, often wider than the wearer's shoulders, went with the straight, slender line. Fastened on top of the mass of hair with long hatpins, it was usually piled high with ornamental flowers, fruit or feathers. Another, less popular, style was for a tall narrow hat that covered the hair and might be ornamented with a single long feather.

Most women wore a *Veil*, each tying it over her hat and face in her own way. A stronger veil

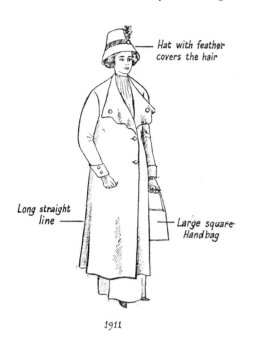

Hat with feather covers the hair

Long straight line

Large square-Handbag

1911

would be worn when motoring, to tie the hat on and keep the dust out.

By the time the War started veils were no longer worn and there was a great variety of hats. They grew smaller as hair styles became simpler, and had far less decoration than before. They could be worn at an angle, and tended to be pulled down low towards the eyes.

ACCESSORIES

MEN

Older men still kept watches in their waistcoat pockets, attached to a chain draped across the stomach. As wrist-watches became popular this chain disappeared.

Walking sticks or short canes were still carried, except when the weather necessitated an umbrella. A white handkerchief was often seen peeping from a gentleman's breast pocket.

ACCESSORIES

WOMEN

Almost until the beginning of the War very long *Fur Stoles* and huge square *Fur Muffs* were worn. Those who could not afford them wore fluffy *Feather Boas*. When the stoles went out of fashion the muffs shrank and had fur tails attached to them. Two kinds of large *Handbag* went with them. Both hung from the wrist on a strap or chain. They were either of leather, flat and square, or of chain mesh. With the advent of the War they grew smaller and softer in shape, following the general line.

CHILDREN

Children's clothes changed slowly. By 1914 a boy, dressed otherwise like his father, wore short pants and socks.

Small girls could still be dressed up in large hats and elaborate kid boots. They normally wore buttoned boots or shoes with ankle straps. Even before the War they were put into short, straight dresses with low, loose belts—a preview of a later fashion. Their hair was still worn long; loose, curled or in plaits. They did not usually have it short until the fashion was established by their elders.

SUMMARY

MEN

Dress

Much as before.
Lounge suits and soft collars worn more.
Collars always white, shirts sometimes striped.
Slips in waistcoats.

Legs

Trousers narrow; a little longer than the leg. Plus-four suits added to the sporting wardrobe. Turn-ups coming in.

Feet

As before. Shoes displacing boots.
Spats still worn with shoes.

Hair

As before. Some beards. Moustaches. Most young men clean shaven.

Hats

  As before.

Accessories

  Canes and walking sticks.
  Watch chains still worn.

WOMEN

Dress

  Tailored two-piece. Blouse and skirt.

Smaller
Hat

Full short
Skirt

1916

Pre-war straight dress, high waist.
Evening dress, neck low front and back; train.
1912 hobble skirt, necessarily slit.
Wartime—fitted bodice, full short skirts.
Coats often shorter than dresses.
After the War—straight line returns.
Loose with little shape. Longer skirts again.

Legs

  Stockings mostly black, though many colours
    available. Cotton, wool, silk. Lace inser-
    tions for evening.

Feet

  Boots and gaiters, finally superseded by shoes.
  High, curving heel. Ornamental straps. Toes
    alternately round and pointed.

Hair

  At first puffed up and out as before.
  Bandeaux and combs.
  Later dressed closer to head. Marcelling.

Hats

  Large—wide brimmed and heavily decorated
    or high and narrow. Veils.
  Later smaller, covering hair, pulled low on
    head.
  Osprey feathers smart.
  Large ribbon bows for girls.

Accessories

  Fur stole and muff. Feather boa.
  Mesh or leather handbags.

CHAPTER XXVII

PEACE AND WAR, 1920–45

WHILE men's fashion continued almost unchanging women's went back to the period before the hobble skirt, ignoring the changes in between, and then swung from one extreme to another until the Second World War brought fashion to a standstill. Informality became more and more fashionable, with manners and clothes growing generally freer and more relaxed while world affairs moved in the opposite direction.

Artificial silk came on the market in the twenties, and it was possible to buy ready-made clothes of good quality for comparatively low prices. So new fashions spread through society more quickly than ever before.

LOUNGE SUIT 1932

DRESS

MEN

Style showed in such constantly changing details as the length of a jacket, the width of lapels and the number of buttons. *Waistcoats* were cut lower and were sometimes squared off at the waist. Shoulders got broader during the thirties, and very square during the War years. The *Lounge Suit*, mostly single-breasted, was the usual wear.

There was much more variety in clothes for sport and informal wear, both in style and material. For instance a tweed coat often replaced the blazer, and the trousers that went with it could be of corduroy or cavalry twill as well as flannel.

Individuality showed most strongly in the choice of the *Tie*, which could be striped or otherwise patterned, and the *Shirt*. White and stiff-fronted for formal wear, on other occasions this could be white or coloured or striped.

In the thirties *Coloured Shirts* with matching collars were worn. The soft collar was rapidly becoming the most popular. Coloured sports shirts with short sleeves were quite usual.

DRESS

WOMEN

There were two distinct cycles of fashion in this period, the change coming precisely at the end of the first decade.

In the early twenties clothes were loose and straight, ending just above the ankle. The waistline, marked by ornament or an unconstricting belt, was far below the natural waist. It stayed low on the hip throughout the decade. A feminine appearance was at a discount; a flat bosom and narrow hips were smart.

Sleeves grew shorter until in the second half of the decade it was quite proper to wear none, even in the street by day.

Evening Dress followed the line of the day dress, sometimes with added drapery and often with a chemise-shaped bodice.

Skirts began to rise in 1924, reaching their highest point (the knee) in 1926–7. The line was simple; the waistline, such as it was, stayed on the hips and any fullness and most ornament appeared below it.

Necklines were sometimes cut extremely low and filled in with contrasting material known as

Bobbed hair

Ornamental Shoes

AFTERNOON GOWN 1923

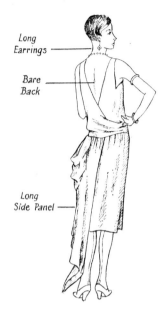

Long Earrings

Bare Back

Long Side Panel

EVENING DRESS 1928

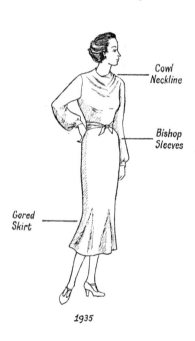

Cowl Neckline

Bishop Sleeves

Gored Skirt

1935

a "modesty vest." Beige was far the most popular colour for outer clothes—yet at this time women began to wear coloured underclothes.

There were some semi-fitting *Coats*, but most were either straight or narrowed a little at the bottom to give a barrel effect. Leather coats were sometimes worn, especially for motoring. Clutch coats, with no fastening, came in. Coats were often fur-trimmed. Silk shawls were often used for evening wraps.

In *Evening Dress*, now as short as day dress, the bare back was introduced—sometimes bare to the waist. In the late twenties an uneven hemline became a feature of evening dress; it varied from a long panel attached to the "waist" at one side, to a full skirt that reached the knees in front and the floor behind.

From 1929 to 1930 fashion changed completely. The loose, straight line was replaced by a curvaceous one with plenty of ornament. Skirts dropped to the lower calf, clothes fitted the figure with the waist in its right place, and shoulders were broad and square. Dressmakers achieved this slim line with a full skirt by cutting material on the cross and using gores. Fullness ideally started from below the hips, although the less sophisticated let it fall from the waist. Fussy necklines and cowl necks, full bishop sleeves and puff sleeves were all popular. There was a soft, almost floppy, look about the clothes of the early and middle thirties.

Jackets that contrasted with the skirt or dress under them were much worn, and so were short *Boleros. Overcoats* might be fitted or loose and swinging; they came to have big collars that could be turned up behind.

Evening dress in this decade always touched the ground. It was often barebacked, and clinging to below the hips. A small "fishtail" train was popular; it would have a small loop for the wearer to hold it out of the way while dancing. The strapless evening dress was an exciting innovation of the thirties that has never gone right out of fashion.

By 1938 there was a subtle change, as though with a premonition of disaster. The general line grew crisper, still following the figure but with less emphasis, and skirts rose to the knee.

June 1941 to March 1949) and brand names were lost in the self-explanatory official one of "Utility."

It became normal to see women in *Trousers*. In the early thirties they were worn, like shorts,

1927

as playclothes and were extremely wide and full. As a simple tailored garment, they proved eminently suitable for wartime life.

Legs

Men

Turn-ups were usual now. Trouser legs got wider in the twenties, going to extremes of width in the smart young men's short-lived fashion of "Oxford bags."

Legs

Women

As skirts got shorter *Stockings* became more important. The most elegant—and expensive— were of transparent silk. When artificial silk arrived everyone who could not afford real silk

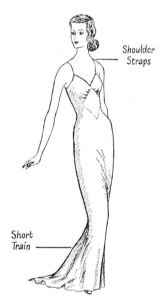

Shoulder Straps

Short Train

EVENING DRESS 1934

During the Second World War fashion came to a standstill. There was no change in style except for the increasingly square shoulders. Materials were scarce, and for the first time in history clothes were officially rationed (from

used it for stockings instead of cotton, lisle or wool. These remained part of schoolgirls' uniform. Nylon, developed during the War and used for military purposes, was ideal for stockings since it could be woven into a hard-wearing, transparent fabric that seemed no more than a film of colour. The few pairs to be had in Britain during the War were expensive and much coveted.

The usual stocking colour was brown or beige —all shades from nearly black through grey to nearly white. They were woven to fit without a wrinkle, and with ornamental clocks; nylon stockings did not have clocks.

FEET

MEN

Shoes displaced *Boots* for ordinary wear, and brown was worn more than it had been; black patent always went with evening dress. Some men wore suede shoes, or the two-tone "co-respondent" type; these were considered rather vulgar.

FEET

WOMEN

Shoes, like stockings, were now an important article of dress. There was great variety, from low-heeled heavy brogues to high-heeled court shoes. High-buttoned walking shoes were still worn at the end of the First World War, but when skirts rose they went out of fashion, as did the tango shoe with its ribbons criss-crossing to above the ankle.

Toes were usually round. Heels got higher, becoming narrower as they did so and losing the curved, waisted look. Vamps were at first cut fairly high, or filled in with straps—T-straps, ankle-straps, etc.—all buttoned. Ankle straps were popular for little girls. When the War began, low, open sandals were correct informal summer wear.

HAIR

MEN

Men wore their hair short, nearly all had it cut "short back and sides." A side parting was usual.

During the War, Air Force pilots had a tradition of very wide "handlebar" moustaches. Others were cleanshaven.

HAIR

WOMEN

Hair styles got progressively shorter, from the bob to the shingle (above the hairline at the back), the most extreme style being the Eton Crop, as short as a man's. The usual length was about ear level, with a half curl flicked forward on to each cheek. Hair was either sleek or well waved and curled, often waved down on to the forehead. The permanent wave appeared in the twenties.

Longer hair came into fashion with longer skirts. It was usually curled at the ends at least, and by 1939 was ideally shoulder length. The basic styles were loose, piled on top of the head, or rolled neatly round the head; sometimes when it was loose there was a roll in front to add height. Little girls often had their hair bobbed, wore fringes and usually had a ribbon bow or slide.

Throughout the War, when clothes were functional, hair remained long and loose however inconvenient (although in uniform it had to be above the collar).

HATS

MEN

The summer straw went out of fashion. The *Trilby*, a soft felt with a long dent in the crown, was the most common headgear. A few men stuck to *Bowlers*. *Top Hats* were still formal wear—black at night or for mourning, grey during the day.

HATS

WOMEN

Now women had cut their hair off, hats hugged the head. They were simple, with little decoration, and often had no brim, like the *Cloche*. They were pulled right down to the eyebrows in the twenties—this even applied to wedding veils. Around the turn of the decade brims were often turned down behind.

When fashion became more ornamental so did

hats. In the thirties they were all shapes and sizes, though never approaching the gigantic styles of 1910. Many had little *Eye-veils*. There were larger brims, and the *Halo Hat* was popular. Hats and berets were either worn right off the face, or tilted over one eye.

Hats were a wartime casualty. In those years it was common to tie a scarf over the head, peasant fashion, or knot it into a "turban" where hair could be tucked out of the way.

Make-up

Cosmetics, now safe to use, became respectable during this period and a fashionable face was an important part of one's appearance.

In the twenties a broad, square face was the thing, with wide-set large eyes and a rosebud mouth. Women were still learning how to make the best use of cosmetics. In the late twenties and the thirties eyebrows were extensively

1926

plucked; sometimes quite erased and a different-shaped brow painted on.

A longer face was desirable in the thirties, with a high forehead and high, arched thin brows. Make-up was less obvious, except for the dark

red lipstick. In the War years lipstick was considered the most important cosmetic.

By the late twenties coloured nail varnish had arrived. Some women painted their toenails as well as their finger nails.

TAILORED SUIT 1936

Accessories

Men

The walking stick and cane dropped out of use.

Accessories

Women

In the twenties a long cloth scarf was often wound round the throat with its ends fluttering behind. Long strings of beads and long earrings went with the simple line and short hair; bandeaux were worn, and ornamental slides were sometimes fixed in the hair. Bare arms made bracelets popular, and "slave bangles" were often pushed up above the elbow. A single large ostrich feather was often carried as a fan with evening dress. This was the era of the long cigarette holder.

A popular accessory of the thirties was the short fox fur stole with legs and head (complete with glass eyes) attached. This was draped round the neck and shoulders, or slung over one

Longer hair roll on top

1938

shoulder. A silk scarf, too, was often knotted into the neck of a dress or jacket.

During the War large handbags on a long strap that could be hung on one shoulder were popular.

SUMMARY

MEN

Dress

Much as before. Mostly S.B.
Soft collar superseding stiff one.
Knotted tie with long ends the most usual.

Legs

Turn-ups usual.
Fad for wide trouser legs in the 1920s.

Feet

Laced shoes.
Suede, and two-tone as well as one-colour leather.

Hair

Short back and sides. Side parting. Clean-shaven.

Hats

As before. Summer straw goes out of fashion; trilby superseding other hats.

WOMEN

Dress

1920s Straight and loose, low waist.
Sleeveless day dresses.
Skirts short after 1924.
Uneven hem and bare back for evening dress.
1930s Figure fitting clothes, soft and fussy.
Square shoulders.
Long skirts, rising to the knee for the War.
Fishtail train and low back for evening dress. Strapless evening dress.
Variety of play suits.
Trousers much worn in the War.

Legs

Silk stockings—and artificial silk.
Beige; with clocks.

Shoes

High-fastened shoes go as skirts rise.
Round toes. Curved heel. Straps.
Button fastenings.
Vamps cut lower, heels higher and straps go, in 1930s.

Hair

1920s: Short—bobbed or shingled, straight or permed.
Flicked on to cheeks.
Often waved on forehead.
1930s: Hair allowed to grow.
Curled, especially at ends.

Either hangs loose to shoulders, or put up
with curls on top of the head, or rolled
round the head.
War: Long, loose hair.

Hats

1920s: Hug the head, pulled down to the
eyes.
1930s: Brim turned down behind.
Variety of styles perched on the head at an
angle.
Eye veils.
War: Little worn. Head scarves and turbans.

Cosmetics

Much used.
1920s: Square face, big wide-set eyes.
1930s: Longer face, high thin brows.

Accessories

1920s: Long scarf, beads, earrings.
Ostrich feather with evening dress.
1930s: Fox fur stole.

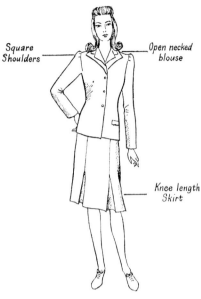

Square Shoulders

Open necked blouse

Knee length Skirt

WARTIME TAILORED SUIT

CHAPTER XXVIII

THE POST-WAR WORLD, 1945–65

IN 1947 the cycle of women's fashion started again. As after the First World War it returned to the last serious pre-war style. Afterwards the length of skirts fluctuated—and so did the length of women's hair.

Long tie
No waistcoat

Trilby Hat

LOUNGE SUIT 1958

As for men, there was still no basic change in their clothes, but the trend to greater freedom and informality continued. They clung to their very broad, padded shoulders for some years after the War.

During these years nylon was followed by other artificial materials which imitated natural ones more or less successfully, and added convenient qualities of their own. Their advent, added to the proliferation of chain stores selling the latest fashions in good quality at low prices, meant that almost anyone who wished could always be in the height of fashion. In its way, a social revolution.

One result of this was that style, by the middle fifties, was more a matter of age than of money or class. Many young people of both sexes, in their teens and early twenties, followed fashions unlike those of their elders and more conservative contemporaries. Sometimes their styles, which changed very quickly, achieved a wider acceptance and sometimes not. This Adolescent Fashion is still very much with us in 1965.

DRESS

MEN

One lasting result of wartime austerity was the *Two-piece Suit* with no waistcoat. In the early fifties smart men wore *Waistcoats* that contrasted with their suits. Yellow was popular, but some gay dogs wore brocade.

A slightly larger range of colour was permitted in the now ubiquitous *Lounge Suit*. The soft collar was worn by most men, and there were many passing fashions in *Shirts*—various stripes and colours came and went. There was also a much wider and gayer choice of *Ties*. The bow tie, which had been nearly eclipsed by the long-ended knot except for evening dress, was worn by more people now.

In the sixties a short *Fleece-lined Jacket* of leather or suede was much worn, particularly for motoring.

Adolescent Fashion, still based on the traditional suit, rang quite violent changes on it— *Jackets* were straight and full, or cut very high, or made without collars, etc. Black leather jackets were one of their longer-lived styles.

The brilliantly gay *Leisure Shirt* introduced from America became generally popular, as did the *T-shirt*. In the early sixties these were worn outside the trousers.

Bathing Suits, which before the War had covered the torso (with the upper part often largely cut away), were now largely reduced to *Trunks*.

DRESS

WOMEN

In 1947 the "New Look" arrived and women somehow changed their appearance to follow the fashion in spite of clothes rationing. Like the clothes of the thirties these emphasized the lines of the figure, with a tightly fitting waist and skirts (usually full) down to the lower calf. The only differences were that shoulders were no longer square but followed the natural shape, and that all fullness sprang from the waist. Hips were emphasized, and three-quarter sleeves became common.

By 1950 however loose straight *Top Coats* were as smart as fitted ones.

Two years later *Skirts* began to rise; this continued slowly until in 1965 they touched the knee and sometimes rose above it. Adolescent Fashion was experimenting with skirts inches above the knee by then.

NEW LOOK 1947

In the late fifties styles changed again and a straight, waistless dress (often sleeveless) came back into fashion. This simple, uncluttered line was similar to that of the twenties. The main differences were that the line was unbroken and

SUMMER 1939, STILL SMART IN 1945

In the middle fifties skirts were either very full, with stiff, frilly petticoats, or so tight they made walking difficult (this was often overcome with a tiny pleat at the bottom). Tight, straight skirts remained an accepted feature of fashionable dress.

Low cut Shoes

WAISTLESS DRESS 1958

that skirts got narrower, if anything, below the hips. The idea was not to disguise the figure but to hint clearly at it; no belt was worn. After a few years semi-fitted dresses became smart, but the close-fitting dress was still not considered

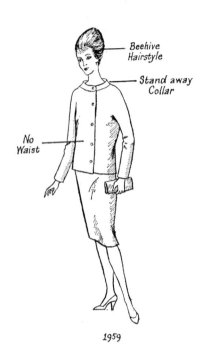

Beehive
Hairstyle

Stand away
Collar

No
Waist

1959

truly elegant in 1965. Top coats and suit jackets followed the same line, the latter being short and straight above a straight skirt, which could be either tight or pleated.

A feature of this fashion was that the neckline, often round, was cut to stand away from the neck. Collars were few, even on top coats. About 1960 there was a fashion for coats made of suede and leather.

Evening Dresses, ever since the 1947 New Look, could either touch the ground or be the same length as day clothes. Often the only difference was in the material.

The two-piece *Bathing Suit* was seen before the War but the *Bikini*, which only covered the necessary minimum, arrived in the early fifties. Although it was considered rather shocking at first, it came to be thought normal for the young and shapely.

LEGS

MEN

Trousers lost some of their pre-war fullness. Smart young men went through a phase of wearing them really tight. Close-fitting jeans, another American importation, were often worn on active but informal occasions.

LEGS

WOMEN

As soon as it was generally available nylon became the only material for *Stockings*. They were made both with and without seams; the vestigial clocks vanished.

Colours were the same as before, only the shade varying with fashion. In the early sixties Adolescent Fashion introduced two styles which were generally accepted for a short period—black stockings, and stockings woven in an openwork pattern.

Trousers were worn more than ever, informally; some people tried wearing them in luxurious materials as an exotic evening dress. Adolescent Fashion took up jeans too; and then all trousers were cut very tight, often ending above the ankle. These were followed by elasticated trousers, held by a strap under the foot.

FEET

MEN

Besides the regulation *Laced Shoe* a slip-on kind was worn. Adolescent Fashion introduced shoes with excessively long sharp pointed toes.

FEET

WOMEN

At the end of the War there was a short-lived fashion for wedge heels and then one for ankle straps, followed by a longer-lived one for open or peep-toe shoes and sling backs—this last was a shoe with nothing but a strap round the heel.

Vamps were cut lower, and the most elegant shoe was a plain court. Fastenings were usually laces or buckles, rarely buttons. Toes, round at first, became sharply pointed and this fashion stayed, with a short interruption by a season of square toes, for about ten years after which the rounded toe re-appeared. The very high, thin heel known as the stiletto came in with the pointed toe and stayed as long; lower heels came in with rounder toes.

Summer sandals became fragile-looking affairs of a few narrow straps. Shoes of all colours were worn.

HAIR

MEN

For most men "short back and sides" was the only style, but they were on the whole fussier about their hair. Some younger men began to wear *Beards*.

Adolescent Fashion set great store by hair styles. Beginning in the fifties with an elaborate quiff and sideburns (hair growing down in front of the ear) it developed into the long-haired styles of the sixties. These varied with individuals' taste from just a few inches to shoulder-length. Many professed to think this effeminate, but the idea spread until most men were wearing their hair a little longer—and in 1965 the Army eased its Regulation about the shortness of soldiers' hair.

HAIR

WOMEN

At the end of the forties women cut their hair off. The fashion was for very short, curly hair but it soon went out in favour of straight or slightly waved hair, usually combed off the face. In the next few years those who had long hair wore it in a chignon.

For the rest of the period the fashionable length fluctuated, the one constant being that it must not lie flat but be "bouffant," i.e. look exceptionally thick and springy. Older women usually kept to short styles; if they had long hair it was worn in a bun or roll. High fashion in hair styles constantly changed, and false hair was respectable. It became common to dye one's hair.

Adolescent Fashion wavered between very short and very long hair. Among the more outstanding styles which lasted for some time was the "beehive," which looked something like Nefertiti's crown and was achieved by back-combing and then moulding the solid mass into shape, and hair worn very long and loose (sometimes with a fringe) and preferably quite straight.

HATS

MEN

Men's hats, like women's, were something of a wartime casualty. Those who wore them followed pre-war styles.

HATS

WOMEN

A hat was no longer an essential part of a woman's street costume. There was considerable choice of style for those who did wear them.

MAKE-UP

Fashions varied more in make-up than in clothes. It was possible to obtain a really natural look which changed with fashion from peaches-and-cream to a golden glow, and so on. Eye make-up became more elaborate, and was often deliberately obvious. Adolescent Fashion, of course, had its own styles, at one time favouring pale, even white, lipstick and at another eschewing cosmetics altogether.

ACCESSORIES

Artificial Jewellery was much worn, as a costume accessory rather than as jewellery in the real sense. Some of it was beautifully designed. Earrings might be worn at any time; there was a craze for ear-piercing in the fifties, although this was not necessary as earrings were often made with clips and screws.

Necklaces were much worn with the plain dresses of the fifties and early sixties. Popular types were: very long ropes of pearl beads shortened with a knot, "bibs" of several rows of beads, and a medallion or large pendant on a long chain.

Spectacle Frames were made in such a variety of shapes and colours (both sunglasses and the medical kind) that they were chosen for their style.

SUMMARY

MEN

Dress

Mostly S.B. but D.B. coming back.

More variety of colour—dark grey, dark blue and very dark tweed now decent town wear.

Two-piece suit.

Very square shoulders soon die out.

Fancy waistcoats early fifties.

Bow tie more popular. More gaudy long-ended ties.

Leather top coats.

Variety of gayer leisure clothes.

Legs

Trousers narrower.

Hair

As before for older men, longer for others.

Hats

As before, but fewer men wear them.

WOMEN

Dress

1947 New Look—Figure fitting, long, full skirts. Then loose and three-quarter coats.

1950s: Skirts begin to rise. Tight short skirts come in. Stiff petticoats for full skirts.

Late 1950s: Loose waistless dresses; narrow skirts.

1960s: Semi-fitting dresses. Skirts up to the knee.

Round, standaway necklines. Few collars.

Legs

Transparent nylon stockings.

Fashions for black and patterned stockings.

Trousers much worn, at first similar to men's later close-fitting.

Feet

Wedge heels. Peep-toes. Sling-backs. Round toes.

Mid 1950s: Pointed toes. Stiletto heels.

Mid 1960s: Round toes, lower heels. Bare "strappy" sandals.

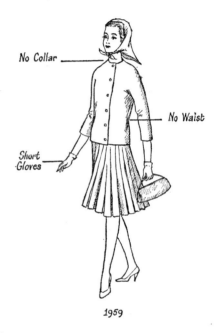

No Collar

No Waist

Short Gloves

1959

Hair

Cut short in the late 1940s. Thereafter length fluctuates.

"Bouffant." Very short or very long. Many styles simultaneously. Backcombing widely used. Dyed hair common—and respectable.

Make-up

Fashionable looks change frequently.

Elaborate eye make-up.

Accessories

Much costume jewellery. Earrings.

Early 1960s a large medallion on a long chain almost uniform with young women.

Stylish spectacle frames.

CHAPTER XXIX

CLERGY AT MASS

ECCLESIASTICAL costume, more than any other type, is most often wrongly shown on the stage. It falls into three categories, according to whether it is worn for Mass, for Choir services, or for the street and home. It is further subdivided by the persons, cardinals, bishops, or priests, who wear it. Throughout the Middle Ages ecclesiastical costume met with little change, but there have been modifications during modern times, and there is an interlude from the Reformation until the middle of Victoria's reign, when certain garments fell into temporary disuse. The modern Roman Church in addition to medieval vestments wears new garments derived from late Italian sources.

The secret of attaining beauty of form in mass vestments is to cut them on a generous scale so that ample folds give both ease to the wearer, and plenty of play of light and shade.

The chasuble has slightly followed current secular fashions in its cut through the centuries. Thus, when the Rococo and Baroque styles in architecture were invented, the chasuble followed them in principle. That is to say, that these styles were based on the curve rather than the straight line, so the chasuble became what was known as "the fiddle back"; its sides were cut away in a curve inwards to the body, starting on the shoulders and ending in a bow fronted bottom edge. This fiddle back has gone out of fashion with the passing of the corresponding architectural phase, and is now seen only in antique vestments. This period was that of the eighteenth century.

Earlier in England, during the seventeenth century, the chasuble had been cut down but it took a straight line from the shoulder, and there was no curve. Concurrently with this mode, the orphrey, which had formerly been Y shaped, was altered to a single column on the front and a cross on the back. This was the Renaissance style.

The fully cut Y shaped orphrey type is the medieval and present-day Gothic style.

This cutting down affected also the dalmatic which in the seventeenth and eighteenth centuries lost its sleeves, which were reduced to rather wide epaulets covering the shoulders, but not stitched

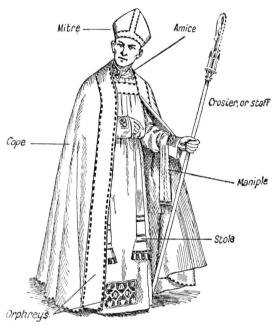

BISHOP (SOLEMN SERVICES)

together under the armpit. This change was probably due to the increasing splendour of the materials which were often cloth of gold and silver, heavily encrusted with gold lace bullion and silk embroidery.

Again, if great accuracy is desired it is possible to indicate the particular period not only in the shape of the vestments, but also in their material and decoration. While the medievals liked conventionalized floral brocaded designs, or plain velvets, the seventeenth century used cut velvets from Genoa and the East and Jacobean styles, while the eighteenth century favoured the secular "all over" floral patterns on natural lines.

Valuable suggestions for vestments can be gleaned by a visit to the Ecclesiastical Section of the Victoria and Albert Museum, South Kensington, London, and it may be appropriate here to add that many costumes from the late seventeenth century to our own day can be seen in the London Museum, which is now housed at Kensington Palace.

DRESS

The *Cassock* is a ground-length, close-sleeved coat, double-breasted, fastening with a single button at the shoulder and another at the waist, and made of black cloth, except for bishops, who wear magenta or purple, and cardinals, who wear scarlet. It has a shoulder cape without a hood, and about 1850 became a single-breasted garment fastened down the centre with numerous small buttons. In modern times for informal use bishops and cardinals wear it in black piped with their respective colours, along the cape edge, the cassock vertical edge, and with the buttons in colour.

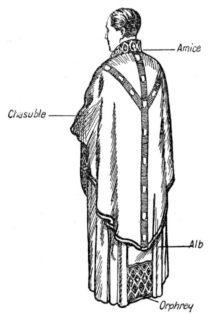

PRIEST AT MASS

The *Alb* is a ground length white shirt with loose sleeves to enable it to slip over the cassock.

The *Stole* is a long strip of embroidered or coloured silk or other material, about $2\frac{1}{2}$ in. wide, and reaching to just below the knee. It is tucked in by the girdle at the waist and worn in different ways by the various orders. A bishop wears his

straight down, a priest crosses it over the breast, and a deacon has it over the left shoulder and loosely tied under the right arm at the waist, the ends hanging down the right side of the body.

The *Amice* is an oblong piece of linen, 36 in. by 24 in., to which two tapes are attached at the

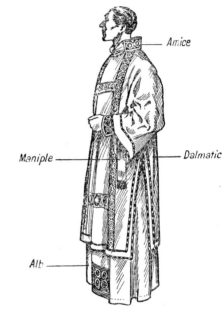

DEACON (SOLEMN SERVICES)

upper corners. It is placed behind the neck and shoulders. The tapes are carried round the neck to the front, across the back and round the waist in front, where they are tied. It has an oblong patch of embroidery, called an apparel, appliquéd at back of neck and brought over the outer garment.

The *Girdle* is a linen woven rope tied round alb and stole at the waist.

The *Maniple* is a miniature stole about $3\frac{1}{2}$ ft. long worn on the left arm at the wrist.

The *Chasuble*, when placed straight out on a table, is vesica shaped, that is the shape of two Gothic arches placed together with their points outwards and meeting each other at a straight line drawn just below their chords. It is, in other words, an oval shape with its longer ends sharply pointed. It is adorned in a Y shape, with bands of embroidery back and front at the seams, which are called *orphreys*. They may also take the shape of a cross on the back and a pillar on the front, this type being late Medieval. It should be

BISHOPS

As Cardinal   At Mass

In Choir and Processions   Outdoors

fairly full, hang in good folds, and be made of light silk, with a hole for the neck.

A set of Mass vestments (chasuble, stole, maniple) should match in material and embroidery. Its colours are restricted to red, green, violet, and white, with black for funerals, and gold, or yellow as an optional shade, for other occasions. In the Middle Ages colour restrictions were few, and almost any colour or combination of shades is permissible.

The *Dalmatic* is a tunic with sleeves reaching to the forearm, and having two vertical bands of embroidery (orphreys) down front and back, joined by two horizontal bands. Like all the Mass vestments it is a survival from Classical times, and follows the lines of the Roman tunica. It is fringed along its edges.

The *Tunicle* is a similar garment to the dalmatic, except that it has its two vertical bands joined by one short horizontal band of embroidery at the top. Both Dalmatic and Tunicle sometimes have at the shoulders long tassels which fall on the back, not on the chest.

Gloves were at first of white silk with jewels on the back and wide tasselled gauntlets. To-day they are of coloured silk. In Georgian times they were of white or lavender, with gauntlets fringed with gold bullion.

The *Pallium* is of white lamb's wool, adorned with crosses in gold or purple, about 1½ in. wide, with about five crosses on the pendant portion hanging down in front of the chasuble, and four on the shoulder parts. It is worn over the shoulders, and hangs down in front in a loose tie.

The *Pastoral Staff* or *Crosier* may be of ivory, gold, silver, ebony, or other decorated material, in the shape of a shepherd's crook, and of Gothic or Renaissance design. Just below the crook a linen scarf, long enough to cover that part of the staff that is held by hand, is hung from a metal ring. It is designed to protect the finely wrought work from damage by the hands. The bishop bears it with his left hand.

The *Archbishop's Cross* is a processional cross about 8 ft. high, made of similar materials to the crosier. It is borne in the left hand.

Both staff and cross may be carried by chaplains, in which case they hold it in front of them with both hands. The bishop merely carries it in his

left hand so that he may bless the people with his right hand.

The *Mitre* is a hat of silk or velvet and contains an inner cap, in front and at the back of which are placed triangular upstanding pieces of

THE PAENULA (CLASSICAL CHASUBLE)

material decorated with bands of embroidery and jewelled.

At funerals the bishop wears a plain white linen or silk mitre; on other occasions a decorated coloured one; on great feasts one plated with gold and jewels.

The bishop's *Ring* is generally of amethyst. It was worn on the middle finger of the right hand in the Middle Ages, but is now worn on the third finger.

HOW TO WEAR THE CLOTHES

The order in which these clothes are put on is—
Cassock.
Amice.
Alb.
Stole.
Girdle.
Maniple.
Chasuble, or dalmatic or tunicle.

The bishop wears, over the alb and under the

chasuble, a thin silk dalmatic and tunicle without embroidery—generally of golden colour.

A medieval bishop wore stockings of linen, later of silk, and shoes, at first of open work, but later, in the fourteenth century, fastened with

Girdle — Amice — Sash — Alb

SERVERS

strings and adorned with a Y-shaped band like the chasuble band.

If clergy are represented in connexion with a High Mass the priest is assisted by a deacon and a subdeacon. All will wear vestments of the same colour and decoration.

If late Renaissance vestments are required, the chasuble is cut away at the sides and curved like a fiddle back and the sleeves of dalmatic and tunicle become merely large epaulets hanging about 6 in. over the shoulders.

Mass vestments are practically never worn in the street, nor are dalmatics, tunicles, copes, and mitres, except in religious processions.

FROM REFORMATION TO MID-VICTORIAN

The Mass vestments and the almuce fell into disuse after Elizabeth's time. Mitres and crosiers were worn until Charles II's time. Copes continued to be worn throughout in cathedrals mainly. Bishops retained their gloves, which became white or lavender, fringed with gold bullion.

Episcopal pectoral crosses do not come in till Victorian times.

ACOLYTES

Acolytes and servers at Mass wore cassocks and albs with amices up to the Reformation, and from 1900 onwards they wear either an alb or a cotta—which is a waist length surplice with tight sleeves to just below the elbow—edged with lace at option.

Bishops, if not celebrating, may attend at Mass in cope and mitre, and they also wear these for processions, whether in church or in street.

SUMMARY
FOR MASS

Cardinals may be either bishops or priests and wear the clothes of those orders at Mass.

Priests

    Cassocks—black, double-breasted; single-breasted since 1850.

    Alb—long white ground length shirt.

    Stole—long embroidered shoulder strip. Crossed in front.

    Amice—linen oblong.

    Girdle—linen rope.

    Maniple—small stole on left arm

    Chasuble—elliptical silk cloak.

Bishops

    The same with the addition of—

    Mitre—cap with triangular revers.

    Gloves—gauntleted.

    Pastoral staff—shepherd's crook.

    Processional cross borne before him at option.

    Stole is not crossed in front.

    Dalmatic } of thin silk.
    Tunicle }

    Ring—right middle finger—amethyst.

Deacons

    The same as priests, save for a dalmatic instead of a chasuble, and stole worn over left shoulder under right arm.

Subdeacons

    The same as priests, save for a tunicle instead of chasuble and no stole.

Archbishops

    Same as bishops plus *Pallium*—white wool strip, and use pastoral staff and processional cross together.

CHAPTER XXX

CLERGY—CHOIR AND STREET

BY choir dress is meant the vestments that are worn at the daily services other than the Mass. In the Medieval period these included matins and evensong, or vespers, besides the "little hours," which were similar, but shorter, services of psalms and readings which occurred at stated intervals during the day. They are still held by the religious orders and the present Roman secular clergy.

By Sacramental vestments other than the Mass are meant the dresses worn for baptisms, confirmations, marriages, and funerals. For these the same garments are worn, but the stole replaces the almuce or the tippet and hood. For royal functions and solemn services of all kinds, both priests and bishops wear a cope, and the bishop his mitre.

The distinction should be clearly drawn between what the clergy wore out of service time in the medieval period and in modern times.

A further difference may be noted in the distinction of modern outdoor clerical dress as between the Roman and English Churches and Nonconformity.

In Catholic countries modern Roman clergy wear the same non-service dress both out of doors and within. In other countries Roman and Anglican clergy wear the same dress within doors, but a different one outside. The Cassock is the indoor one; secular lounge suits being the street wear.

Again the medieval garments have been modified into the modern Italian versions which are now current wherever the Roman Church exists; this change affects both choir and mass vestments, as we shall see.

There is at the present an unfortunate divergence in the cut of the same vestments, owing to historical reasons connected with the secular modes current.

The greatest care should be taken to dress clerical persons correctly according to their time, place, or occupation, as otherwise results may be achieved which will be ludicrous to churchmen.

Clerical costume, more often than not, is unconsciously travestied on the stage and in pageants.

The costume for services of the early Christian clergy was that of Imperial Rome, and reference should be made to the Roman chapter. It consisted in the main of a long white dalmatic

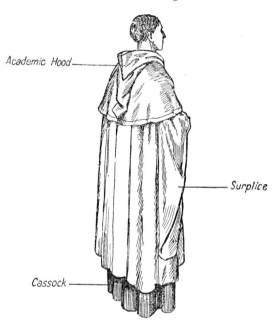

PRIEST (CHOIR SERVICES)

reaching to the ankles, with thin purple stripes. This was the dress of a deacon. A priest or bishop wore over this a classical chasuble (the Paenula) as portrayed in the previous chapter.

Naturally for street wear the clergy in the days of persecution dressed as laymen, Roman, Jewish, or whatever their nationality might be.

CHOIR DRESS

The *Cassock* has been described.

The *Surplice* is of linen, reaching below the knees, and has wide, open sleeves of the shape that the name denotes. At the neck it is gathered into a circular band, which is rather wider than the neck itself. In the Middle Ages the surplice was made full, with beautiful folds, and with long sleeves. In Tudor times a fashion came in to make the sleeves identical both back and front so that their edges were true to each other. Previously the front edge was less than the rear edge, and the style was more graceful.

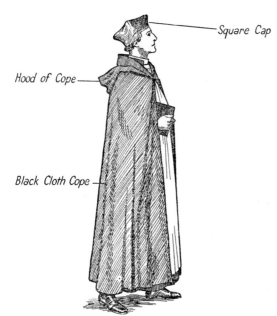

Square Cap

Hood of Cope

Black Cloth Cope

PRIEST (OUTDOOR SERVICES)

The *Almuce* was a dark cloth hood lined with fur, with long ends hanging down in front over the surplice, and with a roll collar. It came in about the thirteenth century, mainly for warmth in the then unheated churches. The fur part was worn outside, canons and dignitaries having grey fur, usually squirrel. The *Tippet*, in the fifteenth century, took the form of a scarf, still worn cloth-side inwards, but with a sable-fur lining turned back and rolled over from the inner edge as it lay on the body. In summer the lining was of silk. All graduates wore it. Lesser clergy wore, instead of an almuce, a tippet and hood of black cloth. The *Hood* should be of medieval shape, which was a full cape covering the shoulders, with a small peaked hood attached to its back. This shape is much more beautiful than that of the modern hood, which has degenerated in a curious fashion

owing to the wearing of wigs in later times. The wigs would not allow the narrow natural opening of the hood to pass over them, so the openings were widened, with the result that the hood gradually came to rest half way down the back. The cape portion was narrowed till it became a mere string round the neck, the original fullness being relegated to a formal appendage on the back. If you take a modern academic hood and pull it up over the shoulders, spreading it out, you will find that it recovers its original shape as far as the diminished cut allows, the oblong flat part going round the shoulders and the pocket portion becoming the peak of the hood. To-day it is being increasingly worn in its older and more comely shape.

The *Cope* is a semi-circular piece of silk, highly decorated with bands, called *orphreys*,

Priest's Gown

Scarf

Gown

Cassock

PRIEST (WALKING DRESS)

right along the straight edge, and with a "hood" on the back. This hood has become merely a formal shield-shaped piece of velvet, decorated with embroidery. The cope is fastened in front, just across the chest, with a clasp, called a morse. This is of material, except for bishops, who are allowed to wear morses of precious metal.

BISHOPS

The *Cassock* should be of magenta or purple, double-breasted until 1850, when it became single-breasted.

The *Almuce* must be of grey fur in winter and silk in summer Bishops in medieval times often wore, first, the surplice and then the *Rochet* over it. The rochet was a long white linen shirt, not quite as long as an alb, with loose, but not balloon sleeves. The cassock sleeve was usually turned up over it to form a dark band at the wrist. In the eighteenth century, until about 1900, the sleeves became balloon-shaped by stiffening the material, which was of lawn, till it burgeoned out in the ridiculous shape that was so often caricatured. The sleeves were attached to the chimere, which otherwise disappeared. This ballooning has passed away now, and the bishops have returned to the older type. The *Chimere* was a silk overcoat of ground length, open in front all the way down. In modern times it is sometimes held together across the chest by a string. It has no sleeves, and when the white rochet sleeves are pulled through it, it gives the well-known "magpie" effect. No academic hoods should be worn with the chimere; they are often incorrectly added. Its colour is black satin or silk, but red ones are worn on certain high days. Bishops wear either cope and mitre or rochet and chimere, but never a combination.

HATS

The *Square Cap* was at first of loose black cloth or velvet, its seams forming four ridges along the top, not accentuated, and it fitted with ear-flaps closely to the head. In Charles I's time it developed into the "Bishop Andrewes Cap" by widening the upper portion till it became a loose, square shape attached to a band, which fitted the head. In the Universities this process of thinning the height and widening the sides was developed until it became the modern graduate's cap, which is a mere "mortar-board" of stiff cardboard covered with cloth, and square in shape, fitted on to a stiff skull cap, longer at the back than the front, and with a long tassel on top. The tassel must be worn hanging over the front side, and *not* at the back. Another development that came about in the seventeenth century was away from the wide, loose type of

Bishop Andrewes to the stiff close fit of the *Biretta*. This is now worn by most modern clergy. It has its seams turned into stiff, high, semi-circular ridges on three (not four) sides of the top, and is collapsible. The side that has no seam ridge must be worn on the wearer's left.

Rochet

Rochet

Chimere

Scarf

BISHOP (WALKING DRESS)

This is easy to remember if you bear in mind that to take it off with the right hand requires a ridge to clasp. In the Middle Ages a skull cap, rather full on top, was alternatively worn.

Hats, whether mitres or biretta types, are worn at services during readings and psalms, but not during prayers; also on ingress and egress to the choir.

The *Mitre* has already been described.

IN THE STREET

During medieval times the clergy were somewhat lax about wearing strictly clerical costume, and often dressed as laymen in gay clothes. Indeed, regulations had to be made by Parliament to prevent their adorning themselves with ornamental daggers, which were felt to be "the limit." The higher clergy of cathedral and college were the chief offenders in dress. During the medieval period and down to George III's day the customary outdoor dress was cassock, gown, hood, and square cap. Graduates also added the tippet. In Georgian times the square cap gave way to the wig, and the gown blossomed out into full bishop sleeves. The cassock was fastened by a broad waist band, and bands instead of the neckcloth or cravat were added at the

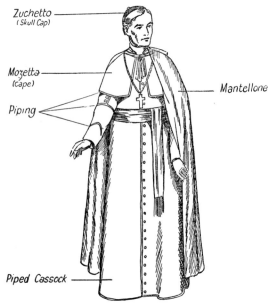

Zuchetto
(Skull Cap)

Mozetta
(Cape)

Piping

Mantellone

Piped Cassock

ITALIAN PRELATE (WALKING DRESS)

neck. The cassock was of silk, at any rate for the richer clergy. The hood and tippet were not worn out of doors.

At the end of the eighteenth century this ancient street dress was abandoned, and the clergy wore dress similar to that of other professional men. This consisted of breeches, and a black, cut-away coat, a white collar and neckcloth, and a top hat, the wide brims of which were tied with side strings to the crown. This costume has been retained to our own day by bishops, but not by ordinary clergy.

The Roman Catholic clergy dressed as laymen from Elizabeth's day till Victoria's, after which they followed the Anglican clergy in dress.

Street dress for priests changed in Victorian times into frock coat and trousers. The head-gear varied. A silk hat was worn till about the 90's, then a clerical flat felt hat till about 1914, then a black felt trilby to our own time. The

frock coat has died out save on formal occasions, when it, or a cut-away morning coat and striped trousers, may be worn with a silk top hat.

Neck-wear followed lay custom till early Victorian times, when a white neckcloth was worn; later it changed to a white bow tie. The modern Roman dog-collar came in about 1870. Below it was worn a stock instead of a tie. The stock was made of black for priests, magenta or purple for bishops, and scarlet for cardinals.

MODERN ROMAN DRESS

For bishops and cardinals an informal full dress consists of a black cassock buttoned and piped with colour—magenta for bishops, scarlet for cardinals. Many Anglican bishops follow the same custom. The cassock is single-breasted, with numerous buttons right down the centre, and with a shoulder cape, also piped, as are the cassock edges and the sleeve edges.

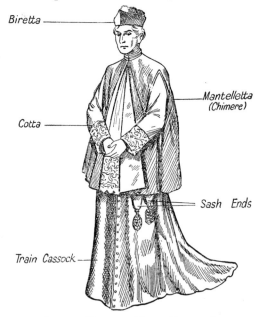

Biretta

Cotta

Mantelletta
(Chimere)

Sash Ends

Train Cassock

ITALIAN PRELATE (CHOIR SERVICES)

Full dress consists of cassock and cape with a train all in magenta for bishops and in scarlet for cardinals. Over all a great caped cloak with narrow collar is worn when travelling. On occasions of great ceremony, the cappa magna (a hooded and caped trained cloak) is worn.

Modern Italian modifications of the ancient

dress are worn by the Roman Catholic bishops. Thus the chimere is now the mantelletta—a knee-length, wider, and looser garment. The bishops wear skull caps called zuchettos under their birettas. All are of magenta—those for cardinals are of scarlet. The cassock has a train, and lace-edged cottas supplant the surplices. Pectoral crosses depend from long chains of green cord or gold, and are fastened at the neck, the chain hanging in two loops on the breast.

SUMMARY
RELIGIOUS ORDERS

Monks

Tunic. Ankle length, sleeved, no front opening or buttons.

Cowl. Large loose gown, sleeved or not (see below) with hood.

Saxon. Sleeved. 6 inches wide at wrist.

9th–11th century. Sleeveless. Bell shaped to ankles, or slit at sides for arms, or slits linked together at intervals.

11th–13th century. Sleeved. Wide "surplice" sleeves reach to knee.

15th century. Sleeved. Wider "surplice" sleeves reach to below knee.

Hood. Saxon. Long point at back.

9th–11th century. Short.

11th–13th century. Widened to shoulders.

15th century. Widened to elbows.

Scapular. Replaces cowl when working. An apron, back and front, circular neck hole, sleeved or sleeveless (see below).

8th century. Sleeved, knee length, 2 side links.

13th–14th century. Sleeveless, ankle length, 1 side link. Covers upper arm.

15th century. Sleeveless, ankle length, 1 side link. Covers arm to elbow.

MONASTIC VARIATIONS

Benedictines (Black monks)

White or black tunics till 14th century, when all black. Black cowl, hood and scapular.

Cluniacs (Black monks)

Black in England and Germany; brown in France. Cowl sleeveless with slits linked at intervals.

Cistercians (White monks)

White tunic, cowl and hood. Black scapular. Cowl sleeves wide to knee.

Carthusians

White tunic, cowl, hood and scapular. 1 link to scapular. Tight sleeved cowl.

FRIARS VARIATIONS

Franciscans (Grey friars)

Brown first, then grey. Close sleeved tunic, no cowl, long pointed hood to waist, short cloak, knotted white cord girdle. Barefoot. Scapular.

Dominicans (Black friars)

White tunic, hood and scapular. No cowl. In church and outdoors a black cloak and hood to elbow.

Carmelites (White friars)

Black tunic, hood and scapular. No cowl. Tight sleeved tunic. White cloak and hood outdoors.

Augustinians

Black. Side sleeves to knee.

Friars of Sack

Simple sack of coarse brown cloth, pointed hood. White scapular. Wooden sandals.

Pied Friars

Black and white.

Friars of Our Lady

White tunic, black cloak and hood.

Trinitarians

White tunic, hood, scapular. Red and blue cross on breast, also on left side of white cloak. An heraldic cross moline.

CANONS VARIATIONS

Premonstratensians (White canons)

White tunic and wide sleeved rochet. White biretta. White fur tailed almuce over arm.

Austins (Black canons)

Black tunic. Tight sleeved rochet girdled. Black cloak and small hood. Black biretta.

Gilbertines

Black tunic. White cloak and hood lined lambswool.

Knights Religious

Jerusalem

Armour. White sleeveless rochet. Sword belt over. Black cloak with S. John's Cross on left breast. Pilgrim's hat.

Templar

Armour. Rochet. Sword belt. White cloak with cross on left breast.

Abbesses

Long cowl girdled, loose-sleeved cassock. Under this tight-fitting sleeves of under dress. Barbe or chin cloth. Mantle cope-shaped. Veil. Ring optional.

Abbots

As their order. Some privileged to wear a mitre. All had pastoral staff. Ring optional. In Parliament slightly trained cape open in front.

Rosaries were worn by all orders on the girdle, and cassocks were double-breasted. Modern religious habits still unchanged unless the order is a modern one. For Parliament, long cape open at front, slight train.

Nuns

As in the corresponding male order with cloak over head instead of hood. Gilbertine nuns wore black, with white cap, black cloak and hood to shoulders worn over cap.

For Choir

Priests

Cassock.
Surplice.
Almuce, or tippet and hood.
Cope—optional.
Square cap or biretta.

Bishops

Cassock.
Grey fur almuce.
Surplice and/or rochet, with either—
chimere and square cap, Bishop Andrewes cap or biretta—or cope and mitre.

For Sacraments (except Mass)

Bishops and priests wear a stole, instead of almuce or tippet and hood. For state and solemn sacraments both may wear a cope as well.

For Street

Priests

Cassock.
Gown.
Tippet.
Square cap—black cloth, or biretta.

Bishops

Cassock.
Chimere.
Scarf or tippet—sable-lined.
Square cap—black velvet, or skull cap—magenta.

CHAPTER XXXI

ARMOUR FASHIONS SUMMARIZED

AS armour is in little demand either for stage or other purposes to-day, I append a brief summary of its principal styles, which will be useful for pageant work or other occasions, primarily so that readers may know what to look for when obtaining a suit. Armour is nearly always hired for such purposes, but it is advisable that the hirer should be able to tell whether he has got the right type of armour. A knight in Norman mail would look foolish in a Tudor setting. With this as an introduction, the pictures and letterpress tell their own tale.

GREEK

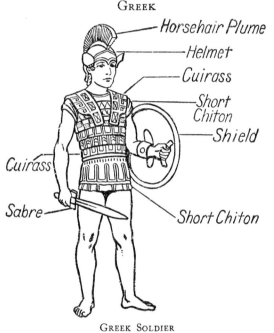

GREEK SOLDIER

THE SURCOAT PERIOD—1272–1307

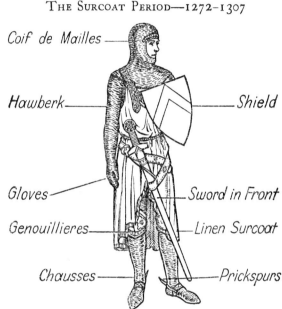

SIR JOHN DAUBERNON, 1277
(Stoke Dabernon, Surrey)

Greek soldiers are occasionally required for the ancient Greek plays and the works of Shakespeare. Roman soldiers were very similar and the block given here is self-explanatory.

SAXON AND NORMAN

The men's armour was composed of mail in chains, rings, or scales sewn sometimes on to leather, at others hung over a leather jerkin. The shield had a six inch boss projecting from its centre, and was kite shaped as in the Bayeux Tapestry, or circular in the more old fashioned North. The Normans wore a pointed helmet with a nose guard.

Complete chain mail of *Hawberk* (body and arms), *Coif de Mailles* (hood), *Chausses* (stockings), *Gloves* (undivided for fingers).

Genouillières (knee pieces) were made of steel or cuirbouille (leather) and strapped over the mail.

Linen Surcoat—worn fairly loosely over all, sleeveless. It reached to below the knee, was fringed at the bottom, and was slit up the front to the waist, where it was tied with a cord.

Shield—small heater (flat iron) shape, or concave, shaped to the body.

Spurs—long prick type fastened by straps across the insteps.

The Transitional Period—Plate and Chain—1307-1320

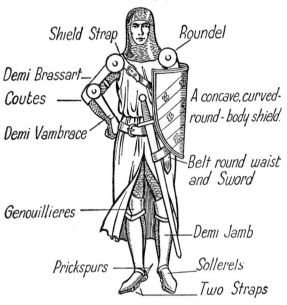

Shield Strap
Roundel
Demi Brassart
Coutes
A concave, curved-round-body shield.
Demi Vambrace
Belt round waist and Sword
Genouillieres
Demi Jamb
Prickspurs
Sollerets
Two Straps

Sir William Fitzralph, c. 1320
(Pebmarsh, Essex)

Ailettes—worn on the shoulders, were optional. They were square pieces of leather covered with silk, decorated with the arms of the wearer, and fringed.

Sword—large cross-hilted in a decorated scabbard. It was hung in front, or a little to the left, by a broad belt over the hips.

Mail—was made either in interlaced circles or banded, and sewn to a foundation of leather in parallel rows.

As before, but with *Plate Armour* worn over the chain mail, viz.

Coutes on the elbows.

Demi Plates on the upper (Brassarts) and forearms (Vambraces).

Roundels (circular plates with spikes or knobs on the shoulders and in front of the elbows).

Jambs (shin plates).

Sollerets (small oblong overlapping plates on the upper part of the foot).

Belt—round waist.

Shield—large concave. *Spurs*—prick.

All plate armour was fastened by straps over the chain mail.

Chain Mail changes from covering the whole of the limbs to bands in rows on a leather foundation.

Pourpoint—fringed dress of rich material embroidered, or

Gambeson—a linen shirt. Worn first.

Hawberk (body and arms)—now the lower edge is pointed showing the undergarment (*Hauketon*); it has shorter sleeves. Worn second.

Hauketon—a padded garment stitched in parallel downward lines to give protection from chafing. Worn third.

The Cyclas Period—1320-50

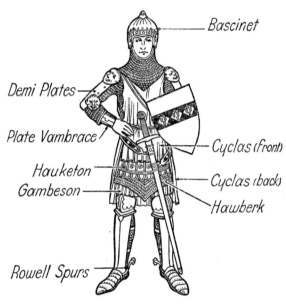

Bascinet
Demi Plates
Plate Vambrace
Cyclas (front)
Hauketon
Cyclas (back)
Gambeson
Hawberk
Rowell Spurs

Sir John de Creke, 1325
(Westley Waterless, Cambs.)

Cyclas—closer fitting than the surcoat, shorter in front than behind, where it reached to the knees. Slit and laced at the sides instead of the front. Sleeveless. Worn fourth.

Bascinet—the hood disappears in favour of a steel Bascinet.

Vambraces of plates were worn over the forearms.

Spurs—rowell type instead of prick, i.e. a circle of sharp points revolving at the end of the spur shaft.

Sollerets—as before.

Shield—small, flat.

A mixture of chain mail and plate armour.

Bascinet—a pointed steel cap.

Camail—tippet of mail, chain or banded, laced to the bascinet, covered neck and shoulders.

Mail Shirt—sleeveless Hawberk, only visible at the lower edge and sometimes at the armpits. Much shorter than before, worn under cuirass.

Steel Cuirass—neck to waist. Worn over mail shirt and under jupon.

Jupon—tight fitting short sleeveless tunic of leather, covered in velvet or silk.

Armdefences—small steel epaulets called Pauldrons (shoulders), Brassarts (arm plates), and Coutes (elbows).

THE CAMAIL PERIOD—1350–1400

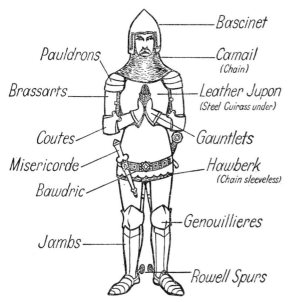

SIR NICHOLAS BURNELL, 1382
(Acton Burnell, Salop)

Gauntlets—steel or leather.

Cuisses (thigh plates)—steel, covered with satin.

Genouillières (knee pieces)—small and plain.

Jambs (shin plates).

Sollerets (toe pieces)—sharp and pointed.

Spurs—rowell type.

Shield—almost disused.

S.S. Collar—worn over shoulders in a broad loop.

Sword—cross hilted. Plain scabbard. Fastened at left side with Bawdric, and hung behind.

Bawdric—broad straight decorated belt worn over the hips. It was enriched with metal work.

Misericorde—short dagger without a guard.

THE LANCASTRIAN PERIOD, 1400–55

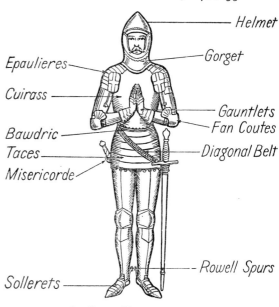

SIR SIMON FELBRIGG, 1416
(Felbrigg, Norfolk)

Complete Plate—no Mail.

Gorget—steel encircling the neck vice Camail.

Helmet—lower and rounder vice Bascinet.

Coutes (elbow plates)—fan shaped.

Bawdric (belt) and *Jupon* (tunic)—cease to be worn, revealing the

Cuirass—steel back and front, plain, round in front, with

Taces—broad steel hoops like a short skirt, about six together.

Sword Belt—now transverse from waist to left side.

Gauntlets—jointed, but sometimes no fingers.

Sollerets—as before.

Spurs—rowell type.

Tuilles—two small plates buckled to the lowest tace, optional.

Epaulières—shoulder plates larger than the old Pauldrons.

THE YORKIST PERIOD, 1455—85

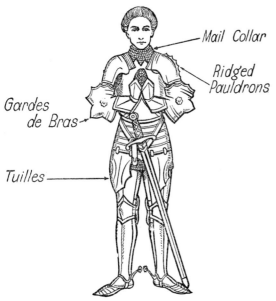

SIR WILLIAM VERNON, 1467
(Tong, Salop)

THE TUDOR PERIOD, 1485-1550

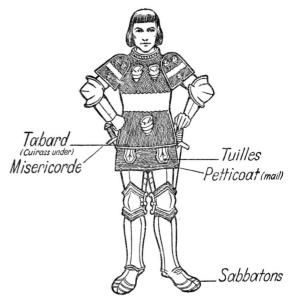

JOHN SHELLEY, 1526
(Clapham, Sussex)

Very fantastic shapes and unsymmetrical modes. Hair worn short, but later flows on the shoulders. Various extra plates made the suit very heavy.

Pauldrons—*ridged* shoulder plates vice epaulières.

Gardes de Bras—extra plates on the Coutes, which differed for right and left arms, and were very large.

Mail Collar—vice Gorget.

Collar—of suns and roses, broadly worn on shoulders.

Lance Rest—sometimes screwed to left side of cuirass.

Tuilles—made longer.

Head—usually bare. Salade or Shell Helmet.

The period is one of peace for soldiers, the fighting was mostly naval, and the tournaments had passed out of fashion.

Cuirass—returns to its first simplicity but is ridged down the centre.

Tuilles and Pauldrons—are still worn.

Shoes—sabbatons with broad toes were in the form of a shoe; vice sollerets.

Spear Rest—a small hook screwed to the right of the breast.

Tabard—embroidered with armorial bearings, with short stiff sleeves on which the arms were repeated. Ceased to be worn about 1550.

Petticote—or shirt of mail worn below the tuilles.

THE ELIZABETHAN PERIOD, 1550–1620

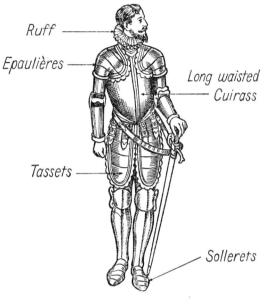

SIR JOHN WINGFIELD, 1584
(Easton, Suffolk)

THE CAROLINE PERIOD, 1620–50

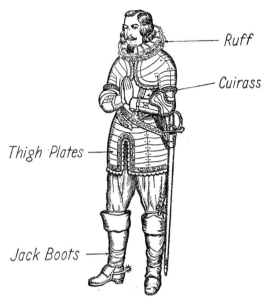

SIR EDWARD FILMER, 1638
(East Sutton, Kent)

Armour was less used. The only purpose it seems to have served was to provide a dignified vesture for the family portrait. It was worn by officers in naval fights on board ship, but rankers wore cap, doublet, coat, trunkhose, shoes and stockings, usually of uniform hue.

Cuirass—becomes long waisted, still ridged in centre.

Epaulières—supplant Pauldrons, and are without ridges.

Taces (skirt)—entirely disappear.

Tassets—many plates buckled to the cuirass, the lowest being rounded off, reaching nearly to the knee and fastened to the breeches by straps.

Ruffs—round neck and wrists.

Sollerets—become less square toed.

After the Great Rebellion in Charles I's reign armour became obsolete and was rarely seen except occasionally as a part of ceremonial dress, but during the Civil War it was, of course, much in evidence and further illustrations will be found on pages 66 and 67. Armour was worn by the officers and less often by the rank and file, who relied on their thick buff leather jackets. The pike and morion are characteristic of this period, but the former leg armour was not worn

Cuirass—a demi suit.

Thigh Plates—laminated.

Knee Pieces—small.

Jack Boots.

Helmet—comb morion.

APPENDIX
DIAGRAMS SHOWING THE EVOLUTION
OF STYLES

MEN

1. Saxon men wore simple tunics, cloaks, and leggings.

2. Norman men lengthened tunics and sleeves, and added short-sleeved over-tunics.

3. Plantagenet men lengthened the over-tunics, slit them at the side, and removed the sleeves.

4. Edwardian men reversed the trend by making sleeves long, tunics short, and wearing hats back to front.

5. Richard II men introduced parti-coloured costumes and added ragged edges to the old styles.

6. Richard II men later reverted to long gowns and turned hoods into hats.

7. Henrician men sobered the cut into long plain robes.

8. Yorkist men turned back to short tunics, widely open with puff sleeves. Hats changed from bizarre to severe.

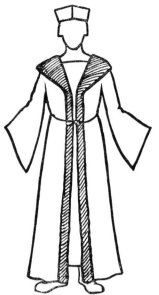

9. Henry VII men added broad fur collared coats, and adopted squared caps and shoes.

10. Henry VIII men made everything square, shortened the coats, and added hanging sleeves.

11. Elizabethan men slimmed, shortened, and puffed trunks and doublets. Square hats became round. Ruffs came in.

12. James I men lengthened trunks into padded breeches and wore pork-pie hats.

13. Charles I men unstuffed the breeches, length-ened doublets, and added lace collars, flat hats and long hair.

14. Puritan men dressed in triangles.

15. Restoration men first wore Eton jackets, petti-coat breeches, puffed sleeves, many bows, and flowing wigs.

16. Restoration men later wore many-buttoned frock coats and sailor hats.

17. Dutch William men found the coats too tight and unbuttoned the bottom half. Wigs became stiff.

18. George II men disclosed waistcoats, flared skirts, and shortened wigs. Square hats became three-cornered.

19. George III men first adopted slimmer figures, shortened waistcoats, and tightened their wigs.

20. George III men later removed the lower front of the coat, added revers, and standing collars. Top boots became customary.

21. Empire men made breeches into trousers, and lessened revers.

22. George IV men swelled trousers into peg-tops and wore top hats.

23. 1850 men wore short double-breasted black coats instead of colours, and check trousers.

24. 1880 men decided to be thin, and frock coat and top hat were universal.

WOMEN

A. Saxon women wore long skirts, three-quarter-length tunics, and veils at the back. Wrinkled sleeves were typical.

B. Norman women developed surplice sleeves.

C. Plantagenet women buttoned their sleeves and made gowns fit closely.

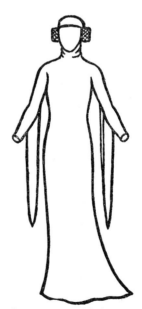

D. Edwardian women added hanging sleeves to gowns and side nets to hair.

159

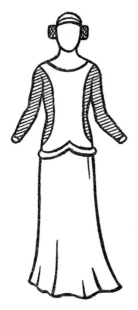

E. Richard II women adopted a sleeveless half-coat.

F. Henrician women raised neck-openings, and invented heart-shaped hats.

G. Yorkist women wore fur-edged and high-waisted gowns, low necks replaced high cnes. Hats were horned.

H. Henry VII women discarded horns and took to gable hats. Neck openings were squared, and sleeves widened.

J. Henry VIII women added huge sleeve-revers, split skirts in front, and wore simple caps or gable hats.

K. Elizabethan women donned crinolines, great ruffs and men's hats.

L. James I women made crinolines into cart-wheels, and wore pork-pie hats.

M. Charles I women became slimmer, closed the split skirts, and added little skirts to bodices.

N. Puritan women dressed in triangles

O. Restoration women opened necks, discarded bodice-skirts, puffed sleeves, and split skirts in front.

P Dutch William women narrowed skirts, tightened and cut sleeves to elbow length, and added bustled over-skirts and high lace caps.

Q. George II women reduced bustles to panniers, added trains, and wore Dolly Varden hats.

R. George III women first reverted to balloon skirts and split them. High white wigs replaced hats.

S. George III women later drew over-skirts and trains into bustles, and covered the neck with full fichus.

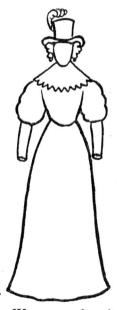

T. Empire women thinned down to Greek styles.

U. George IV women adopted flared skirts and sleeves, and wore feathered top-hats.

V. 1840 women widened sleeves, slimmed waists, and wore coal scuttle bonnets.

W. 1850 women swelled into crinolines and puffed sleeves. Poke bonnets or round hats were worn.

X. 1860 women tucked up skirts in front and narrowed their hips.

Y. 1870 women tucked up skirts in Your places.

Z. 1875 women suppressed hoops in front, thus throwing skirts into loose bustles.

AA. 1880 women reduced bustles to a formality.

BB. 1885 women made bustles into mere sashes and bows.

CC. 1890 women exaggerated sleeves into puffs and epaulets.

DD. 1890 women wore short out-door jackets.

INDEX

ABBESSES, 143
Abbots, 144
Acolytes, 138
Aesthetic Movement, 98, 99
Alb, 136
Alfred Jewel, 16
Alice in Wonderland, 38, 104
Almuce, 138, 139, 140
Amice, 136
Aniline Dye, 108
Apron, 32, 52, 65, 78
Archbishop's Cross, 137
Armour—
   General, 5, 6, 20
   Greek, 5, 6, 145
   Saxon, 145
   1272–1307, 145
   1307–1320, 146
   1320–1350, 146
   1350–1400, 147
   1400–1455, 147
   1455–1485, 148
   1485–1550, 148
   1550–1620, 149
   1620–1650, 149
Aumônière, 22

BAG Pocket, 22, 30
—— Wig, 79, 80
Balandrana, 21
Baldric, 30, 35
Band, Falling, 62, 68
Bandeaux, 120
Bands, Tudor, 50
Barbe, 41, 46
Basil Leather, 21
Bathing Suit, 130
Baudekin Silk, 20
Bayeux Tapestry, 11, 14, 144
Beau Brummell, 87
Beaver Hat, 27, 90
Beehive Hat, 42
Bell-bottom Trousers, 100, 114
Belt. See GIRDLE.
Beret, 127
Bertha Collar, 114
Bicorne Hat, 82
Bikini, 132
Biretta, 46, 141
Birrhus, 8
Bishop Andrewes Cap, 141
—— Sleeve, 50, 90
Bismarck Moustache, 105
Blazer, 118
Bliaud, 17

Blistering, 49, 52
Blouse, 119
Boa, 121
Boater Hat, 71
Bodice, 60, 64, 69, 78, 90, 95, 100, 105, 109
Bolero, 125
Bonnet, 91, 96, 106, 115
Boot Hose, 61
Boots, 9, 32, 51, 61, 65, 70, 82, 120
——, High, 22, 148
Bowl Crop, 36, 40
Bowler Hat, 94, 96, 99, 101, 106, 120, 126
Bow Tie, 94
Breeches, 17, 22, 32, 52, 56, 60, 64, 68, 69, 78, 89, 90
Brocade, 24, 50
Brocella Cloth, 21
Brooch, Cloak, 16, 19
Brown Shoes, 114
Buckle, Shoe, 78
Buffon, 83
Bulla, 9
Burel Cloth, 21
Burnet Cloth, 20
Buskins, 70
Bustle, 98, 99, 103, 109
Butterfly Hat, 38, 39, 41
Buttons, 29, 89
Bycocket Hat, 41
Byron, Lord, 88, 89
Byrrhus Cloth, 21
Bysine Cloth, 20

CAESAR, 7
Calcei, 9
Caligae, 9
Canions, 56
Canons, 143
Cap, 13, 18, 22, 31, 66, 113, 115
Cape, 10, 16, 21, 26, 50, 55
Caped Overcoat, 90
Cappa Magna, 142
Capuchon, 21, 27, 31, 32
Carbatina, 5, 10
Cardigins, 118, 119
Cashmere, 95
Cassock, 119, 124, 142
Caul, 9, 29, 31, 36, 38
Causia, 9
Chain, 46, 47
Chapeau Bras, 79, 82
Chaperon, 31
Chasuble, 8, 135, 136

Chatelaine, 96, 97
Chausses, 17, 32, 145
Checklatoun Silk, 21
Chemise, 17, 32, 45, 50, 55
—— Dress, 119
Chignon, 82, 100, 101
Chimere, 124
Chin Band, 22
Chiton, Doric, 3, 4
——, Ionic, 3, 8
Chlamys, 4
Chopines, 56
Cicero, 7
Ciclatoun Silk, 21
Circlet. See DIADEM.
Clavi, 7
Clergy—
   Eighteenth century, 125
   Medieval, Chapter XXIX and XXX
   Modern, Chapter XXIX and XXX
   Roman, Chapter XXIX and XXX
   Victorian, 142
Cloak, 4, 5, 7, 8, 16, 17, 21, 24, 30, 39, 45, 60, 69
——, Brooch, 16, 19
Clogs, 30, 36, 56
Cloth Hat, 106
Coalscuttle Hat, 91
Coat, 60, 64, 68, 69, 72, 74, 77, 81, 89, 90, 94, 101, 104, 105, 110, 123
Cocked Hat, 72
Codpiece, 40, 50
Coif, 22, 66
Collar, Linen, 55, 56, 62, 68, 77, 104, 113, 118
Colour, Lack of, 109
Commode, 73
Conical Hat, 32
Constantine the Great, 7
Cope, 121, 123
Coronet, 9
Corset, 4, 50, 55, 91, 100
Cotehardie, 25, 26, 29, 32, 35
Courtesans, Greek, 5
Couvre-Chef, 19, 22
Crakowes, 30, 40, 42
Cravat, 94, 100
Crêpe de Chine, 93
Crespine, 31, 37, 38
Crinoline. See HOOP.
Crosier, 137, 138
Cross Gartering, 14, 23

Crusades, 19, 20, 23
Cucullus, 8
Cuirass, 145, 147, 148, 149
Cyclas, 26, 146

DAGGER, 52
Dagging, 27, 29, 32, 35
Dalmatic, Civil, 7, 21
——, Ecclesiastical, 135, 138
Damask, 20
Dances, Greek, 5
Dandies, 87
Diadem, 9, 13
Dinner Jacket, 108, 113
Diplois, 4
Disraeli, 87, 88
Dolly Varden hat, 83
Dorelet Cap, 31
Doric Chiton, 3, 4
d'Orsay, Count, 87
Doublet, 39, 45, 49, 59, 64, 68
——, Italian, 55
Dragoon Moustache, 101
Drawers, 94
Dundreary Moustache, 101

ECHELLE Trimming, 82
Edward II's splendour, 24
—— VII, 112
Elizabeth, Queen, 54
Empire Style, 82, 89
Epaulet, 55
Eton Crop, 126
—— Jacket, 59, 68
—— Suit, 115
Eugenie, Empress, 93, 94
Evening Dress, 110, 113, 114, 118,
   119, 123, 124, 125, 132
Eyebrows, Plucked, 31
Eye Veils, 126

FACE Cloth, 113
Fan, 57, 59
—— Collar, 62
Farthingale, 55, 59
Fauntleroy, Lord, 108
Feathers, 41, 51, 57, 66, 71, 96, 114
Fez, 41
Fibula, 4
Fillet, 31
Flannel Shirt, 113
Flared Coat, 74, 77
Flounce, Greek, 8
Flounces, 93, 94
Flowered Pattern, 73
Fob, 88, 96
Forked Beard, 30
—— Hat, 38
Franco-Flemish Hat, 46
François Premier Sleeve, 88, 90, 99,
   105

French Hood, 51, 52, 56
Friars, 126
Frock Coat, 90, 94, 100, 104, 113, 118
Frontlet, 37, 41
Fruit in Designs, 40, 50
Full Bottomed Wig, 74
Fur, 13, 16, 21, 25, 27, 35, 37

GABLE Hat, 46, 51
Gaiters, 120
Garter, 61
——, Cross, 14, 23
——, Order of the, 27
Gauze, 21
Gigot Sleeve, 88
Gilray, 88
Gipciere, 30
Girdle, 4, 7, 8, 12, 21, 22, 25, 26, 30,
   47, 50, 52, 110, 114
——, Church, 136
Glengarry Bonnet, 108
Gloves, 23, 110
——, Bishops, 137, 138
Gorget, 27, 31
Gown, 17, 21, 22, 25, 26, 30, 32, 39,
   45, 50, 55, 57, 60, 61, 64, 65, 69
Greenaway, Kate, 87
Grosvenor Gallery, 98
Gunna, 11, 12

HABIT Cloth, 113
Hair, Artificial, 19
—— Band, 5, 9, 13, 18, 27, 31, 96
—— Net, 9, 27
—— Side Nets, 22, 26–27, 29, 31,
   36, 37, 96, 101
Halo Hat, 127
Handbag, 121, 128
Hats—
   Barbe, 41, 46
   Beaver, 27, 83, 90
   Beehive, 42
   Beret, 127
   Bicorne, 82
   Biretta, 124
   Bishop Andrewes, 141
   Boater, 71
   Bonnet, 91, 96, 106, 115
   Bowler, 94, 96, 101, 106, 120, 126
   Butterfly, 38, 39, 41
   Bycocket, 41
   Capuchon, 21, 27, 31, 32
   Causia, 5, 9, 10
   Chapeau Bras, 79, 82, 83
   Chaperon, 31
   Coal Scuttle, 83, 91, 96
   Coif, 22, 66
   Conical, 32
   Couvre Chef, 19, 22
   Dolly Varden, 83
   Dorelet, 31

Hats (contd.)—
   Fez, 41
   Forked, 38
   Franco-Flemish, 46
   French Hood, 51, 52, 56
   Friars, 143
   Frontlet, 37
   Gable, 46, 51
   Glengarry, 108
   Gorget, 27, 31
   Halo, 127
   Headrail, 13
   Heart, 29, 38
   Hennin, 29, 37, 38
   Homburg, 113, 115, 120
   Horned, 29, 37
   Juliet, 29
   Kevenhuller, 79, 82
   Lace Cap, 66
   Laurel, 9
   Leghorn, 96
   Liberty, 13
   Liripipe, 27, 31
   Mob Cap, 79, 84
   Montero, 62
   Nebule, 31
   Nivernois, 83
   Opera, 96
   Petasus, 5, 9
   Picture, 106
   Pileus, 5, 9
   Quaker, 83
   Reticulated, 29, 37
   Robin Hood, 22, 32
   Round, 96
   Roundlet, 36
   Skull Cap, 51, 66, 142
   Smoking, 41
   Spanish Turban, 27
   Square Cap, 51, 141
   Steeple, 29
   Straw, 79, 82, 120
   Sugar-loaf, 34, 36
   Sun, 5
   Tall, 37, 56, 57, 101, 120
   Tholia, 5
   Tocque, 101
   Top, 37, 56, 57, 101, 120, 126
   Tricorne, 82
   Trilby, 41, 126
   Tudor, 46, 51
   Turban, 31, 36, 38, 82, 83, 127
   Wimple, 13, 18, 19, 22, 27, 29, 33
Hanging Sleeve, 39
Headrail, 13
Heart Hat, 29, 38
Helmet—see Armour
Hennin Hat, 29, 37, 38
Henry IV, 34
Heraldry, 21, 26, 29
Hessian Boot, 82, 89

Highland Dress, 108
Highwaisted Gown, 40
Himation, 4, 5
Hobble Skirt, 112, 114, 119
Holme-by-Newark, 45, 47
Homburg Hat, 113, 115
Hood—
   Ecclesiastical, 140, 141
   Edwardian, 27
   Greek, 5
   Henries, Three, 37
   Norman, 18
   Plantagenet, 21, 22
   Richard II, 32
   Roman, 10
Hoop, 50, 77,
Horned Hat, 29, 37
Houppelande, 29, 35, 39
Hourglass Waist, 101

IMPERIAL Beard, 95
Instita, 8
Ionic Chiton, 3
Ivanhoe, 12

JACKBOOT, 70, 131
Jacket, 125, 130
James I, 54
Japanese Art, 98, 100
Jeans, 132
Jerkin, 39, 45, 49, 60
Judges, 22
Juliet Cap, 29

KEVENHULLER Hat, 79
Kirtle, 12, 25, 26, 50
Knickerbockers, 118
Knickers, 114
Knights, Religious, 144
Kolpos, 3

LACE Cap, 66
Lacerna, 8
Laurel Wreath, 9
Leaves in Design, 40, 50
Leech, John, 96
Leghorn Hat, 96
Leg of Mutton Sleeve, 88, 90, 110
Leisure Shirt, 130
Liberty Cap, 13
Linen, 66
Liripipe, 27, 31
London Museum, 119
Louis Shoe, 70
Lounge Suit, 94, 96, 100, 104, 113,
   121, 128

MACARONI, 81
Macbeth, 19
Make-up, 127, 132
Maniple, 136

Mantelletta, 142
Mantle, 12, 16, 21, 22, 25, 30
Mitre, 137, 138
Mittens, 19
Mob Cap, 79
"Modesty" Vest, 124
Monks, 143
Montero, 62
Morse, 140
Mortar Board Cap, 141
Mourning, 96
Moustache—
   Bismarck, 105
   Dragoon, 101
   Dundreary, 101
   Handlebar, 126
   Kaiser, 105
Muff, 78, 95, 121
Mules, 51, 70

NAPOLEON III, 95
Nebule Hat, 31
Neck, Shape of opening, 40
Neckcloth, 68
"New Look", 131
Nivernois hat, 83
Norfolk Jacket, 104, 114, 118
Nun, 22, 143

ONE-PIECE Dress, 82, 113
Opera Hat, 96, 104
Orange Hat, 38
Organdie Muslin, 94
Orphrey, 136, 140
Ostrich Feathers, 41, 51, 61
Overcoat, 81, 101, 118, 125
Oxford Bags, 125

PADDED Shoulder, 39, 49
Paenula, 8, 137
Palla, 8
Pallium, Church, 137
———, Civil, 3, 8
Panniers, 77
Pantaloons, 89
Parti-colour, 26, 29, 32, 35
Partlet, 50
Pastoral Fashion, 76
——— Staff, 137
Peacock Shade, 98
Pearls, 61
Peascod Doublet, 55
Peg Top Trousers, 90
Pelicon. See HOUPPELANDE.
Pelisse, 90, 91
Peplos, 4
Peplum, 3
Periwig, 70
Pero, 9, 22
Persian Vest, 68
Petasus Hat, 5, 9

Petticoat, 50, 55, 57, 61, 69, 78, 89,
   90, 94, 95
——— Breeches, 68, 69
Petti-cote, 45
Phaecassium, 9
Philistines, 100
Picture Hat, 106
Pileus, 5, 9
Pinsnets, 51
Plaits, Hair, 13, 27, 32
Plucked Eyebrows, 31
Plumpers, 73
Plus-fours, 118
Pocket, 22, 30
Pointed Shoes, 30, 36, 40
Poke Bonnet, 96
Polonese, 82
Pompadour, 110, 114
Poulaines, 30, 36, 40
Powder and Patches, 76
Pre-Raphaelites, 99
Puffed Sleeve, 60, 98
Pullovers, 118
Puttees, 5

QUAKER hat, 83
Quill, 22

RAMILLIES Wig, 73, 74
Ray Cloth, 20
Red Heels, 61, 65
Religious Orders, 143
Reticulated Cap, 29, 37
Richard of Bordeaux, 21, 29, 34
Ring, Episcopal, 137
Ringlets, 61, 82
Robin Hood, 22, 32
Rochet, 141
Roman Dress Rules, 7
Rosette, 61
Round Hat, 96
Roundlet Hat, 36
Ruff, Falling, 62
———, Neck, 54, 55, 62
———, Waist, 56
Rushes, Floor, 23
Russian Tiara, 27

SACQUE, 78
Sailor Suit, 108, 115
Samite Silk, 21
Sandals, 4, 9, 14
Sarcinet Silk, 21
Sash, 103
Satin, 21, 94
——— Shoes, 114
Saturnalia, 7
Scallops, 27, 29, 32, 35
Scapular, 143
Scarf, 127, 128
Scotch Fisherwomen, 32

Scott, Sir Walter, 11
Shaved Head, 18, 31, 36
Shield—see Armour
Shirt, 16, 39, 44, 49, 52, 59, 64, 69,
    81, 90, 118, 123, 130
Shoes, 4, 9, 13, 18, 22, 23, 26, 30,
    32, 35, 40, 46, 50, 56, 57, 70, 91,
    114, 120, 125, 132
Shorts, 60, 68, 108
Shot Silk, 95
Shoulder, Padded, 39
Side Nets. See HAIR.
Silk, Lyons, 94
Sinus, 8
Skirt, 61, 64, 69, 78, 90, 94, 101,
    103, 105, 109, 112, 113,
    118, 123, 128, 131
——— Turned-up, 32
Skull Cap, 51, 66, 142
Slashing, 39, 44, 46, 49
Slaves, Greek, 5
Sleeve—
    Bishop, 50, 90, 110
    François Premier, 88, 90, 99, 105
    Gigot, 88
    Hanging, 39
    Leg of Mutton, 88, 90, 110
    Puffed, 60
    Slit, 19
Slit Sleeve, 19
Smock, 17, 32
Smoking Cap, 41
——— Jacket, 104
Snood, 13
Snuff Box, 72
Socks, 120
Soleae, 9
Sombrero, 61
Spanish Cape, 55
——— Turban, 27
Spats, 120
Spatterdashes, 70
Spotted Muslin, 107, 114
Sprigged Pattern, 73
Spurs, 61, 145, 147, 148
Square Cap, 51, 141
Startup, 22, 23
Stays, 4, 50, 55, 91
Steeple Hat, 29, 41
Stephane, 9
Stick, Walking, 42, 76
Stirrup Hose, 70
Stock, 90
Stockings, 17, 18, 22, 32, 50, 56, 61,
    78, 82, 89, 120, 125
Stola, 8

Stole, 119, 121, 127, 128
Stomacher, 45
Straw Hat, 79, 82
Striped Tights, 45
Strophion, 4
Sugar Loaf Hat, 34, 36
Sumptuary Laws, 7, 24–25, 27
Sunhat, 5
Super Cotehardie, 25, 30, 35
Supertunic, 3
Surcoat, 20, 21, 25, 30, 145
Surplice, 139
Swallow-tailed Morning Coat, 118
Sword, 81

TABARD, 22, 29, 147
Tailcoat, 104
Tall Hat, 37, 56, 57, 94, 96, 106,
    120, 126
Tarlatan, 94
Tassets, 60, 64, 148
Tenniel, Sir John, 38, 104
Tholia, 5
Tie, 94, 100, 109, 118, 123, 130
Tights, 22, 23, 24, 25, 26, 30, 32, 35,
    40, 45
Tippet, Church, 140
———, Civil, 26, 30
Tissue Silk, 21
Toga, 7, 8
Top Boot, 82, 89
——— Coat, 119, 131
——— Hat. See TALL HAT.
Toque, 101
Train, 29, 110, 114, 118
Travelling, 21
Tribon, 3
Tricorne Hat, 82
Trilby Hat, 41, 126
Trousers, 90, 100, 104, 114, 120, 125
———, Norman, 17, 18
———, Saxon, 13
Trunk Hose, 56
Trunks, 130
T-shirt, 130
Tudor Cap, 51
Tunic—
    Candida, 8
    Greek, 3, 5
    Greek, length of, 4
    Laticlavia, 7
    Norman, 16, 19
    Palmata, 7
    Picta, 8
    Plantagenet, 21, 23
    Praetexata, 8

Tunic (contd.)—
    Pulla, 10
    Restoration, 69
    Richard II, 32
    Roman, 7, 8, 10
    Saxon, 11, 14
    Sordida, 10
    Virilis, 8
Tunicle, 121
Turban, 31, 36, 38, 82, 83, 89, 90, 127
———, Spanish, 27
Turn-ups, 125
Two-colour Dress, 25, 26, 32
Two-piece Dress, 113, 114
Two-piece Suit, 119, 128

ULSTER, 99
Underclothes, 124
Underdress, 45

VANDYCK Beard, 36, 61
——— Collar, 59
Veil, 36, 37, 38, 41, 56, 110, 120, 126
Vest, 49, 68, 89, 90
Vestments, Distinction between Choir
    and Mass, 139
———, How to Wear, 138
———, Pattern of Church, 135

WAISTCOAT, 68, 72, 77, 78, 95, 100,
    104, 105, 118, 123, 128
Waist, Hourglass, 101, 103
———, Ruff, 56
———, Wasp, 101, 103
Wedding Veil, Greek, 5
Whisk Collar, 56
Whiskers, Side, 92, 106
White Waistcoat, 104
Wig—
    Bag, 79, 80
    Full Bottom, 74
    Periwig, 70
    Ramillies, 73, 74
Wilde, Oscar, 98
Wimple, 13, 18, 19, 22, 27, 29, 33
Woolmerchants, 47
Wreath, Hair, 5, 9
Wrinkled Sleeve, 11, 14, 17

YELLOW starch, 54

ZONA, 8
Zouave, 29, 95, 114
Zuchetto, 143